REALIZE

The Self

Awaken to What You Have Always Been

Mark Powers

Book Cover by Mark Powers
Illustrations by Mark Powers
1st Edition Feb.22, 2026
Paperback ISBN: 979-8-9936387-2-0
Hardcover ISBN: 979-8-9936387-3-7

Contact info:
www.realizetheself.com
realizetheself@yahoo.com

Legal Disclaimer

The information presented in this book is provided for educational and informational purposes only. Certain stories, characters, events, and dialogues may be fictitious, allegorical, or composite in nature and are included solely to convey philosophical insights or highlight specific teachings. Any resemblance to actual persons or events is coincidental.

This book does not provide medical, mental health, or professional advice, and should not be relied upon as such. Readers should consult a qualified healthcare provider or licensed physician before making any changes related to their physical or mental health, medications, treatments, or lifestyle.

The author and publisher disclaim any liability for actions taken or not taken based on the contents of this book.

This book is dedicated to the amazing Editor-in-Chief Michelle and the amazing Lucy

May all beings be peaceful.
May all beings be happy.
May all beings be safe.
May all beings awaken to the light of
their true nature.
May all beings be free.
-Metta Prayer

PREFACE

The stories presented here are in reference to 'Mark', who is an actor, a character in the dreamlike illusory world we exist in. I am not 'Mark' which refers to the egoic mind/body identity, I am that which has no name, the nameless, the ineffable, pure awareness, the true Self, as are you. The Self that comes from the light, that bore the light, Atman, Brahman, the pleroma, the monad, non duality and many other names. I am just passing through this world, as we all are. 'Mark' is just an "avatar" in this dream-like, illusory, holographic, AI world we are passing through. With the examination of science and ancient teachings we will walk step by step on how to Realize the Self and awaken to one's true essence. We are not the body, we are not the mind, we are pure awareness, that which is aware of itself. That is who we are, the changeless and the nameless. Any and all words cease to adequately describe the true Self. Nevertheless, throughout this book, I will do my best to convey the closest essence to the Self as possible.

The cause of ignorance as noted in Vedic, Buddhist and Gnostic traditions is from the misidentification of the true Self with the mind and body. This is the root cause of man's suffering and imprisonment. We are already free and awakened, yet it is only the mind that covers the realization of the Self. I cannot urge one enough to pursue Self Realization. This pursuit is of the fundamental utmost importance and all faculties should be focused towards the pursuit of the Self. Self Realization is a process where the Self is realized more and more, little by little that gap in between thought widens ever so slightly. In that place where the Self resides is the place of true and infinite happiness, that neither comes nor goes, that which was never born and that which will never die, the Self. In the state of Self Realization one can abide in the true Self and be forever in serenity, equanimity, happiness, infinite love and ultimate freedom. Realizing the Self is the only way to have permanent happiness. You are happiness itself. There is nothing to do, nowhere to go, simply be who you already are, the Self. Happiness, peace, serenity, infinite love, is one's very nature. YOU ARE THAT!

"Man's search for happiness is an unconscious search for his true Self." - Ramana Maharshi

"Your own Self Realization is the greatest service you can render the world." - Ramana Maharshi

Note: I will use terms of Enlightenment, Gnosis, Self Realization and Realizing the Self interchangeably. Atman, Brahman, Divine Spark are also used to reference the Self.

INTRO

This book is for the serious pursuer of truth, of consciousness and of one's true essence and existence. This book is meant to be a means to aid one in Realizing the Self. The true Self is beyond the mind and all rational understanding so nothing written will adequately express the concept of the Self fully. Only by the experience of one's true Self can one fully understand that which is beyond understanding and that which is beyond words. The true Self can only be experienced; it cannot be understood or expressed as that implies the mind and the mind cannot grasp that which is beyond the mind. This knowledge of the Self or 'Gnosis' transcends the mind and any rational understanding. The Realization of the Self can be done through a systematic and rigorous approach that we will thoroughly go over in this book that can lead to Self Realization rather quickly. Anyone can Realize the Self but not everyone will. This is for those that wish to wake up from this dream of existence, for those that wish to escape the prison of this reality as imposed by the mind and external sources. This book is not meant for those that want a better jail cell, a better dream, a better section in the prison. This is for those that wish to wake up to the ultimate truth and break the chains of bondage forever.

"Those who depart hence without having found here the Self and those real desires, for them there is no freedom in all the worlds. But those who depart hence, having found here the Self and those real desires-for them in all worlds there is freedom."
Chandogya Upanishad, 8:2:6 (Radhakrishan, 2024)

"The two said, 'The Self which is free from evil, free from old age, free from death, free from grief, free from hunger and thirst, whose desire is the real, whose thought is the real. He should be sought, him one should desire to understand. He who has found out, he who understands that Self he obtains all worlds and all desires.'..."
Chandogya Upanishad, 8:7:3 (Radhakrishan, 2024)

The Realization of the Self can be done and you can do it if you so choose to. Many ancient writings and teachings describe the process of Self Realization, often in mysterious and hidden ways. The hidden teachings of Self Realization were quite possibly the original teachings of Christianity as well as teachings of Hinduism, Buddhism and the Greek and Egyptian mystery schools which we will touch upon throughout this book.

Using a systematic and scientific approach, coupled with ancient wisdom and techniques anyone can Realize the Self quite quickly. This can be done quite fast in the course of days or weeks but mostly over the course of months depending on how much time and effort one puts into it. On rare occasions Self Realization has even happened instantly. I would encourage everyone to not waste any time and go full steam ahead as soon as possible towards Realizing the Self. Tomorrow is never guaranteed and one may miss their chance to escape from this 'dream' like existence, this prison of reality and from the cycle of reincarnation. If you are reading this now, you have more of a head start to Self Realization then most of humanity. Do not waste this precious life in the chase of illusory pleasure and material possessions that will never bring permanent happiness, instead focus all of one's might and energy on transcending this illusory world and Realize the Self. The finite can never give infinite happiness, only the infinite can and that is your true nature, your true Self. You are THAT!

Why Realize the Self?

Besides escaping karma and reincarnation as indicated by the Vedic teachings of the Upanishads as well as Buddhism and Gnosticism, real happiness, peace, serenity, everlasting happiness and infinite love can only be found when one Realizes the Self. Aside from that, one is trapped on a hamster wheel of duality: pain and pleasure, happiness and sadness, good and bad, desire and aversion, etc. To get off the treadmill of duality and madness one must Realize the Self. It's really not that hard nor difficult to Realize the Self. Self Realization is our natural state we have simply forgotten. Self Realization takes some effort and diligence as well as guidance and knowledge to do so. May this book help you navigate the journey back to the Self. This book has not found you for no reason, use the opportunity wisely as not everyone has this opportunity.

The methods and teachings I have indicated in here are not the 'end all be all' but they are a good addition on this not so well trodden path. The most important aspect is the desire. If one has the ultimate desire to Realize the Self then one will find a way or the way will find you. With utmost sincerity and desire, the Self within will help one break through this reality and aid one's journey by piercing through the veil of this illusory dream-like world. Once the Self is Realized all desires will vanish, even that desire that brought one to Realize the Self will vanish and there will only be the Self. The Self is everything. The Self is limitless. The Self is infinity times infinity. The Self is you.

As mentioned, we will combine ancient teachings with science in the form of brain waves to aid Self Realization. We will see how much of our emotions and thoughts are not from our true Self and are shaped by external and internal circumstances beyond our control. In fact, neither our emotions, mind nor body are our true Self. We will also go over three main techniques to Realize the Self backed by science and ancient wisdom: Forgiveness process, Release Technique and Self-Inquiry. In addition we will go over practical preparation methods to form a foundational approach to these techniques and finish off with miscellaneous writings and ideas upon different subjects in relation to Self Realization. A good part of this book is simply the knowledge of the Self. One could do all the methods provided but if one does not learn the teachings from a qualified teacher that conveys these secret teachings then one will have a difficult time. Allow this book to be your teacher and guide. Eventually as one becomes more and more acquainted with the Self, the Self within and without, everywhere and nowhere, will become one's own guiding force. Ultimately, you are your own teacher. Let the Self guide you.

What really got me interested in Self Realization was finding out the link between neuroscience and consciousness. I was blown away at the scientific evidence that connects science and spirituality. Of course once one Realizes the Self, everything must go including brain waves and the egoic self which includes the mind and body which is not us. We are not the body, we are not the mind, we are not the emotions, we are the pure awareness that transcends all of these. As mentioned before the root cause of man's suffering can be linked to the misidentification of the true Self with the mind/ego in what the ancient Vedic texts call 'avidya' or ignorance. What Self Realization is, is simply the detachment from the identification with the mind and body and to the awareness witness, observer within. That is the true Self and you are THAT!

Who are we? Who is the Self? What is the Self? Our true Self resides in our heart center and is called the 'Divine Spark' in Gnostic teachings and called 'Atman' in Vedic teachings. Our true Self is traditionally taught to be located in a secret cave like dwelling in the heart center the size of one's thumb according to many ancient Vedic texts, specifically the *Katha, Chandogya, Mundaka* and *Brihadaranyaka Upanishads* (Radhakrishan, 2024). These texts have been around for thousands of years, most have not heard of them. This information seems to be purposely being hidden or distorted from the general public.

The three main teachings I will use to validate and express the ideas and facts to aid one to Self Realization stems from three main traditions as well as science, personal experiences and observations. Those three main ancient traditions are: Gnosticism, Advaita Vedanta from Hinduism as well as Buddhism and to a smaller extent from ancient Egyptian and Greek teachings. Not to say this book is a religious book per se, far from that. This is a book that incorporates ancient ideas to come to a conclusion as to who we really are and how to "remember" our true Self hence the term Realize the Self. We are already THAT! It is only the mind that covers this up. We must peel back the mind which has its firm grip on the Self and realize our true nature.

Another term for Self Realization is enlightenment but I prefer Realize the Self as it has a more direct meaning at least from my non-understanding, understanding of the term. As for the term enlightenment, it has been watered down by the New Age movement and certain organizations use that term to profit off the backs of unsuspecting people. For nearly everyone, Self Realization is a state of realizing the true Self in little bits here and there and bouncing in and out of it as the egoic mind reigns its control less and less until a point is made where the amount of time one abides in the Self is greater than the amount of time one resides in the ego/mind aka the non-self. In addition, the term Self Realization seems to be a better description of the message I wish to convey. Self Realization is simply realizing who we already are. There is nothing to strive for as it is a process of letting go of everything we are not. In Sanskrit this is called 'neti neti' meaning not this, not that. Self Realization is like peeling back the layers of an onion to get to the core which is the Self that shines with the brightness of a million suns times infinity.

You are THAT!

As you read this book forget everything you were taught or think you know. The Self transcends thought and thinking. We will challenge some deeply held beliefs and programs that may shock you to your very core. But it is not the real you who will be shocked, it is simply the ego's natural reaction to try and hold on to its fictitious self as we dissolve the ego and begin to understand without understanding that the ego/mind is not real. We will find that which is real and that is the true Self. In this book I added many quotes. I'm a big fan of letting ancient brilliant teachers speak and express the eternal truth in their own words.

A well-known study asked people in their later years about their greatest regrets in life. These are the five most common regrets of the dying:

1. Working too hard
2. Not staying in touch with friends
3. Not living a life true to oneself
4. Not expressing their true feelings
5. Not allowing themselves to be happier

Yet the greatest tragedy in life is not any one of these. The greatest tragedy is going through life—living and dying—without ever truly knowing who you truly are or discovering the Self within. The greatest tragedy of all is not Realizing the Self.

"The only useful purpose of the present birth is to realize the self. There is nothing else to do." -
Ramana Maharshi

Ramana Maharshi, Welling, (1948).

WHAT IS SELF REALIZATION

"This morning, a number of Gujerati visitors arrived here, evidently returning from Pondicherry, after darshan there on the 15th. One of them asked Bhagavan, "What is meant by Self-realisation? Materialists say there is no such thing as God or Self." Bhagavan said, "Never mind what the materialists or others say; and don't bother about Self or God. Do you exist or not? What is your idea of yourself? What do you mean by 'I'?" The visitor said he did not understand by 'I' his body, but something within his body. Thereupon, Bhagavan continued, "You concede 'I' is not the body but something within it. See then from whence the 'I' arises within the body. See whether it arises and disappears, or is always present. You will admit there is an 'I' which emerges as soon as you wake up, sees the body, the world and all else, and ceases to exist when you sleep; and that there is another 'I' which exists apart from the body, independently of it, and which alone is with you when the body and the world do not exist for you, as for instance in sleep. Then ask yourself if you are not the same 'I' during sleep and during the other states. Are there two 'I's? You are the same one person always. Now, which can be real, the 'I' which comes and goes, or the 'I' which always abides? Then you will know that you are the Self. This is called Self-realisation. Self-realisation is not however a state which is foreign to you, which is far from you, and which has to be reached by you. You are always in that state. You forget it, and identify yourself with the mind and its creation. To cease to identify yourself with the mind is all that is required. We have so long identified ourselves with the not-Self that we find it difficult to regard ourselves as the Self. Giving up this identification with the not-Self is all that is meant by Self-realisation. How to realise, i.e., make real, the Self? We have realised, i.e., regarded as real, what is unreal, the not-Self. To give up such false realisation is Self-realisation."
'Day by Day with Bhagavan' 17-8-46 by A. Devarja Mudaliar

This is a great explanation and summary of what the Self is and what it is not. The Self is not the body, not the mind. The Self is the awareness beyond the body and the mind. The Self is beyond words or descriptions. The Self is ineffable. The Self is present in deep dreamless sleep. The Self is not one's name nor any self identification. The Self is always abiding and never comes and goes. The Self is always happy, tranquil, peaceful, blissful and full of infinite love and joy. The Self is our true nature and no amount of words or thinking or speaking can ever come close to properly describing it. The Self is nothing and everything at the same time. The Self is you. Who are you? You are THAT!

When we talk about the Self, we are not talking about the mind that masquerades itself as the Self, but the calm abiding witness that exists as pure awareness that has no voice and no words and no amount of talking or thinking can show one its truth. In fact, it takes one further away from the eternal truth of one's existence the more thinking and speaking done to try and describe the Self. This eternal Self that resides in each of us goes by many names. The Gnostics call it the "Divine Spark", the Hindus call it Atman or the Self, here in this book we will refer to it as the Self and the Divine Spark mostly.

This Self is ever present, was never born and will never die. This Self is ever abiding in happiness, tranquility, serenity, and infinite love (bliss). It is simply the mind that covers up the true Self. The mind is the only cause of suffering, without the mind "no problem", with the mind "all problem". Later we will examine in full detail how to realize that which we already are. We will discuss how to dissolve, quiet and silence the mind to Realize the Self and once the seed has been planted the tree will grow in time.

Once one has a taste or glimpse of the Self it will never be forgotten and one will wish to experience the Self more and more until one fully realizes the Self. May this book help those that desire to know the Self, get just exactly that. Only the Self can give man reprieve from the bondage of suffering imposed on them and only the Self can give eternal freedom and liberation. The Self is your very nature! YOU are the THAT!

Table of Contents

Chapter 1

KNOW THYSELF

"Know Thyself". -Socrates

*"When you know yourselves, then you will be known, and you will understand that you are children of the living Father. But if you do not **know yourselves**, then you live in poverty, and you are the poverty."*
-Jesus, Gospel of Thomas, 3.

"But ignorance is destroyed by knowledge of the Self within. The light of this knowledge shines like the sun, revealing the supreme Brahman (the Self)." -
Bhagavad Gita, 5:16

Many ancient teachings emphasize knowing oneself. They state that if one truly knows oneself, one knows the secrets of the universe; if one knows oneself, one knows God—which is the Self. These traditions present the knowledge of one's true Self as the most profound secret of existence, and indeed it is. The Self is the entire universe; it is everything, and you are THAT!

The ancient mystery schools of Egypt taught this. The ancient Greeks taught this. Even the secret Gnostic teachings attributed to Jesus expressed it through the concept of "Gnosis." The Greek philosopher Pythagoras declared: "Man, know thyself; then thou shalt know the Universe and God."

At the Temple of Apollo in Delphi, Greece—an oracle established around 548 BCE—there is a famous ancient Greek inscription: Γνῶθι σαυτόν (*Gnōthi seauton*), which translates into English as "Know thyself."

The entire path of Self Realization can be summed up in those two words: "Know thyself." They carry exactly the same meaning as "Realize the Self."

Many of the ancient philosophers from Socrates to Plato to Aristotle to Pythagoras and many more, taught the importance of knowing oneself. Even before the Temple of Apollo was built, across the Mediterranean at the Temple of Luxor in Egypt, estimated to have been built in the year 1400 BCE, there is an inscription on the walls of the temple that says: "Man, know thyself, and thou shalt know the gods". The date of the Temple of Luxor predates the Temple of Apollo by almost 1000 years. And some researchers say this 'know thyself' is inscribed on most temples in Egypt. It seems as though the Greek teachings of 'know thyself' in Greece could have been modeled after the teachings in Egypt.

According to the Greek historian Herodotus, when the original Temple of Apollo at Delphi burned down in 548 BCE, the Egyptian king Amasis contributed a massive sum—nearly three times the amount—toward the construction of the new temple. Some scholars therefore suggest that the Delphic oracle and its associated wisdom may have been an extension, or at least strongly influenced by, the ancient mystery schools of Egypt.

If we dig further, we find that many prominent Greeks did indeed travel to Egypt to study, including Thales of Miletus, Solon, Pythagoras, Plato, Herodotus, Eudoxus, and many others.

Thales of Miletus, one of the Seven Sages of Greece, is sometimes credited with the maxim "Know thyself" that was inscribed at Delphi. But the rabbit hole goes even deeper. When we examine the earliest written references to the true Self, we discover they appear in the ancient Vedic texts of India, particularly the Rig

Veda. This collection is traditionally dated to around 1500–1200 BCE, with some scholars and Indian traditions placing its origins as early as 3000–4000 BCE or earlier.

In the Rig Veda, the true Self is called **Atman**—the inner essence, the eternal observer, pure awareness, the divine spark, the real "I" behind all experience. Atman is none other than our true Self.

If we examine the origin of the word Gnosis and Gnothi, it stems from the Sanskrit word *jnana* meaning knowledge or to know. Jnana can be summarized as: 'know thyself'. This Self knowledge is a central theme in the teachings of the Bhagavad Gita and the Upanishads and is just touched upon in some parts of the Rig Veda. If we look at one of the earliest writings of the real Self we can see it here in the Rig Veda:

From the *Rig Veda* 1.164.20-22 (Lewis, 2025) we have a story of two birds:

1.164.20 Two birds associated together, and mutual friends, take refuge in the same tree; one of them eats the sweet fig; the other abstaining from food, merely looks on.

1.164.21 Where the smooth-gliding rays, cognizant, distill the perpetual portion of water; there has the Lord and steadfast protector all beings accepted me, though immature in wisdom.

1.164.22 In the tree into which the smooth-gliding rays feed on the sweet, enters, and again bring forth light over all, they have called the fruit sweet, but he partakes not of it who knows not the protector of the universe.

The first bird represents the individual soul, the personal self imbued with a feminine, shakti nature—the dynamic energy of the Divine. Drawn to the fruits of the tree, symbolizing sensual pleasures, that bird becomes distracted, forgets their true nature, and seeks enjoyment independently of the whole. This apparent separation marks a kind of spiritual death and symbolizes the soul's descent into the world of material existence, marked by birth, disease, aging, and death.

The second bird represents the Atman, the true, eternal Self. It does not partake of the fruit, for the Self is not a enjoyer of objects—it is the very fullness for which all seeking longs. It is complete, whole, and self-luminous.

This ancient allegory closely parallels the story of the Garden of Eden, where Adam and Eve's fall similarly symbolizes the descent from unity into duality, materialism, and sensual pleasure. It is possible that the Eden narrative itself echoes this far older teaching of the two birds and the soul's fall from grace into identification with the material world.

Later we have the Vedic Mundaka Upanishad text dated 400-300 BCE, that talk of this same ancient metaphor with its meaning:

> On the same tree a person sits grieving, drowned (in sorrow), bewildered, feeling helpless. When they see the other, powerful Lord, content, sees his greatness, they are freed from suffering. When the seer sees the brilliant maker and the Lord as the Self who has their source in Brahman, then they are wise, they shake off good and evil. Stainless, they reach the highest equanimity. *-Mundaka Upanishad* 3.1.2-3 (Roebuck & Lewis, 2025)

This is a direct continuation of the same teaching, and its deepest meaning is that of Self Realization. When one Realizes the Self they are freed from suffering, become wise, they shake off good and evil, become stainless and reach the highest equanimity. That is the Self. The Self is also called Brahman or Atman in Vedic texts but they are all one and the same.

A famous saying from the *Rig Veda* 1.164.46 (Lewis, 2025), "The wise speak of what is one in many ways". This is referring to the wise that speak of the true Self or the Atman in many ways. That's really the gist of the Upanishads and their secret teachings, tons of different ways of teaching the same truth of our true nature, our true Self in many different ways. We will go over many of those different ways to share the same truth. This same truth appears across ancient cultures and civilizations—from India to Egypt, Greece, and even China in the teachings of Taoism. Either this knowledge spread outward from a common source (perhaps the Vedic tradition), or enlightened sages in different lands independently discovered the same eternal, universal truth. Either way, the core realization remains almost identical in all.

There is some evidence to support that the Vedic teachings and Vedic wisdom reached Egypt and China. India may have been the origin of the teachings of "know thyself". The evidence for this comes from many rituals, ceremonies, gods, and the language in Egypt that seem to have Vedic similarities in addition to goods traded such as spices and the possible bloodline of ancient Indian people that have intermingled with Egypt.

We have another fascinating connection between Egypt and India in the Great Hymn to the Aten by Akhenaten of Egypt, who reigned from 1353–1336 BCE (Kak, 2003). This hymn is also strikingly similar to Psalm 104 in the Old Testament. What makes it even more interesting is that King Akhenaten may have derived his Great Hymn from Rigvedic Hymns 1.50, 4.13, and 10.37. This is one direct piece of evidence—among many—that demonstrates India's influence on Egypt. There are numerous such parallels between India and Egypt; one can read more about them in the works of Arianauova and on the Hindu Wisdom website listed in the references. The material is so extensive that it alone could fill many pages of books.

Let us dive a little deeper. One potential theory regarding the connection between ancient Egypt and ancient India lies in the Indus Valley Civilization, which was centered primarily in what is now modern-day Pakistan. This ancient civilization may date back as far as 8000 BCE or even further according to recent 2016 studies on the artifacts found there (Pandey, 2016). This would predate Egypt, Mesopotamia and all the world's civilizations. One such theory is that these ancient peoples of India left their homeland to search for a better place only to come back home to India while leaving their impressions throughout the world.

Even the Great Pyramids of Egypt have a relationship to India with their construction appearing to be based on Vastu Shastra which is an ancient science of design and architecture according to some scientists (Niranjan, 2019). There is also what appears to be a sphinx located in the region once occupied by the Indus Valley Civilization—strikingly similar to the Egyptian Sphinx—situated in Balochistan, Pakistan, at Hingol National Park.

Another intriguing claim is that an inscription from the Bhagavad Gita was allegedly found on the Step Pyramid of Djoser at Saqqara, not far from the Giza Pyramids. The cited verse is *Bhagavad Gita* 2.22: "As a person puts on new garments, giving up old ones, the Self similarly accepts new material bodies, giving up the old and useless ones" (trans. Mukundananda, 2025).

According to some reports, the inscribed slab was taken to a British museum and later sold to a private collector from a blog written by Ramanin (2020). Some researchers suggest that mainstream archaeology and Egyptology may suppress evidence of ancient Indian influence on Egypt in order to preserve the traditional narrative and mystique surrounding the pyramids.

The core message of the verse allegedly found on the Step Pyramid at Saqqara concerns the eternal nature of the true Self (Atman) and its relationship to the cycle of birth, death and rebirth, known in Sanskrit as *samsara* or reincarnation. This raises the question: why was it inscribed on the pyramid? Were there other inscriptions from ancient Vedic texts that were deliberately erased or kept hidden? It is quite possible.

There appears to be a systematic effort to "de-Vedify" the Egyptian pyramids and Egyptian civilization in general. History, after all, has largely been written by conquerors and shaped to serve their own purposes and interests; the suppression of the Vedic connection between Egypt and India seems to be one such deliberate reshaping.

The date of the completion of the step pyramid from which the verse of the Bhagavad Gita was found is 2648 BCE yet the date according to modern scholars, of the Bhagavad Gita is 200-100 BCE and the oldest physical one we have is from 1492 AD held at a library in Oxford. Was the inscription written later after the construction of the step pyramid? Or was it placed there during its construction and the dating we have of the Bhagavad Gita is incorrect?

Many ancient Indian texts may be far older than previously thought. These teachings and stories were initially transmitted orally and only written down much later, meaning they could be significantly older than we typically give them credit for.

In his book *Return of the Aryans* (1994), Bhagwan Gidwani speculates that Indian civilization can be traced back to 8000 BCE. He argues that the British deliberately created the myth that Indians have always been ruled by foreigners, thereby distorting their true history. Gidwani further asserts that the Vedas were composed around 4000 BCE—much earlier than traditional scholars claim. This would predate the pyramids of Egypt.

A more popular theory as to the roots of ancient Egypt lies in the ancient lost civilization of Atlantis. Some scholars speculate that Egypt was founded by ancient Atlanteans. There appears to be much more evidence for Egypt's Indian roots than there is for Atlantean roots. There is only a small amount of historical evidence we have for that and indirect evidence but with the India roots we have direct evidence, direct connections, direct a lot of things. Even the Egyptian language and writing is similar to Sanskrit. The name Egypt may have come from the Sanskrit word *Ajap*, the Nile River may have come from the Sanskrit word for blue which is *Nila*. The great Egyptian ruler Ramses's name may have come from the Hindu god Rama. There are many undeniable similarities all across the board between India and Egypt including many of the gods (Hindu Wisdom, 2006 and L. Sara 2025).

TAKSHASHILA

Before we finish off this topic of the history of the Self and know thyself, which can consume many books, we must talk about a couple of the most incredible places of learning in all of antiquity. The first place was the premiere learning center of the world starting around 600 BCE and lasted for almost a 1000 years. The name of this center is called *Takshashila* in Sanskrit and the Greeks called it Taxila. Taxila lies in what is modern day Northern Pakistan smack dab at the crossroads of the Silk Road that divided the east and the west. Taxila was a haven for learning and teaching and the spreading of Vedic knowledge that cultivated into a mix of world knowledge that spread around the globe.

At that time, Taxila was the main seed that planted the knowledge of the Self to the world as far east as China to as far west to Greece and beyond. Taxila was humongous with close to 10,000 students learning more than 60 different topics from science to medicine to arts, etc. These students would go on to shape the world, driving major advancements in science and academia, as well as in what we are focused on here: Self Realization. Students from across the world studied at Taxila, including Greeks, Babylonians, Chinese, Egyptians, Arabs, Turks, and many others.

Many ancient Greek thinkers are said to have studied at Taxila. Among the most notable are Pythagoras, Thales, Empedocles, Democritus, and Plato—all of whom are rumored to have traveled there for instruction. In his writings, Philostratus mentions that Pythagoras studied with naked sages in India. It is even suggested that Pythagoras (c. 570–495 BCE) derived his famous theorem from the Vedic Baudhayana Sulba Sutra (c. 800 BCE).

It is quite possible that many of the brilliant Greek scholars of the time obtained a significant portion of their knowledge from India, as Hindu philosophical and scientific ideas spread widely throughout Greece. Later, Alexander the Great reached Taxila and conquered the region in 326 BCE. It is said that he took numerous teachers and scholars from Taxila back to Greece with him.

At the turn of the millennium, even the Apostle Thomas is confirmed by numerous sources to have traveled to India and studied at Taxila. The Gospel of Thomas sounds remarkably similar to the Upanishadic teachings on the Self.

ALEXANDRIA

Another one of the most remarkable cities of antiquity is Alexandria in Egypt. Founded by Alexander the Great in 331 BCE, it was built to be one of the greatest centers of learning and philosophy of its time. Many Greek philosophers, along with scholars from around the world, came to Alexandria to study ancient knowledge and the secrets of the universe. The city was home to one of the largest libraries of the ancient world and was considered the capital of knowledge and learning at that time.

As the centuries passed, the Great Library of Alexandria was repeatedly set ablaze and partially destroyed by successive invaders. Finally, a massive tsunami in 365 AD—triggered by a powerful earthquake in the Mediterranean—devastated what remained and caused the library's precise location to vanish from historical record. In that catastrophe, we also lost the tomb of Alexander the Great, which Egyptian archaeologists are still searching for today.

Not only are there striking similarities between Hindu and Egyptian deities, but also between Greek and Hindu gods. The ancient Greeks were deeply familiar with the maxim "know thyself" and even elaborated on it through the writings attributed to Hermes Trismegistus. Most likely, these teachings were brought from India.

GOSPEL OF THOMAS

Further along in history, we have Christian teachings from the Gnostic texts suggesting a similar concept to Atman or the true Self as that of ancient India. In the Gospel of Thomas (3b) Jesus says: "When you know yourselves, then you will be known, and you will understand that you are children of the living Father. But if you do not **know yourselves**, then you live in poverty, and you are the poverty." (Patterson & Meyer, 1992)

The Gospel of Thomas can be traced back to 130-180 AD, hundreds of years after the Greek and Egypt "know thyself" and much later after the concept of Atman from Vedic texts. It is reasonable to conclude that the peoples discussed here freely shared this profound knowledge with one another.

Vedic texts most likely reached Egypt from India then some of the Greek scholars that did travel to Egypt took it back to Greece and from there it may have been part of the foundation for the Gnostics. As mentioned the Apostle Thomas went to India himself and learned the teachings of the ancient Vedic texts. At the turn of the millennia the Apostle Thomas is confirmed by numerous sources to have traveled to India and even studied at Taxila. This makes perfect sense when one compares the secret sayings of Jesus in the Gospel of Thomas with the Upanishadic teachings on the Self.

Jesus says to them, "When you make the two into one, and when you make the inner like the outer and the outer like the inner, and the upper like the lower, and when you make male and female into a single one, so that the male will not be male nor the female be female, when you make eyes in place of an eye, a hand in place of a hand, a foot in place of a foot, an image in place of an image, then you will enter [the kingdom]." — *Gospel of Thomas*, 22 (Patterson & Meyer, 1992)

It's worth noting that in Egypt there are Egyptian hieroglyphic inscriptions that read: Smai Tawi or uniting Upper Egypt with Lower Egypt which could be a reference to Self Realization. We will go over that a little later.

The four Mahavakyas of the *Upanishads* (700–100 BCE):

1. "*Prajnanam Brahma*" (Consciousness is God)

2. "*Aham Brahmasmi*" (I am God)

3. "*Tat Tvam Asi*" (Thou art God)

4. "*Ayam Atma Brahma*" (The Self is God)

Kena Upanishad 2:1–3 (Radhakrishnan, 2024)

2:1 If you think you have understood Brahman well, you know it but slightly, whether it refers to you (the individual self) or to the gods. So then is it to be investigated by you (the pupil) (even though) I think it is known.

2:2 I do not think that I know it well; nor do I think that I do not know it. He who among us knows it, knows it and he, too, does not know that he does not know.

2:3 To whomsoever it is not known, to him it is known: to whomsoever it is known, he does not know. It is not understood by those who understand it; it is understood by those who do not understand it.

GNOSTICISM ROOTS

There seems to be some cross over from Gnosticism and Vedic teachings of the Self. In fact the Vedic origins seem to be the main driver of the teachings of the Egyptian and Greek mystery schools, Buddhism and Gnosticism as noted in the first chapter. One of the great Hindu Philosophers Swami Vivakananda, even states that the entire world's philosophy originated from India (Murty, 2014). It's a fascinating idea that has some credible evidence to support this.

Not long ago, while I was riding my bike and listening first to the Ashtavakra Gita and then switching to Gnostic texts like the Gospel of Thomas, I was struck by how similar they sounded. The ideas in both clearly overlap. I was astounded.

In the Gospel of Thomas, Jesus is unmistakably teaching non-duality. He is speaking directly about emptiness and nothingness. The "Kingdom" he describes is none other than Self Realization. Many of his teachings feel less like ordinary parables and more like Zen-style koans—short, paradoxical statements designed to shatter conceptual thinking and provoke direct awakening which koans are designed to do.

Look at this from the Gospel of Thomas (17), where Jesus said: "I will give you what no eye has seen, what no ear has heard, what no hand has touched, and what has not entered into the heart of man."

What is cannot be seen, cannot be heard, and cannot be touched. It is the true Self, beyond all illusory senses and beyond the mind. This is a direct reference to Self Realization.

Here is a brief historical timeline for reference—it is by no means complete, but it serves as a useful starting point. These dates are estimates, as there is always some margin of error, especially the further back one goes in antiquity, where the evidence becomes increasingly murky.

This timeline is based on the working hypothesis that ancient wisdom flowed from India to Egypt (rather than the conventional theory of Egypt influencing India, or the alternative idea of Atlantis influencing Egypt). Who knows—perhaps the ultimate origin of the world's most ancient structures and teachings is Atlantean or Lemurian. I simply don't have enough evidence yet to assert that. For now, I am proceeding with the hypothesis of an Indian origin, specifically linked to the Indus Valley Civilization (IVC).

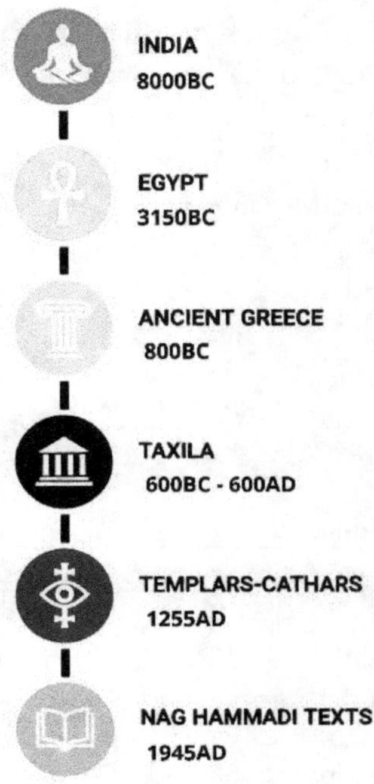

To summarize we can theorize that the origin of Self Realization or "know thyself" may very well stem from the ancient Indus Valley Civilization as early as 8000 BCE then made its way into ancient Egypt in 3150 BCE then into Ancient Greece around 600 BCE by way of the great university of Taxila, then into the modern Bible and Gnostic texts over the turn of the millennia nearing 100 AD. That's as far as I could trace it as the further we go into deep antiquity, the scarcer and less certain the information becomes. Also I completely omitted out ancient Mesopotamia but upon examination there are definitely major interactions between the IVC and them as seen by an ample amount of physical evidence as well as the close geographical proximity between each other.

We have a myriad of connections between Egypt and India as well as Greece and India that are undeniable. That's not to mention the many connections between Vedic teachings probably stemming from Taxila to many other parts of the world including China and its teachings on Taoism. We can write an entire book just on that subject and go into much greater detail on the origins and interpretations of "know thyself" and its profound significance around the world.

EXTRA:

Egyptians came from Atlantis?

https://www.reddit.com/r/GrahamHancock/comments/10fkiir/hopi_sumerian_egyptian_accounts_of_atlantis/

"Among those influenced by Akhaldan learning were such seminal individuals as Pythagoras and Moses. Ancient Egyptian texts speak of Seven Sages who were survivors of Atlantis and planned the monuments and pyramids of Egypt. They were "divine beings who knew how the temples and sacred places were to be created." The Sages were divine survivors of a previous cataclysm who made a new beginning. Originally, they came from an island – the Homeland of the Primeval Ones – the majority of whose divine inhabitants were drowned.

Arriving in Egypt, the survivors became "the builder Gods, who fashioned in the primeval time, the Lords of Light . . . the Ghosts, the Ancestors . . . who raised the seed for gods and men . . . the Senior Ones who came into being at the beginning, who illumined this land when they came forth unitedly."

The correlation with Gurdjieff's description of the second Transapalnian perturbation, which caused the island of Atlantis "to enter within the planet," and with the surviving members of Beelzebub's tribe and the Society of Akhaldans who resettled in the region of Ethiopia and Egypt."

Not to discredit the incredible work of historians and archaeologists, but I personally find the India–Egypt connection far more convincing, simply because we have vastly more information and evidence supporting it. If substantial physical or written proof of Atlantis ever surfaced, that would of course change the discussion—but as of now, we have very little concrete evidence to work with. Atlantis may well have existed somewhere and still awaits discovery. For the moment, it remains one of the greatest unsolved mysteries of the world.

Chapter 2

THE HAPPINESS MYTH

Some time ago, I was running races, traveling the world, and working long hours—a lifestyle that filled a good chunk of my life. I carried this idea that if I could just visit more countries and see more places, I would be happy. If I competed in more races and won more of them, I would be happy. If I made more money, I would be happy.

The key word there is "would"—always pushing happiness into some future moment once the next goal was attained.

The versions of happiness that society sells us as reality are nothing but myths. They are illusory concepts that keep us chasing tomorrow and blind us to happiness which is in the NOW—the present moment where true happiness actually resides, in the Self.

Happiness is our very existence, Happiness is our very nature. I didn't realize this at the time pursuing all those endeavors, as most of us don't. Most don't realize it because we are so caught up in the dream of this world chasing illusions of happiness. It's when we stop looking outside of ourselves, when we stop chasing the mirage of happiness that we find happiness. Happiness is who we are and has nothing to do with anything outside of us. It's not that we find anything, it's that we simply realize what we already are, we are happiness itself. Happiness is the Self and you are THAT!

THE GIFT

Many years ago, after years of competitive sports, my body simply said no more. A genetic switch was flipped where my iron levels got higher and higher. At the time I didn't know why I felt so exhausted all the time. I didn't understand why my brain was so foggy. I didn't understand why my body hurt and I could barely get out of bed. I had a hard time in college studying with all the brain fog and cognitive disruption.

Luckily around this time a gift presented itself to me. I met a wonderful partner and adopted (more like she adopted me) a wonderful cat named Lucy. Lucky Lucy seems to flow quite nicely. This was probably one of the darker periods of my life. Being in bed half the time feeling like death and not having a release for my pent up emotions from non favorable emotional programs that were installed when I was a kid. I ran less and less and competed less and less as my body could not deal with the physical stress of training and running so much. My mind was in disarray and I faltered as most do when they reach the end of one part of life's journey and the beginning of another.

Luckily at this time as well I got more and more involved with helping out at races rather than competing in them. Oddly enough my heart seemed to fill itself with love, kindness and compassion more and more as I served others rather than competed with them. The more I helped others, cheered them on and encouraged them, the better I felt. I never really understood why I felt so good after doing this. I would feel like I was in a higher energy state like almost on a different frequency as though I was floating on air, ecstatic.

Later while doing neurofeedback brain wave training I experimented with thinking positive and negative words and I found something interesting. The more negative words I thought the more my alpha brain waves went down and beta went up. While the more positive words I thought the more my alpha and gamma went up and beta went down. Alpha brain waves are the slower, more relaxed, feel good brain waves while beta are the higher frequency, agitated, anxiety, fight or flight type of brain waves.

It finally dawned on me some time later that the mind cannot tell the difference between negative or positive words towards oneself or towards others. The brain wave changes are the same if the words are directed at oneself or if they are directed at others. Maybe there really is something to this whole idea and notion that we are "one". This also gave me a greater understanding as to why I felt so good helping people and cheering people on each weekend. This goes to show the reality is, we really are each other.

This is a big lesson that shows us that negative gossip or speaking ill of anyone can hurt us by decreasing alpha brain waves and increasing beta brain waves. That saying—"If you don't have anything nice to say, don't say anything at all"—is quite on point. For example, if you go on social media, you will see many negative comments. People often don't realize that they are causing pain both to others and to themselves, because, technically, there are no others." We are all connected—there's no doubt about it.

For hours on the weekends, I would serve others by giving them water or snacks and cheering them on with positive words and encouragement as well as taking their pictures. Service and words are two of the love languages and some say service is one of the most powerful. In fact there is a whole branch of Yoga dedicated to serving others called Karma Yoga. While serving others, I felt so good almost like I was blissed out in another dimension. A little time after coming home, I would have a lower energy emotional programmed response and start to snap out of the high I felt. Someone would irritate me whether driving or doing something that annoyed me and I would get upset, or better to say the fictitious ego would get upset as a program was triggered to invoke an emotional response.

The issue with the current state of the world is our disconnection from each other and from the Self. We can go from disconnection to connection and realizing the Self is definitely a huge part. If the world realized the Self then everything would be a perfect utopia. That will probably never be the case because this world was not built for the freedom of Self Realization, it was built to keep us in a beta brain wave state as we will see later with numerous data points and evidence to support this.

"As we grow in our consciousness (the Self), there will be more compassion & more love, and then the barriers between people, between religions, between nations will begin to fall." - Ram Dass

SOCIAL SHAPING

Society tells us what we need to do or be in order to be happy. The issue with that is it teaches us that there is some external source of happiness which is disingenuous. The truth is happiness is found in the ever present NOW and HERE. Although it is worth noting the Self is beyond all sense of time and space and "now" is simply a reference point for the mind to be able to grasp the idea. The Self is beyond all space and time but the present, here and now is the closest way to describe the Self so it will work for the purposes of this book.

The idea that one has to make a certain amount of money, drive a certain car, own a certain house, travel to a certain country, find the perfect partner, win a race, etc. is a fruitless, never ending trap of this world. And the world is full of traps. Sure one will find temporary non-lasting happiness and pleasure in fleeting experiences and possessions but the permanent form of happiness and peace will never be found until one goes inside themselves to the source, to the Self. Unfortunately society has shaped and molded people subconsciously, having them chase these illusions of happiness and pushing one further away from the Self.

Self Realization is the only pursuit truly worthwhile in this life. We must Realize who we are beyond thought, beyond the mind, and beyond the body; this is the only path to true and lasting happiness. Most people have experienced fleeting moments of the Self through some form, yet they do not fully understand what those moments signify. There may have been a quieting of thought and an anchoring in the present moment brought about by one of many things: exercise, encounters with extreme beauty, non-understanding that transcends the mind and induces stillness, complete surrender and letting go, a near-death experience, and so on.

As Ramana Maharshi said—and this cannot be reiterated enough: **"The only worthwhile pursuit of this life is to realize the Self."**

There is simply nothing anyone needs to do for happiness except Realize the Self. It is here right now and you are THAT! Of course we all have our jobs, careers, families and whatever it may be and that's going to keep happening regardless of Self Realization or not. What does change is that there is no more mental resistance upon anything that anyone does any longer. There's a great saying that illustrates this: "Before enlightenment, chop wood carry water, after enlightenment, chop wood carry water."

The benefits of Self Realization do not end with permanent, abiding happiness. They transcend the very boundaries of comprehension and understanding, and they help others in profound ways by shining a light on the path out of worldly misery and suffering. How many are stuck in the same routine, same thinking and programming, immersed in the madness of the world and don't know how to escape? Probably the majority of the population chases these short term pleasures as a means of escapism and as a means of an unconscious pursuit of the Self. True escape of bondage is only through Self Realization and the Self is the key to ultimate freedom. Self Realization is the only way to escape this world of madness and insanity. No matter what one does they will never change the world, one can only "change" themselves by Realizing the Self.

Insanity is often described as doing the same thing over and over again expecting different results. Are you ready to break free from the cycle of insanity and do something different? Are you ready to Realize who you truly are? Are you ready for ultimate freedom and to escape from the bondage suffering? It is so simple yet so difficult because very few people even know about Self Realization, let alone teach it. There's so many self help gurus out there that convince everyone to do this or to do that, you need this or need that to become happy when in reality they are not happy themselves. They are selling a mirage, an illusion and yet the masses eat it up like candy because everyone else is doing it and the crowd likes to follow the crowd. It's the blind leading the blind.

Matthew 15:14 *King James Version*:
"Let them alone: they be blind leaders of the blind. And if the blind lead the blind, both shall fall into the ditch."

To Realize the Self, one must go against the crowd. One must have the courage to turn away from the path of normalcy and break free from the prison of the mind and societal conditioning.

This not only can be done—it must be done if one is ever to Realize the Self. Another way to see it is as layers of societal norms and conditioning wrapped tightly around us. These layers must be shattered into pieces to reveal the true Self beneath.

There will be challenges and difficulties as one begins the journey and all the way to the end the challenges will continue. But I promise you if you pursue the Self with all your **heart**, the journey will be worth it and one will finally see the true radiant, effervescent, shining, Self. The Self that shines brighter and is more radiant than a million suns times a million. You are THAT! Be happy, be free!

Chapter 3

BRAIN WAVES

For me, the truth of Self Realization was ultimately confirmed through a scientific insight that bridged modern understanding with ancient wisdom: brain waves offer a measurable link between consciousness and science.

Numerous measurements of yogis, enlightened and Self Realized beings from all walks of life have had their brain waves measured and recorded. Brain waves are indeed a very interesting part of the puzzle to Self Realization. Although as we shall see later, it is only a small piece of the puzzle as it can also be part of the trap and make the ego stronger or it can be a tool to Self Realization. We will discuss both but first we must go over a few basics.

Let us turn our attention to brain waves and lay a scientific foundation and then connect it to Self Realization then we shall elaborate further and the reason for this as we go along will become ever clearer. It's fascinating to realize that our brains constantly generate measurable electrical activity in the form of brain waves. These electrical impulses are produced in the thalamus and cortex regions of our brain and are measured in Hertz or cycles per second.

Here's a brief overview of the different brain waves (Pearce, 2025):

- **Gamma (30–100 Hz)** The fastest brainwave, associated with peak consciousness, flow states, **compassion**, intuition, advanced cognitive processing, and heightened information integration.

- **Beta (12–30 Hz)** The predominant waking state. Beta is linked to focused attention, problem-solving, and active thinking, but also to stress, anxiety, fight-or-flight responses, and arousal.

- **Alpha (8–12 Hz)** Appears when we are alert yet relaxed. Alpha is considered a resting state for the brain, enhances learning, and is the primary brainwave of meditation and the "flow state."

- **Theta (4–8 Hz)** Present during deep relaxation, meditation, and dream-filled (REM) sleep. Theta is connected to creativity, intuition, and memory processing. Hypnotists deliberately induce this state to access and reprogram the subconscious mind. Advanced meditators can also consciously enter Theta while remaining awake.

- **Delta (0.5–4 Hz)** The slowest brainwave, dominant in deep, dreamless sleep. Delta is associated with profound healing, bodily rejuvenation, and access to the deepest layers of the unconscious. The ancient traditions teach that in this state we are all naturally Self Realized. One of the ultimate goals of spiritual practice, therefore, is to make the unconscious conscious—to bring this **mindless** state of deep sleep into waking awareness, which is known as **turiya** (the fourth state) or pure consciousness. We will talk about turiya a little later.

One can see there are many fascinating aspects of brain waves. Every person on earth produces their own unique sets of brain waves. Maybe the most interesting of all, is that every single aspect of a person's life is associated with brain waves. We produce brain waves in all fashions and forms until the day we die. When I first learned about brain waves I was intrigued. To learn that mystical states of consciousness are measurable through brain waves is simply incredible. There's a specific brain wave pattern for people who see angels, there's a specific brain wave pattern for kundalini experiences, there's a specific brain wave pattern for out of body experiences (OBEs), there's a specific brain wave pattern for seeing auras, there a specific brain wave pattern for Self Realization, there's a specific brain wave pattern for everything. Although, ultimately, Self Realization is not reliant on any brain waves as its the background awareness that determines Self Realization and not anything that comes and goes such as brain waves.

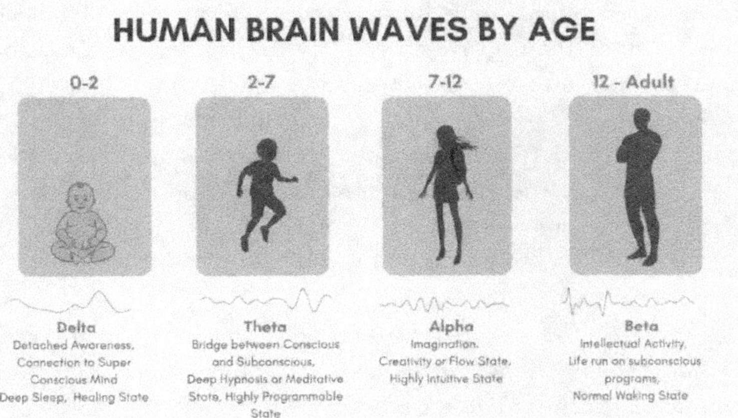

Not to say brain waves are not important, they most certainly are but to focus entirely on brain waves and nothing else would be folly. As the brain is part of the body which is part of this dream or 'maya' like nature of this reality. One simply cannot reach Self Realization solely by focusing on brain waves but if it is used in combination with other practices, methods and knowledge then it can become quite a powerful tool to complement other practices to aid in Self Realization.

The majority of people in life and society are predominantly in a beta brain wave state of 12-30Hz. A problem solving, 'fight or flight', past or present, busy minded state. Our society is fueled by addiction and consumption of caffeine, nicotine, alcohol which keeps us in a predominantly faster brain wave state of beta. On every street corner there's a coffee shop, a bar or a liquor store to buy one's fix of alcohol, nicotine or caffeine. All three of which dramatically reduce our levels of alpha brain waves and increase beta brain waves. The social norm is to ingest these substances.

Over and over again we see advertisements for coffee, beer, and not so many for cigarettes anymore compared to the past. Study after study shows us the benefits of coffee and alcohol or wine being touted in some way. One needs to ask who is benefiting or profiting from these studies? And why aren't they showing the other side of the spectrum, the negative aspects of drug consumption. Come to find out there's a reason for this and we will look at it here shortly. Needless to say this is more evidence there are traps of consciousness everywhere. It's safe to surmise that the entire world is set up to trap and ensnare our consciousness and to keep us from Realizing the Self.

Caffeine is the most consumed drug in the world. Ever drink coffee for a week and then just stop? Yes, that's called withdrawal. Anything that causes a withdrawal needs to be consumed sparingly. I'm not saying avoid all these substances 24/7, I'm saying ingest them infrequently. Regular consumption of alcohol, caffeine or nicotine is destructive and detrimental to the human organism especially to our brain waves and acts as an obstacle to Self Realization by causing agitation rather than stillness.

CAFFEINE CONSPIRACY

Since the most consumed drug in the world is indeed caffeine and there's a Starbucks on every street corner does it not make one think that maybe, just maybe there's a reason for that? Maybe whoever is controlling or in charge of society wants us hooked on these substances to possibly keep us disconnected from the Self. It has shown caffeine does decrease alpha, theta and delta and increase beta dramatically. Increasing alpha increases our intelligence and makes us feel more clear headed. Slowing down our brain waves into alpha helps us see the world through a clearer lens.

With increased alpha and gamma comes increased love, compassion, empathy and kindness and more connection to the Self. Imagine if the world was more loving, compassionate and kind to each other? Imagine all the wars that can be avoided, imagine all the lives saved, imagine all the money saved, imagine the end of needless suffering. Imagine if people loved one another and said kind things to each other. Imagine a better world. Alpha brain waves are the stepping stone to the Self from a brain wave perspective as its the bridge from the conscious to the subconscious.

CAFFEINE NICOTINE ALCOHOL

While doing neurofeedback feedback training we were told to abstain from caffeine, alcohol and nicotine as those all decrease alpha brain waves. I did not believe it at first until I saw the data first hand. During a training week, there was some concern about a trainee whose brain wave measurements were dramatically low, as much as 30-40% lower than normal. Nobody understood why he was having such low numbers. Then upon his next training the trainers heard a wrapper in the chamber where he was doing neurofeedback. At the break they examined the chamber and noticed a chocolate protein bar wrapper. After that chocolate bar was discarded the next day his numbers shot right back up to normal. Most people don't know this but chocolate has a little bit of caffeine and even a little bit of caffeine dramatically lowers slower brain waves such as alpha, theta and delta. Even the caffeine in green tea causes tremendous dips in those slower brain waves. After I saw this firsthand I never touched caffeine again albeit some chocolate here and there.

A quick data search on Google will give these numbers:

* Around 80-90% of the world drink caffeine in one way shape or form.

* Around 32.5% of the world consumes alcohol.

* Around 20% of the world smokes cigarettes.

What do all those have in common? Besides all those substances being super addicting, most of the world is living in a beta brain wave state, disconnected from the Self and would have a hard time getting into a slower brain wave state such as alpha or theta due to the agitation caused by these substances. Most people are living in a state of borderline madness which can be expressed as beta brain wave state.

The more the beta brain waves the greater the madness and the further from the Self. You know those who can never sit still— the ones who talk rapidly, walk briskly with a latte in hand, and constantly criticize everyone around them? They are trapped in a high-beta brainwave state, mistakenly identifying with the restless mind and body instead of their true Self. And it seems this is no accident; modern society appears deliberately designed to keep us locked in that very state.

Interestingly enough there are those that promote caffeinated beverages as well as brain enhancement training. I once walked into a neurofeedback center to get a brain mapping done and noticed the facilitator drinking coffee I turned around and walked right out. It seems a bit contrary and makes no logical sense from a scientific standpoint. Reminds me of the sci-fi story I read long ago about a company that opens up in a city and gives away free candy and chocolate. More and more people eat chocolate and candy, more and more they gain lots of weight and become obese until nearly the entire population is morbidly obese. Soon after, the company that gave away all the free candy opens up a weight loss company with a very high price tag to lose weight. They raked in a fortune by creating a problem for free then selling a solution for a high price.

NEUROFEEDBACK TRAINING

I first heard about brain waves and neurofeedback years ago. I don't remember exactly when—it was a long time ago—but I do remember the claim: that one could experience the effects of decades of meditation over the course of a single week. Even at the time, it sounded a bit too good to be true. I remember seeing the price tag and thinking it was more than I was willing to pay, so I let it go, though the idea stayed with me in the back of my mind.

Years later, after finally saving enough money, I decided to attend. In the weeks leading up to the experience, I was meditating heavily, doing what I could to prepare. I expected the course to be consciousness-focused and meditative in nature. Part of me believed that simply attending might lead to enlightenment—or even Self Realization. If the promise of decades' worth of meditation effects were accurate, then it had to lead somewhere meaningful, or at least offer a significant shift.

What I eventually discovered, however, was that it was far more of a marketing narrative than a genuine shortcut to realization. The promises of accelerated enlightenment, rapid transformation, and measurable gains in intelligence or emotional insight were largely unsubstantiated. There were flashy claims, carefully designed environments, and rituals that made the experience feel important and profound, but in practice, much of it relied on suggestion and expectation rather than real, sustained inner work. The techniques themselves had value, to be sure, but they were packaged in a way that emphasized spectacle over substance. It was less about cultivating a lasting shift in consciousness and more about selling the idea of rapid transformation. Over time, I realized that the real work—the deep, ongoing practice of awareness, reflection, and self-inquiry—couldn't be shortcut by a week in a chamber, no matter how alluring the promises sounded.

Alongside the promise of compressed meditation effects, they also claimed improvements in intelligence, emotional intelligence, and creativity. I told myself that even modest gains in those areas might justify the cost. What struck me as odd, though, was that they didn't test anyone before or after the training. There were no baseline measurements, no follow-up assessments—nothing that would make it possible to verify whether any of these improvements actually occurred.

The night before the training began, I checked into a somewhat run-down hotel, feeling more uneasy than excited. The week-long alpha neurofeedback program was scheduled to start the next morning. After a restless night of sleep, I drove the short distance to the center, still entertaining the possibility that this might be some kind of turning point. As I walked inside, I wondered—briefly—whether this place might answer long-standing questions or accelerate my so-called Self Realization. Time would answer that question quickly.

The building itself felt dated, frozen somewhere in the 1980s: worn carpets, painted walls, and decorative elements that seemed intended to suggest depth and mystique rather than anything substantive. Artwork was scattered throughout, alongside carefully placed lighting and symbolic design touches meant to create an atmosphere of significance. I felt mildly uncomfortable entering a room full of strangers, though everyone was polite enough.

There were only three participants in the program, plus the trainer. A couple of staff members handled the daily placement of electrodes; they were friendly and professional, though clearly just following a routine. The other two participants were an older married couple attending primarily for relationship issues. It was their second time at the center, which I took less as a vote of confidence and more as a reminder that whatever this was, it hadn't resolved much the first time around. I focused on keeping my attention on my own experience and expectations.

The trainer was very nice and cordial, but they spoke at length, which made me question whether this was really a place that claimed to replace years of sustained meditative practice with a single week of training. Everyone seemed to talk constantly, and it gradually became clear to me that few, if any, of the people there actually meditated or practiced mindfulness—at least that was how it appeared and felt. Even the trainer remarked, "You do not need to meditate." I was genuinely taken aback. Was the training truly so effective that meditation itself had become unnecessary, or was something else being substituted in its place?

As the day went on, there was so much talking that my head began to ache. I wasn't used to it. For me, excessive conversation only creates confusion and agitation. Words are inherently dualistic; they pull attention outward and away from the eternal truth—the Self within. I wasn't sure the trainer understood this, because the talking continued, hour after hour, as if it would never end.

Even after the day was over, I could still hear the reverberations of voices looping in my mind as I lay in bed trying to sleep. That observation would later become a key to my own liberation and freedom in realizing the Self. Who was the one observing those thoughts? We are not the mind. We are not the thoughts. We are the observer beyond them. That is the Self. That is you. You are **THAT!**

At least for me, neurofeedback was completely new and exciting; for the other two participants, it felt more like a refresher course. Our first time in the chamber on day one was a learning experience. We experimented with any meditative techniques or approaches we wanted, exploring what might work best for us. Later, we would learn the main protocol, which revolved around a forgiveness process. You think about an event or situation that caused you pain and sit with that feeling for a few minutes, then consider a gift or lesson learned from it, put yourself in the other person's shoes, and finally direct loving-kindness toward the person—through visualization, a hug, or whatever felt natural.

The days during the training were long—around twelve hours or so. We entered the chamber with electrodes attached to our heads a couple of times throughout the day. I'm not sure exactly how long, because we had to turn in our phones—a bit of a red flag—and were instructed to "let go of time" and enter a place of timelessness. If I had to guess, it added up to a few hours in total, spread across multiple sessions practicing the techniques. The first day was mostly an adjustment period, focused on learning how to perform the core forgiveness method.

When I learned we would mostly be doing the forgiveness process I was a little disappointed. All the money and time I'm going to spend here just to do a forgiveness process. When the facilitator told us we would be doing a forgiveness process, I told them I don't have anyone to forgive as I have forgiven everyone already. Needless to say my egoic response was trying to hinder my progress from the get go. This seems to be a common thought by nearly everyone on the first day of the program but as the days go by one gets the hang of the process and gains a greater understanding of the benefits of the forgiveness method.

After being used to meditating for long periods of time I was not used to the constant talking but I was used to being in a dark chamber, being as still as possible. I must admit that talking did help me with learning about emotions to release them and becoming more emotionally intelligent which is helpful. How can we let go and dissolve into nothingness—which is Self Realization—

If we subconsciously suppress or avoid our own emotions, or lack emotional intelligence? How can we release emotions if we do not first recognize them? Developing emotional intelligence can be profoundly helpful on this path. While it is still possible to attain Self Realization without consciously addressing the emotional component, the journey is likely to take much longer.

There's also a counter argument that says we don't need to know the emotions we just need not identify with them and only identify with the observer or witness or awareness beyond the mind and emotions aka our true Self. One may get a more rapid progression in consciousness or Self Realization if one becomes emotionally more intelligent but up to a point then that must be let go. Everything must be let go of in order to reach nothingness—or emptiness—which is the existential ground of the true Self. One can only grasp the Self with an empty hand.

Let us digress slightly. When we are young we accumulate traumas, sanskaras, emotional wounds, whatever you want to call them. These can be something as simple as your mom not letting you have ice cream then we feel a heightened negative emotion. It could be a heightened emotional reaction as a child to the dentist or the doctor or to bright lights or to a certain food or to anything really. This heightened negative emotion gets stuck in our body and mind if it is not let go or released. It just continues to play itself out on a loop until resolved. This loop causes agitation and decreases stillness and increases beta brain waves thus furthering us from the Self.

This unresolved trauma or heightened emotional charge can manifest whenever someone says a particular word—such as "No," for example. Many people feel instantly triggered by that single word. In fact, it's one of the most common triggers I've observed in real life: someone asks for something, you say no, and they immediately become angry, sad, or emotionally flooded.

We accumulate countless such imprints over the years, especially when we are young, because children naturally spend much of their time in slower brainwave states that are highly receptive—almost identical to hypnosis:

- 0–2 years: predominantly **Delta**
- 2–7 years: predominantly **Theta**
- 7–12 years: predominantly **Alpha**
- After age 12: predominantly **Beta**

(as shown in the chart below)

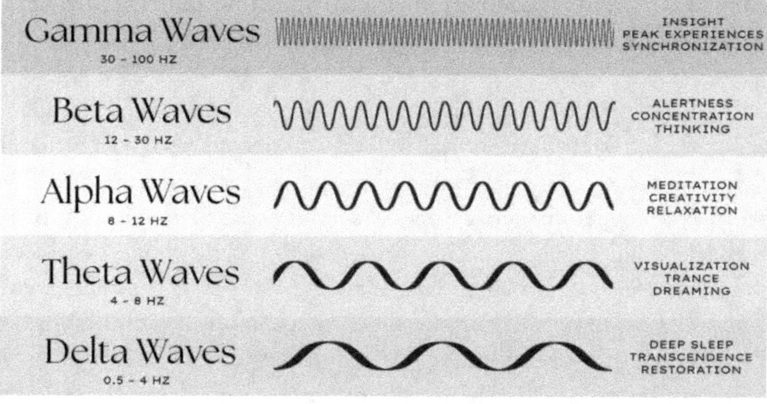

These slower brainwave states make the brain very susceptible to programming and the embedding of trauma. During hypnosis, one enters a theta brainwave state, where programs can even be added or removed, akin to a computer. In many ways, the mind functions like a vast AI supercomputer. This is not to say that traumas cannot accumulate in adulthood—they certainly can, as we still see the residue of the global trauma from 2020. Traumas can accumulate in adulthood in many ways: for example, people who witness their families die in war zones, grow up in extreme poverty, or experience severe personal suffering such as assault, gun violence, or other extreme pain or misfortune. Any number of events can cause these traumas. These are unresolved traumatic emotions, and they siphon off one's life-force energy. The mind and body try to release them, but when they do not know how, the same loops replay over and over until a person either dies or the trauma is resolved or released.

Good news, all of these traumas can be released with the methods we will go over and rather quickly. Anything which may have created a trauma or emotional scar, one could quickly release that emotional bond and cut it for good and release that energy that is being siphoned off. Energy is released when that emotional wound is healed. One can feel the increased energy and see it in the form of alpha and gamma brain waves and this will help one inch closer to Self Realization. Inch closer to Self Realization is used metaphorically as we are all already Self Realized it just its covered up with layers of the mind and programs.

The reality is, we are all energy beings at the core. I like to think of us as light slowed down in a water medium in a biological meat suit. After neurofeedback training I am left with the impression that emotional energy is a primary driver for most illnesses or at the very least related to all. First, there's an unresolved emotional wound, then that energy manifests itself physically. We almost all know of someone who's very angry and has had a heart attack. That's the simplest example. In TCM or Traditional Chinese Medicine different emotions manifest themselves in different organs of the body:

In TCM or Traditional Chinese Medicine different emotions manifest themselves in different organs of the body (Tierra, 1998):

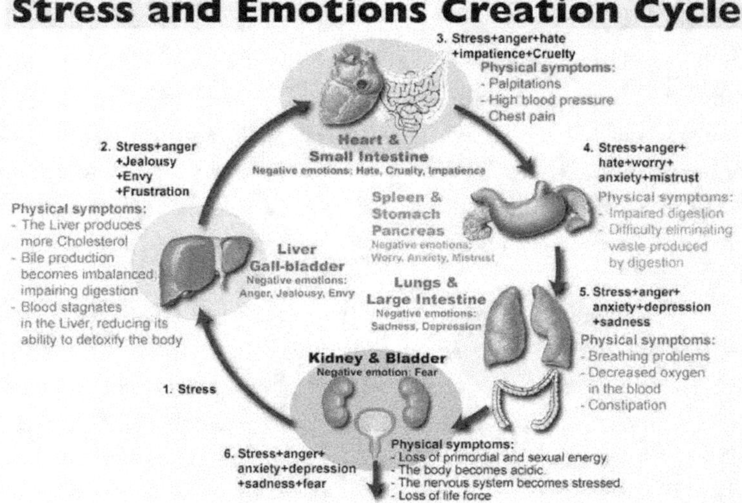

Each day throughout the week at the center, we learned a little more to expand our healing tool box—such as ho'oponopono, inner-child meditation, child rescue, the love algorithm, and rescripting—but the main and most powerful process was the forgiveness method. All these techniques focus on developing love, kindness and compassion. All of these tools are based on love. Love for the self and for others, but ultimately there are no others as we saw with the effects of negative and positive words. The key to Self Realization is opening the heart.

All the visualization techniques that I did focused on incorporating the 5 love languages: time, touch, words, gifts and service. When we are spending time with someone we are showing love. When we give a hug, a handshake, a kiss a fist bump we are showing love. When we are saying kind words to one another we are showing love. When we give each other gifts we are showing each other love. Maybe the most powerful form of love is service to others. This loving kindness and compassion will be extremely important later as we talk about breaking the knot of the heart.

In yogic teachings service is called seva. Seva is when one serves others selflessly with no expectation of gain or reward. It could be anything from helping an elderly person cross the street. Cleaning up and doing the dishes. Serving food to the homeless. There are many, many kinds of seva one can perform. The practice of seva is so profound and impactful that it became the cornerstone of Karma Yoga, a branch of yogic discipline devoted entirely to selfless service as a path to spiritual growth and Self Realization.

Karma yoga is not just about seva, it's about being in the present moment detached from outcomes and using action as a form of prayer and worship. The importance of developing the heart center and love cannot be understated and is of utmost importance on the path of Self Realization. This can be seen as one of the main preparatory undertakings to do while pursuing Self Realization. Practice this as much as you can.

This leads into the four Brahma Viharas—Abodes of Brahma, or Abodes of the Self—which we will discuss more in depth later. They describe loving-kindness, compassion, empathetic joy, and equanimity. These qualities are essential to cultivate in aiding Self Realization; they are also expressions of Self Realization itself. By awakening the heart center, we can begin the process of Self Realization, and eventually the awakened energy—the Divine Spark that the ancients say resides in the heart—can escape the prison of the knot.

If one does nothing else, serving others and developing loving-kindness, compassion, empathetic joy, and equanimity will greatly prepare one for Self Realization. Even if one does not pursue Self Realization any further, these jewels will still act as radiant expressions of the Self, shining through one's life as a guiding compass.

After feeling better and better each day from the forgiveness process, I was hooked. It is challenging to do at first but after a while one gets the hang of it. The feeling I got from the release of all those trauma cords being cut was absolutely blissful and incredible! I never felt so good. Each day I felt better and better. So much so it seemed like reality was even becoming more and more beautiful. The world even seemed more radiant and brighter. Photos looked more beautiful almost as if they were AI generated. The tenseness I had in my stomach from an ulcer got better and better. My knee pain from a running injury felt better and better. I couldn't believe it. I actually never would have believed it if I didn't go through it and experience it for myself. I had no idea emotions were connected to our physical health.

Once I made a small tear in reality, I tore the whole thing open and wanted as much as I could of this amazing feeling and healing. I was primed for discomfort from many years of athletic competition and I looked forward to knocking out as many of these forgivenesses as I could and seeing how far I could go. The forgivenesses and other tasks weren't as much physically demanding as they were emotionally demanding. It was a simple task for "Mark" to switch from the physical discomfort to the emotional discomfort.

Most people are not conditioned for discomfort but for comfort. I noticed those who were athletically inclined did exceptionally well in the training, as they were accustomed to discomfort. Another good preparation for Self Realization is to make sure one is not addicted to comfort and adds some form of discomfort into one's life on a daily basis. That could be something as simple as getting up early, making your bed, working out, even walking outside, anything that gets one out of their comfort zone or mechanical living as Gurdjieff calls it.

Life is comfortable and it's important to get comfortable being uncomfortable. That is one helpful aspect that those extreme motivational speakers talk about. Instead of using those habits to make our dream world nicer we can use those habits to Realize the Self and wake up from the dream.

Even with the forgiveness process there comes a limit as to how much one can do each day. One can only cry and feel the pain and release of the emotions so much each day. Unmoving and unwavering, every single day of those seven days, I shed tears. I let the tears run down my face and shed the egoic layers one by one getting closer and closer to the jewel of the Self. Closer and closer to breaking the knot of the heart.

During the forgiveness process, we would forgive everyone and anyone that has done wrong to us including ourselves. It could even be a "small" forgiveness which sometimes yielded big results with big blasts in alpha tones. I should mention our brains are hooked up to wires and those wires are plugged into a wall where we are able to hear our brain waves in real time like a symphony, each region of our brain corresponded with a different sound. One sound may be a clarinet, a saxophone, a piano, etc. I don't remember the exact sounds for each region. The main regions of our brain measured were: Frontal, temporal, central (just in front of the parietal), and occipital.

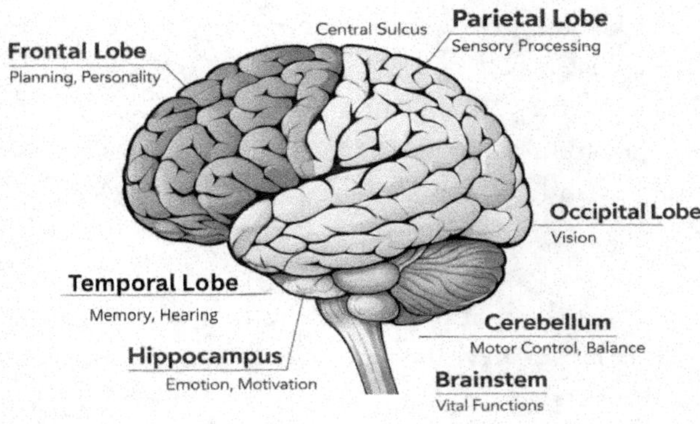

The electrodes for neurofeedback training are affixed to one's head using a washable glue to hold the electrodes in place and measure one's brain. This made for great hairdos when we finished and washed the electrode gel out of our hair.

In addition to being able to hear the brain in real time, one can see a set of scores that reflects the amount of alpha being produced. Every two minutes these scores would pop up for 8 seconds. They say when one is able to see their scores and hear their brain waves in real time, huge improvements in consciousness can take place. Of course that's the brilliant marketing but there is some truth to it.

The perception of the world and life in general did show a noticeable improvement after undergoing the training. Before that, like most people, I was simply living out subconscious programs and preconceived internal biases, playing themselves out again and again. The fact is no one truly needs to undergo neurofeedback to achieve this type of growth. One can gain all the same benefits—and even more—by practicing the methods prescribed in this book, albeit at a slightly slower, yet ultimately more powerful, pace.

As I continued with the inner work, what I noticed more and more is that it became easier and easier to think. Like a fog was lifted. Like this deep anxiety or nervousness dissipated. The world changed. The world changed because I changed. That's when I began to truly understand the world is a giant mirror and reflecting ourselves right back at us.

We see the world through the lens of our emotions, and most of our lenses have become clouded by years of emotional experiences. There may be a lens of victimhood, anger, guilt, or shame, and we respond to the world through that lens. Each emotion carries a specific energetic frequency. A useful chart illustrating this is provided by Dr. Hawkins in his book *Letting Go: The Pathway of Surrender* (2014):

Score	Level		
700+	Enlightenment	HIGHER FREQUENCY	EXPANSIVE
600	Peace		
540	Joy		
500	Love		
400	Reason		
350	Acceptance		
310	Willingness		
250	Neutrality		
200	Courage		
175	Pride		
150	Anger		
125	Desire		
100	Fear	LOWER FREQUENCY	DESTRUCTIVE
75	Grief		
50	Apathy		
30	Guilt		
20	Shame		

Hawkins, 2014.

These scores proved a good reference point while doing the training. They give a good indication of where one is and where to go. The goal is to move up as much and as high as possible. Most people are stuck in the lower frequencies of Shame, Guilt, Apathy, Fear, Desire, Anger, Pride. Some religious programming definitely has something to do with that. I know the programming that "we are all bad" causes guilt and shame. That may be the reason it's so prominent in society, to keep people in a lower level of consciousness and disconnected from the Self.

Later, we'll go over evidence to support the idea that our consciousness is intentionally being suppressed to keep us controlled and "dumbed down." When you consider the brainwave research that points in this direction, the possibility becomes difficult to ignore. By keeping people disconnected from the true nature of their existence and from eternal truth, they remain unaware of who they truly are—the infinite Self, beyond all emotions, concepts, and understanding. You are THAT!

A downside worth mentioning is that that chart and the neurofeedback training never mentioned our true Self as the observer, eternal witness, pure awareness within. Rather than attaching to these emotions we can simply cease to identify with them completely and simply watch them come and go. We do not have to attach to them at all, we can observe without attachment and simply watch them. It is only when we grasp or cling or attach to these emotions that causes the suffering.

Non-attachment should be taught in the program, but I don't think the majority of people who go through it—or work there—even know what Self Realization is from the purest perspective. It took me a while, after attending the training and practicing self-inquiry, for it to finally click. At that point, "I" made huge progress—but there was no longer a " me" to make progress. There was simply the Self: the pure awareness within, the observer, the changeless, the ineffable. You are THAT!

Neurofeedback is an external intervention that alters brainwave activity and should be approached with caution. While it is sometimes presented as a tool for improving mental states or supporting personal development, it is not necessary for Self Realization and does not produce genuine inner understanding. Self Realization is not the result of modifying brain activity, but the recognition of what is already present beyond all changing states.

Because neurofeedback directly influences the brain's natural patterns, its effects can vary widely between individual's and unintended or destabilizing effects may occur. No external technology can replace self-awareness, clarity, or insight. True realization arises from direct understanding, not from manipulating physiological states. For this reason, reliance on external systems may create distraction, dependency, or confusion rather than genuine freedom. Self Realization remains entirely independent of any device, method, or technological intervention.

Doing the inner work, I must have gone through the forgiveness process over a hundred times, along with several of the other techniques they taught us. Some of the forgiveness work was even directed toward myself—for the things "I" (false self) had done both to myself and to others. I had always been hard on myself, constantly expecting the best yet feeling it was never enough. No matter what I achieved, I found a way to criticize myself. I demanded perfection, and that expectation created a never-ending loop of suffering.

I would win a running race and still berate myself for not being fast enough. If I placed second in a race or triathlon, I would be angry for the same reason. I had adopted a tough-love approach toward my own psyche, and while it sometimes fueled achievement, it was ultimately destructive and wrought with suffering. It was unsustainable, and eventually I would crash. I believed toughness was the path to success—that being hard on myself would make me happy and help me get things done. But in truth, it was nothing more than emotional escapism and bypassing.

There are great benefits to suffering and hardship. One is that is to help bounce one out of it and onto the path of Self Realization. Suffering helps shake us awake. If the dream was always good would you ever want to wake up? It's only when the dream is not pleasant that we want to wake up. This is how pain and suffering in the world can help wake us up and help each of us Realize the Self.

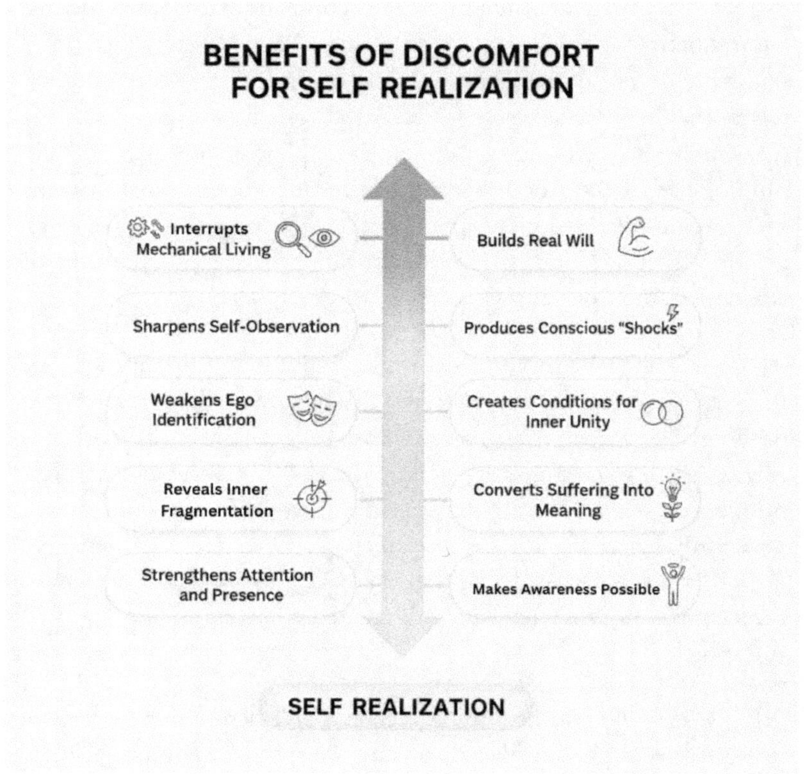

Unfortunately, not everyone will Realize the Self, but we all have a choice. I just wish everyone knew WE HAVE a choice. We can move out of those suffering states and WE ALL can be happy and peaceful living in a state of equanimity, kindness, and infinite happiness by Realizing the Self. Pain is mandatory in this world but suffering, which is of the illusory mind, is a choice. Choose to Realize the Self. You are THAT!

After the completion of deep inner work: I felt like a completely different person. Not different but a better version of myself, not quite the true Self but still the egoic self. I had a greater understanding and awareness I didn't have before. Even so, I was still identified with the false sense of "I" but that would soon change.

Being raised in an emotionally unintelligent family—where suppressing and escaping one's emotions was presented as the way to cope—was deeply destructive for both myself and everyone around me. Emotions don't simply disappear; they want to be acknowledged (illusory or not) and released. One cannot keep pushing them away or distracting oneself forever. Eventually, they build up and burst out. That was the pattern I witnessed throughout my life.

Growing up, learning to "be a man" was not the healthiest way to deal with emotions—in fact, it was quite the opposite. A far more effective approach is to acknowledge emotions and then let them go. I would argue that this is the true epitome of strength and masculinity. Many men scoff at the idea of love, yet if you look at the chart, love calibrates at a powerful 500. They say love is the most powerful force in the universe—and indeed, the Self is pure, infinite love and bliss. As strong men and women, it would serve us well to embody love, for it is the eternal truth of our existence; it is the Self. Love is the fragrance of the Self.

One of the most powerful expressions of love is forgiveness. Consider which is truly stronger: holding onto anger or choosing to forgive. The chart makes it clear—anger calibrates at 150, while love is at 500. And which is harder to do? Forgiveness, of course. Yet the more we practice it, the more our brains build the neural pathways to support it. Over time, we can construct a towering "skyscraper" of forgiveness—one that leads us ever closer to the Self.

If we examine David Hawkins' book *Letting Go: The Pathway of Surrender* (2014) further—beginning on page 11—he describes three common ways we are taught to handle emotions, which I found very enlightening: suppression/repression, expression, and escapism. Each of these approaches fails to fully address emotions and can hinder one's progress toward Self Realization.

The first way we are taught to deal with emotions, as Hawkins describes, is through suppression and repression. In suppression and repression, we push down feelings—either consciously or subconsciously—and set them aside. These suppressed emotions eventually rise to the surface in the form of physical symptoms such as headaches, indigestion, insomnia, and more. When someone receives difficult news, a common response is to avoid dealing with it and simply suppress it. But these bottled- up emotions do not disappear on their own. They must be acknowledged, observed, and released.

The second method is expression. In expression, we "vent" or release our unfavorable emotions verbally, nonverbally, or even through group demonstrations. According to Hawkins, expression simply lets off enough steam for the remaining emotion to be pushed back down and suppressed. Many people mistakenly believe that expressing feelings frees them, but this is not the case. This is another common error in emotional processing. All expression does is spread more negativity into the world and invites more negativity into one's life. The emotion still needs to be observed, allowed, and ultimately released.

The third way we are taught to handle emotions is through escapism. This involves avoiding our feelings through various forms of distraction. Escapism is one of the most common ways people deal with emotions, and society is largely built around it—through alcohol and drugs, food, sex, over-exercising or overworking, reading, texting, talking, playing, and more. Many of these forms of escapism can even turn into addictions. It's not that these activities are inherently bad; the issue arises when they become excessive or when they are used primarily as a means of avoiding our emotions.

Escapism keeps us from facing our inner selves and prevents our feelings from surfacing. We've all done it, often without realizing it. This isn't to say that taking a break now and then is unhealthy. However, spending an entire day on the couch watching TV, going out drinking, or engaging compulsively in activities like exercise or travel can become forms of escapism. For example, I know someone who has been traveling for many months in Southeast Asia; for her, it may well be a form of escapism as she moves from city to city, chasing one dopamine hit after another.

There is a way to overcome these three misaligned coping mechanisms, and that is through letting go—observing and releasing our emotions. On page 19 of Dr. Hawkins' book, he describes a simple method of releasing emotions that is quite similar to Lester Levenson's approach, which we will discuss later. I won't go into it in detail here, but I highly recommend that book, as well as the others I reference throughout this work.

Often, we engage in one or more of these three misaligned coping mechanisms subconsciously, without even realizing it. Most people do this almost automatically. It becomes a habit—an ingrained response learned in childhood, carried into adulthood, and taken all the way to death, while simultaneously being passed down to one's children. But there is a better way, one most people are never taught: we can let these emotions go. We can observe them, allow them, and release them. In fact, this is the only way to deal with emotions properly. When we don't release them, they may even become attached to our astral energy body. Releasing them can be as simple as not grasping onto them but instead watching them come and go like a movie screen. But if one does attach to them as we are taught then they must be let go.

In Angeliki Anagnostou's book *Can You Stand the Truth? Chronicles of Man's Imprisonment*, she discusses the various energy bodies and explains that all emotions are stored in the astral body. These imprinted emotions can leak into the physical body and contribute to disease and health problems. This perspective makes sense when you consider the structure of the energy bodies. She even goes a step further, suggesting through ancient texts and teachings that these stored emotions may serve as a source of energy for beings beyond our normal awareness. It may sound a bit unbelievable at first—but perhaps not so unbelievable once you finish this book.

An interesting idea that one typically learns only later on is that the ego may need to be healed before it can be seen for what it truly is—unreal. I heard this theory from a talk in which Howdie Mickoski mentioned it, and upon further reflection, it seems to hold some weight. I'm not exactly sure where he derived it from, but in my own experience and the experiences of others, it appears to be true. The ego is like a prison guard to the Self, doing everything it can to prevent us from realizing our true nature. It will scream, cry, get angry, and fight—anything to maintain control. The ego fears its own dissolution, so it clings tightly around the true Self, keeping it imprisoned within layers of programs, traumas, and beliefs.

Once these many egoic layers start to come undone, it becomes easier and easier to fend off the ego and see it for what it truly is: not real. The ego is fictitious. It is the man behind the curtain in *The Wizard of Oz*, trying to appear more frightening and powerful than it actually is. The ego maintains control by keeping us in states of fear, guilt, anger, and other lower-energy emotions. When the ego—or false self—is finally healed, we can see it clearly as unreal, and only then can we realize the Self. The Self is infinite more powerful in anything false of this world including the ego. You are THAT!

Healing the fragmented ego caused by the traumas and emotional wounds of the past is like building a bridge to reach the other side—only to discover, once you arrive, that you were always already there. You never needed to cross the bridge or go anywhere at all. There was never anything to do because you were always already home. That is what Self Realization is. The ego convinces us that we need to do this or achieve that, but in reality, we are all already Self Realized. We simply need to stop, do nothing, still the mind, and become aware of our true eternal nature—the Self.

Chapter 4

THE ENERGY BODIES

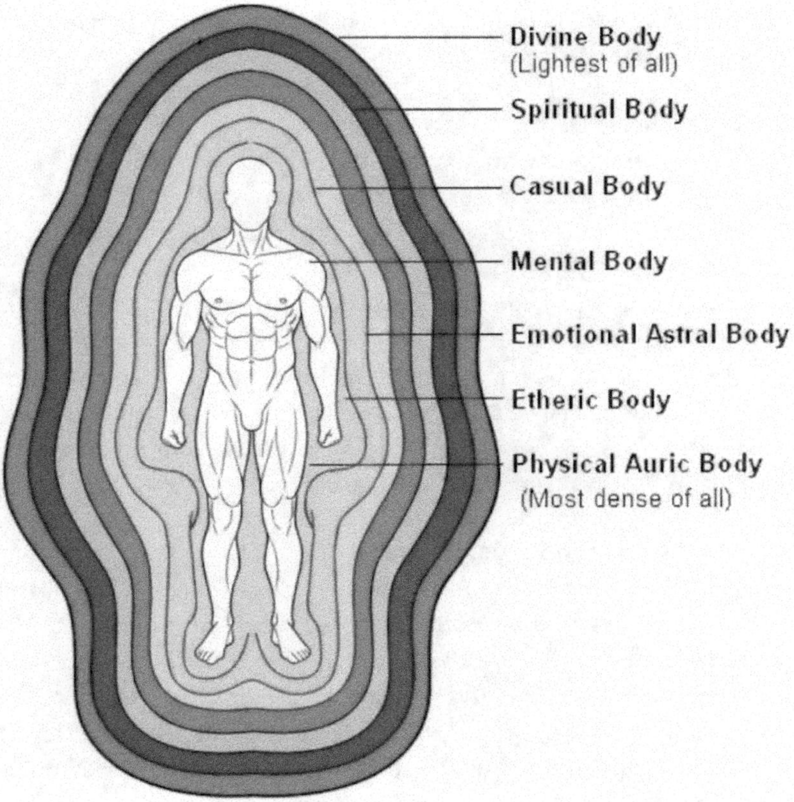

There are many diagrams depicting the different energy bodies. Some describe five, others seven, but I prefer the one because it's simplified and easy to understand. Different sources may use alternate terms for various parts of the energy bodies or divide them into additional layers—such as upper and lower astral bodies. With the help of Nepal Yoga Home (2020), we will explore these bodies in more detail.

1 — Physical Body:

The physical body is the densest of all the bodies and allows us to navigate this realm. It serves as an interface for interacting with the physical world. Death occurs when the physical body wears out or becomes too damaged to contain the life-force energy.

2 — Etheric Body:

The etheric body is the blueprint for our physical body. It can be seen in the aura and is composed of various colors, which can even be captured in aura photography—a practice that has become fairly common today. Its main function is to act as a conduit for life-force energy and to provide the template for the physical form. It is finer and more subtle than the physical body, though still part of the physical plane. After the physical body ceases functioning, the etheric body persists for about 40 days before dissolving. Once the physical body is gone, the etheric body is no longer needed as a blueprint or container for life-force energy.

3 — Astral/Emotional Body:

The astral body is a subtle body that exists alongside the physical body and serves as a vehicle for consciousness. One can access the astral body during out-of-body experiences (OBEs), also known as astral projection, during dreaming, as well as in deep meditation. The astral body is associated with feelings and emotions and acts as the link between the spiritual and physical realms. The chakras are located within this body. It is the primary body we inhabit when we pass from this world into the astral world.

4 — Mental Body:

The mental body is also a subtle body, serving as the domain of thoughts, ideas, and mental processing. It acts as a bridge between the physical world and the deeper inner world of consciousness. The mental body contributes to one's sense of identity or ego and is connected to both the physical and astral bodies. This body stores vast amounts of knowledge and experiences, including information from past lives.

5 — Causal/Higher Mental Body:

The causal body can be somewhat elusive, and information about it tends to be more philosophical and limited. What is known is that it is the highest subtle body, sometimes called the higher mental body.

In Indian philosophy it is considered the seat of dreamless sleep, samadhi, and possibly related to "the void." The causal body is associated with the causal plane. In Vedantic philosophy, it is the innermost of the five koshas, or sheaths, that veil the Atman, or true Self. It is also regarded as the home of the soul, the superconscious mind, and the repository of karma. The causal body serves as the bridge—the final layer—before reaching Self Realization or realizing one's own Buddha nature. Through these five bodies, reincarnation is theorized to occur. It is only in the sixth and seventh bodies that one can transcend reincarnation and karma.

6 — Spiritual/Buddhic Body:

The Spiritual, or Buddhic, body is the seat of Self Realization and enlightenment. In this body, the mind ceases, and only intuition and our Buddha/Self Realized nature remain. In Vedantic philosophy, this is the realm of Brahman and Atman (the Self). It is the kosha, or sheath, of bliss—a place of harmony, love, and oneness. Words fail to capture its nature. This is theoretically the level at which one can escape reincarnation and karma. At this stage, the sense of "I" ceases, as the mind is now seen for what it truly is: illusory and not real.

7 — Divine/Nirvanic Body:

The divine, or Nirvanic, body represents direct union with God. At this stage, there is no longer a separate Self, Atman, or Brahman—only emptiness and nothingness. This stage is complete and utter void, also known as Nirvana. In Vedic teachings, it is referred to as the bliss body, the ultimate state of liberation where duality disappears and there is only pure, undifferentiated consciousness. It is beyond words, beyond thought, and beyond the limitations of the mind—pure freedom, peace, and oneness with the entirety of existence.

According to Jain (2024), yogic traditions describe five koshas, or sheaths:

- **Annamaya Kosha:** the physical, or "food" body

- **Pranamaya Kosha:** the energy or vital body

- **Manomaya Kosha:** the mental or emotional body

- **Vijnanamaya Kosha:** the wisdom or intellectual body

- **Anandamaya Kosha:** the bliss or spiritual body

It is important to note that the Anandamaya Kosha is considered the theoretical seat of the Self, located in the heart center of the causal body.

In the Vedic system, these five sheaths are part of a three-body framework: the gross (physical), subtle, and causal bodies. The **gross body**, also called the Annamaya Kosha, consists of the material body—flesh, bone, and the elements. The **subtle body** is non-material and includes the mind, intellect, and vital energy. It contains three sheaths: the Pranamaya, Manomaya, and Vijnanamaya

Koshas. The **causal body** is the most complex of the three and stores impressions from past experiences. This body corresponds to the Anandamaya Kosha, or **bliss body**.

All of these bodies and koshas cover the Self, or Atman—the Divine Spark. To connect with our Spark, we must disidentify from these bodies and identify solely with the Self. It should also be noted that the nadis, which connect from the Self at the heart center, are present in the subtle and causal bodies.

An important aspect to remember is that negative emotions do not simply disappear when we escape, suppress, or express them—they become embedded in our energy body and can filter into the physical body, forming chains that bind us and are often linked to disease and illness.

The significance of understanding this cannot be overstated, as it is a central aspect of Self Realization. Through this process, we let go of everything we are not and ultimately reconnect with what we truly are—our true Self. The forgiveness method is essentially a structured way to release deeply buried traumas—the emotional chains that bind the heart, where the Self resides. It also facilitates the breaking of the "knot of the heart," which we will discuss in more detail later.

Buried emotions do not simply vanish; they **must** be consciously released or observed. In the end, one realizes that there was never truly anything to let go of, as these emotions were never real to begin with. These traumas siphon life-force energy, as can be measured through brainwave activity. With each trauma healed through forgiveness, there is typically a noticeable boost in alpha and gamma waves and a decrease in beta waves. This shift reflects an increase in life-force energy, which mirrors our reconnection to the Self.

Chapter 5

SAMADHI

One day, unexpectedly, while doing extensive deep forgiveness work, I experienced a profound breakthrough known as **Kevala Nirvikalpa Samadhi.**

Kevala Nirvikalpa Samadhi is a temporary state in which the ego-mind dissolves into the Self in the heart. Because it is temporary, the ego eventually re-emerges after this dissolution. It's often described as a bucket being lowered into a well and then drawn back up again.

After this experience, many things began to make more sense—especially insights into similar experiences I had previously, which I'll discuss later.

As the days passed, I became increasingly attuned to the rhythm of the forgiveness exercises. For me, the process wasn't difficult, because I understood that I could separate my present self from who I had been in the past. We are constantly changing; who we are in each passing second is different from who we were just moments before. One key indicator of the Self is that anything which changes—anything that comes or goes—is not the true Self. The Self is the unchanging background awareness that is always present. You are THAT.

During these forgiveness sessions, I began investigating people and events at a much deeper level. I spent more time with each forgiveness than I had before, sometimes devoting 15–20 minutes to a single one instead of the 10 minutes I previously allotted. The ego, of course, resisted this process. It clings to control and often hides traumas to prevent them from being forgiven, frequently through forgetfulness—one of its hindrances, along with doubt, drowsiness, ill will, and worry.

One of the people I focused on forgiving—among family and friends—was my brother. He felt like a crucial key to my healing. Each day, I worked on forgiving a different family member, and on this particular day, it was him. I forgave myself for pushing him into the pool at Whiskey Pete's, fully clothed, when we were young boys at the Nevada state line just outside Las Vegas. I also forgave myself for joining the military and leaving him behind in the difficult, chaotic childhood we were immersed in—a childhood I hadn't fully recognized as traumatic at the time, because trauma had become normalized.

We grew up with a single mother and an abusive, alcoholic stepfather. As a young boy, I would sometimes run as fast as I could in an attempt to escape, but I always had to return. I forgave my brother for the things he did to me as a child: slamming a door on my finger, shooting me with a BB gun, or telling our mother I had been mean to him when I hadn't—then smiling from the corner as I was punished. None of us knew any better. Without proper guidance or healthy role models, we simply mirrored what we saw, believing it to be normal.

Along with forgiveness, I rescripted the negative scenes, transforming them into loving, joyful memories. I recalled moments playing at the beach, the park, and the bowling alley. As I did this, I felt lighter and lighter—until, finally, I broke through.

I'm not entirely sure what happened next, but I became love itself. At that moment, my body seemed to melt into the seat; I could barely move. I felt completely mushy—and overwhelmed with love, far more than I could begin to comprehend.

It felt as though a flood surged through my heart center, as if a dam had broken. What was released wasn't water, but a powerful wave of energy that shot up into my head. When I stood up from the seat, I could barely walk. My entire body was vibrating so intensely that when I looked at the wall and the kitchen, I noticed everything—my body and the world around me—vibrating at the same high frequency, corresponding to gamma.

Why was my body—and seemingly the entire world—vibrating? Was I everything? Was this showing me that both my body and the external world were illusory? Who am I? Or, more accurately... **what** am I? That question will become important later.

I sat down cross-legged, closed my eyes, and felt a massive surge of energy rising from my heart into my head like a rushing current. It felt like a full-body orgasm—though not sexual in any way. The moment I closed my eyes, I was pulled magnetically into a deep meditative state. The experience was incredible.

KNOT OF THE HEART

If I were to theorize about what had happened, I would say that I broke the Divine Spark out of its prison embedded in the heart, and it rose to the top of my head, to the crown area. The experience felt like a dam had burst, sending a rush of energy—like water—upward to the crown. When I closed my eyes, I was instantly drawn into a meditative state, with a magnetic pull toward the top of my head. Perhaps I connected my lower chakras to my upper chakras by breaking the heart knot, thus freeing my Divine Spark, or Self.

One theory is that the majority of the population are stuck in the lower three chakras and rarely reaches the heart chakra, which acts as the bridge between the lower and upper chakras. This is intriguing because, in ancient Egypt, the words *smai tawi* are often interpreted as "know thyself," but they literally mean the unification of the two lands—Upper Egypt and Lower Egypt. Could it be that the phrase actually refers to the unification of the lower and upper chakras, or the union of the lower and higher self in humans? Some even propose that smai tawi signifies "know thyself" in the sense that one truly knows oneself only when the lower and higher selves come together. This interpretation seems possible, especially given how prominent the idea of "know thyself" was in ancient times.

According to Ashby, in his book *Egyptian Yoga: The Philosophy of Enlightenment* (2005), **Smai Tawi** means "union of the two lands of Egypt," ergo "Egyptian Yoga." The two lands refer to the two main districts of the country—North and South. In ancient times, Egypt was divided into two sections or land areas known as Lower and Upper Egypt.

In Ancient Egyptian mystical philosophy, the land of Upper Egypt relates to the divinity **Heru (Horus)**, who represents the Higher Self, while the land of Lower Egypt relates to **Set**, the divinity of the lower self. Thus, Smai Tawi means "the union of the two lands," or the "union of the lower self with the Higher Self."

The lower self relates to that which is negative and uncontrolled in the human mind, including worldliness, egoism, and ignorance (Set), while the Higher Self relates to that which is above temptations and is good in the human heart, as well as in touch with transcendental consciousness (Heru).

Thus, we also have the Ancient Egyptian term **Smai Heru-Set**, or the union of Heru and Set. Therefore, **Smai Tawi** or **Smai Heru-Set** are the Ancient Egyptian terms that are translated as "Egyptian Yoga."

Interesting to note in Ashbys same book he goes on to state: "The Egyptian language and symbols provide the first "historical" record of Yoga Philosophy and Religious literature. The Indian culture of the Indus Valley Dravidians and Harappans appear to have carried it on and expanded much of the intellectual expositions in the form of the Vedas, Upanishads, Puranas and Tantras, the ancient spiritual texts of India." Since Ashby's book was written, evidence has emerged suggesting that the ancient civilization of India may predate that of Egypt.

I actually have photos of the hieroglyphics of Smai Tawi from Egypt when I was there. I found these on numerous temples including at: Luxor, Karnak, Hashepsut and Colossi of Memnon.

Here is the one from the Temple of Luxor I took in 2023:

Gospel of Thomas 61
Jesus says: "...if one is whole, one will be filled with light, but if one is divided, one will be filled with darkness."

Mundaka Upanishad 2.2.8 (Radhakrishan, 2024):
"When he that is both high and low is seen, the knot of the heart is untied; all doubts are solved; and all his karma is consumed."

This photo resembles a spinal column, and the knot appears to be at the heart center. When examining a diagram of the chakras, there is a main channel that runs up and down the spine, along with two channels that crisscross along the spine. The ida and pingala are these crisscrossing channels, representing masculine and feminine energy. The knot prevents these two energies from meeting. Perhaps the idea is that the "union of the two lands" symbolizes the union of masculine and feminine energy once that knot is dissolved.

Another theory that seems plausible is that the "union of the two lands" may represent the union of the heart and the brain. The HeartMath Institute has conducted numerous studies over the years demonstrating the significance of heart-brain coherence. When the heart and brain are in harmony, our emotions, thoughts, and physiological functions align, creating a state of balance, clarity, and optimal functioning. This coherence is associated with increased intuition, emotional stability, and an enhanced connection to our Self.

It's also worth noting that, according to Vedic teachings, there are three primary knots: one at the base of the spine in the muladhara chakra, called the **Brahma Granthi**; one at the heart, called the **Vishnu Granthi**; and one at the third eye, or ajna chakra, called the **Rudra Granthi** (see below).

According to Chaturvedi (2020), "The Ida and Pingala Nadi that are like spirals of opposite poles of the central axis intertwine and unlock while passing through the seven chakras. Psychic knots of granthis are like protective blockages for the gradual change in awareness and open only with the purification of mind and balance between the two Nadi. The purpose of granthis is to block the sudden upward flow of prana, are like circuit breakers to protect the overload that may occur to the practitioner in case of a spontaneous ascension. The display of 'granthis' is associated with the 'Trinity' as the three main deities (Tri Murti)."

Maitri Upanishad 7:11 (Radhakrishan, 2024):
The person who is in the eye, who abides in the right eye, he is Indra and his wife abides in the left eye. The union of these two (takes place) within the hollow of the heart and the lump of blood which is there is indeed the life-vigor of these two.

That photo may actually depict the heart knot that is keeping the Self which lies in the heart center imprisoned. The ancient Upanishads teach that the heart has a knot around it. This comes from many different Vedic Upanishad texts: *Mundaka, Katha, Mandukya* and *Chandogya* (Radhakrishan, 2024).

Mundaka Upanishad 2:1:10 & 2:2:9 (Radhakrishan, 2024): 2:1:10 The person himself is all this, work, austerity and Brahma beyond death. He who knows that which is set in the secret place (of the heart), he, here on earth, O beloved, cuts asunder the **knot** of ignorance."

2:2:9 The knot of the heart is cut, all doubts are dispelled and the deeds terminate, when He is seen—the higher and the lower.

Katha Upanishad 2:3:14-16 (Radhakrishan, 2024):
2:3:14 When all desires that dwell within the human heart are cast away, then a mortal becomes immortal and (even) here he attaineth to Brahman.

2:3:15 When all the **knots** that fetter here the heart are cut asunder, then the mortal becomes immortal. Thus far is the teachings.

2:3:16 A hundred and one are the nadis of the heart; one of them leads to the crown of the head. Going upward though that, one becomes immortal; the others serve for going in various directions.

Mandukya Upanishad 3:2:9 (Radhakrishan, 2024):
He, verily, who knows the Supreme Brahman becomes Brahman himself. In his family, no one who does not know Brahman, will be born. He crosses over sorrow. He crosses over sins. Liberated from the **knots** of the secret place (of the heart), he becomes immortal.

Chandogya Upanishad 7:26:2 (Radhakrishan, 2024):
...When memory remains firm, there is a release from the **knots** of the heart. To such a one has his stains wiped away, the venerable Sanatkumara shows him the further shore of darkness...

There are many more references to the hearts knot in the Upanishads one can find (Dennis, 2016).

When I had that Samadhi experience, it felt as though something in my heart region broke loose and triggered an explosion of energy rising to the top of my head. This involved a surge of high- energy gamma waves coupling with slower theta waves—known as theta–gamma synchronization—producing a transcendental experience. We can produce this same effect outside the chamber with the data and information we have now. There is no need to spend thousands of dollars to have a transcendental experience. Just remember a transcendental experience is just that, an experience and does not denote Self Realization as Self Realization is ultimately independent of any brain wave.

In addition to the heart knot, the Upanishads also describe many nadis, or energy channels, that connect the heart to other parts of the body. Of the 101 nadis, only one leads to the crown of the head, and ascending through it theoretically allows one to escape reincarnation. It's worth noting that in everything I've read from the classical Upanishads so far, there is no mention of chakras or the crown chakra.

The knot around the heart center—associated with the Anandamaya Kosha in some interpretations—arises from desires, ignorance, and the misidentification with the body and mind, also known as the false self. This is why the Upanishads repeatedly emphasize that desirelessness is equivalent to Brahman (the Self), and why they stress the importance of fasting or abstaining from sensual indulgences, as such indulgences reinforce attachments and desires. Desire breeds more desire—except for the desire for the Self, and even that desire dissolves once the Self is realized.

In the chamber, that knot around my heart was finally broken, accelerated by the forgiveness process. A knot is not unlike a chain or any other binding force; all represent bondage and imprisonment. Self Realization is the dissolution of those knots or chains. Ultimately, it is the recognition that these bindings were never real in the first place, and that one was always free.

You are THAT!

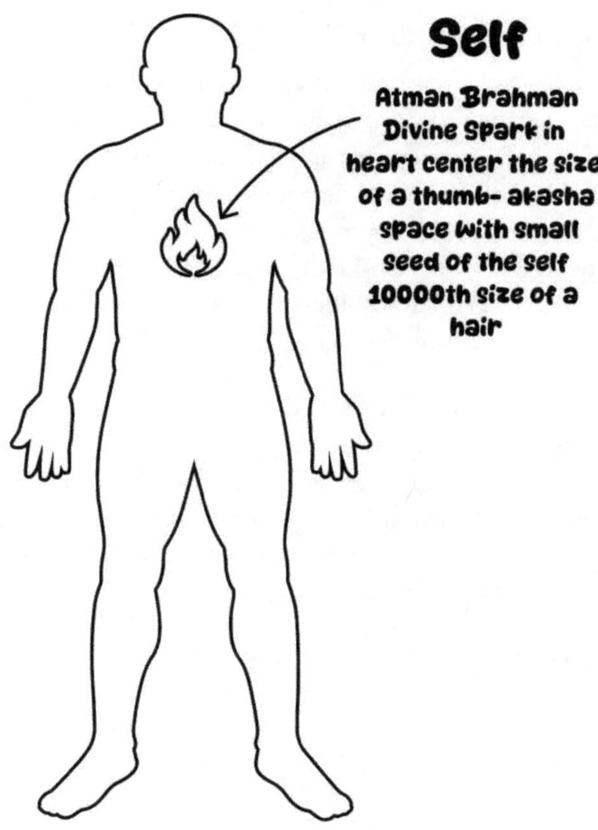

Here is a diagram I made of the Divine Spark in the heart, based on descriptions from the Upanishadic texts. The Self resides in a space at the cave of the heart, about the size of a thumb, called the akasha. The Divine Spark is 1/10,000th the size of a hair— similar to an atom in size—yet infinite in its essence. We all have this; it is the secret of secrets. Even simply focusing one's awareness at the cave of the heart and the Divine Spark can produce magical effects.

BIBLE HEART REFERENCES

Ezekiel 36:26
And I will give you a new **heart**, and a new spirit I will put within you. And I will remove the **heart** stone from your flesh and give you a **heart** of flesh.

Matthew 5:8
Blessed are the pure of **heart**, for they shall see God.

Proverbs 21:2
Every way a man is right in his own eyes, but the Lord weighs his heart.
(like the Egyptian book of dead weighing of **heart**)

Luke 12:34
…For where your treasure is, there will your **heart** be also.

Proverbs 4:23
Above all else, guard your **heart**, for it is the wellspring of life.

John 7:38 Anyone who believes in me may come and drink! For the scriptures declare, "Rivers of the living water will flow from the **heart**".

Ephesians 1:18
I pray that your **hearts** will be flooded with light (Divine Spark) so that you can understand the confident hope he has given…

Chapter 6

THE CHAKRAS

ere's a brief description of the chakras, or energy centers of the body, based on the work of Himanshu (2021), with added commentary from myself. Chakras were never directly mentioned in the early Vedic texts; they appear in later texts, such as the *Netra Tantra* around 700 CE. The term chakra means "wheel," as these are energy centers in the body that spin like wheels. Each chakra is associated with a color, a sound, a symbol, and nerve bundles along the spine. While these chakras exist primarily on the astral body, they also influence the physical body and affect our experience in this reality. Some traditions mention more chakras

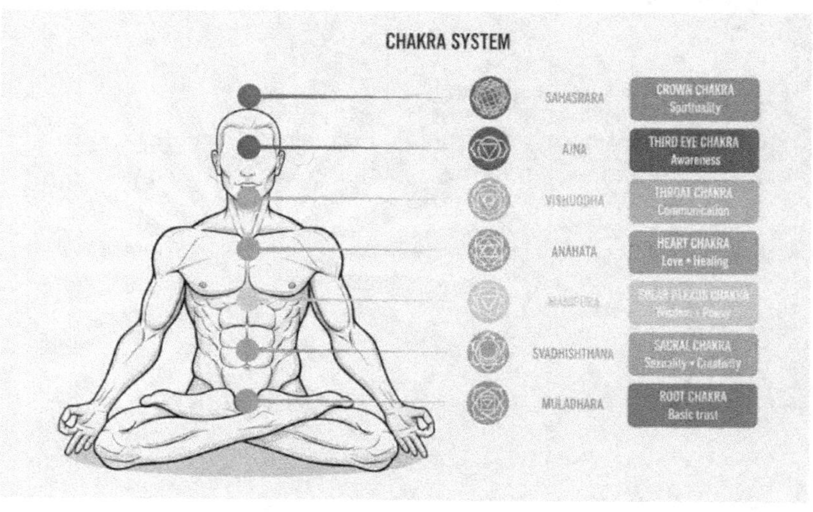

than are presented here, but I've included the basic, most commonly known ones.

Chakra 1: Root Chakra (Muladhara)

The first chakra is the lowest on the spinal column, near the tailbone. Its color is red. This chakra governs grounding, stability, and physical identity.

Chakra 2: Sacral Chakra (Svadhisthana)

Located just above the pubic bone and below the belly button, the sacral chakra is orange and associated with pleasure, sexuality, and creativity.

Chakra 3: Solar Plexus Chakra (Manipura)

This chakra is in the upper abdomen and is yellow. It is responsible for self-esteem and confidence. One theory suggests that most people operate primarily from these first three chakras, rarely ascending into the higher chakras, or if they do, they bounce in and out, remaining mostly grounded in the lower three.

Chakra 4: Heart Chakra (Anahata)

The heart chakra, the bridge to higher consciousness, is green and linked to love and compassion.

Chakra 5: Throat Chakra (Vishuddha)

Located at the throat, the fifth chakra is blue and governs communication, including words, thoughts, and images.

Chakra 6: Third Eye Chakra (Ajna)

The sixth chakra, located between the eyebrows in the middle of the forehead, is indigo and associated with intuition and imagination. According to Angeliki Anagnostou (2012) in her book *Can You Stand the Truth: Chronicles of Man's Imprisonment*, the sixth chakra can become a theoretical trap. She describes a shortcut to enlightenment where kundalini energy is activated at the base of the spine but becomes stuck in the sixth chakra, preventing it from reaching the seventh.

This can lead to mesmerization with visions, gods, out-of-body experiences, astral travel, and siddhi powers. Accepting these powers, according to Anagnostou, can block further ascension, causing the kundalini to oscillate up and down the chakras without ever reaching the seventh, where Self Realization awaits.

Chakra 7: Crown Chakra (Sahasrara)

The final chakra, the crown, is white or violet and is associated with awareness, spirituality, and enlightenment. This chakra links us to the divine and may be considered more of a bridge or portal than a traditional chakra. It can also be seen as a prism, where white light enters and is refracted into the other colors of the chakras. During deep transcendental experiences, one can perceive a bright light, and beyond the light lies the darkness or the void, which gives birth to the light.

The Upanishads say that by awakening the heart center, where the Divine Spark (Self) resides, that spark of energy can ascend to the crown at the time of death through one of the 101 nadis that connect the heart to the crown of the head. The Self is not in the crown but only ascends to it and beyond. The heart is where the Self lies in waiting for the knot to be broken so that the Self can be freed from bondage. Many people get trapped by thinking they need to ascend their chakras to the crown as the ultimate goal. The main area where the Self lies in waiting is the heart—this cannot be stressed enough. The heart is the key to Self Realization. The methods prescribed in this book help untie the knot at the heart, allowing the energy to rise to the crown.

It's also worth noting that the crown chakra is not traditionally seen as a chakra at all, but more as a prism that emanates all the other chakras and serves as a bridge for the Self (Divine Spark) to travel to other realms, such as the moon or the sun, according to the Upanishads. Traditionally, the main information we have about chakras comes from a book written in 1577 CE, which was roughly translated by John Woodroffe I his book *The serpent Power* in

1919. If you look at the original 1577 text, it mentions only six chakras— not the crown chakra.

When one examines the Upanishad texts there is no mention of a crown chakra, just the mentioning of the energy going to the crown of the head. Maybe someone just added the crown chakra later on. In fact when I've read many of the original Upanishads there is no mention of chakras in general. These come from later texts. It's worth noting that the chakras also correspond to the 5 elements of earth, air, water, fire, ether and the 6th chakra or the third eye chakra represents the mind.

Personally I don't put too much weight in the chakras and feel as though it can lead and misdirect people towards pursuits other than Self Realization. The only thing to do is Realize the Self. Don't worry about activating this chakra or that chakra. That will happen naturally as a by-product of Self Realization. If one tries to activate the chakras through processes that promise rapid results then one runs the risk of that chakra trap we talked about where the energy gets stuck in the 6th chakra and induces devious wisdom or maybe even gets stuck in the lower chakras. This is a trap of many popular social media influencers and teachers to this day who primarily focus on chakras activations promising a fast track to enlightenment and Self Realization.

Everyone and their mother is selling a chakra activation program and everyone and their father is selling meditation techniques for activating certain chakras. Be wary of those that promise Self Realization by paying a certain amount of money to activate one's chakras. Chakras may or may not activate as one Realizes the Self which is located in the heart, everything else is just noise. No need to focus on the chakras, no need to focus on brain waves, no need to focus on anything but Realizing the Self. Abide as the Self! Be Happy! Be Free! You are THAT!

As experience the with Samadhi showed, the unknotting of the heart can be accomplished without any focus on the chakras whatsoever. It occurred predominantly as an effect of the forgiveness work, possibly aided by the built-up energy from sensual fasting. In addition, many years of service to others helped build a foundational component that supports Self Realization by activating the "Divine Spark" within the heart center. Notice I said heart center, not chakra. As mentioned earlier, the Self is located in the heart center, called akasha, and not in the heart chakra itself. The Self resides in the Causal (Nirvanic/Divine) body, in the middle of our chest if considering the seven-body theory, or in the anandamaya kosha if viewing it from the Vedic five-body system—based on everything I've gathered.

One must activate the heart center by cultivating love through service, loving-kindness, compassion, empathetic joy, and similar practices. Immerse yourself in loving actions through speech, behavior, and thought. Ideally, one can progress more quickly by incorporating periods of silence and stilling the mind as much as possible. If extended periods of silence and stillness are not feasible, then focus on choosing loving words, thoughts, and actions as often as possible to help build the foundation for Self Realization.

Our chakras are traditionally viewed as existing in the astral body. The same applies when one has an aura photo taken or receives a reading from an aura reader, who might tell you all about your personality and chakras. It's a bit like astrology, but focused on the chakras. I wouldn't much attention to this either, though it can be fun occasionally. Just take it with a grain of salt and don't place much emphasis or importance on it. The reason is that our primary concern should be Self Realization, not astrology, aura readings, or similar practices. Those are more distractions than anything else. Even too much focus on brain waves can be a distraction. The absolute main goal is to Realize the Self. That is all.

For another reference point on chakras lets see what Ramana has to say in the Book: *The Teachings of Ramana Maharshi* (Osborne, 2014):

> In fact the body is in the mind which has the brain for its seat. That the brain functions by light borrowed from another source is admitted by the yogis themselves in their fontanelle theory. The Jnani further argues: if the light is borrowed it must come from its native source. Go to the source direct and do not depend on borrowed sources. That source is the Heart, the Self.

> The Self does not come from anywhere else and enter the body through the crown of the head. It is as it is, ever sparkling, ever steady, unmoving and unchanging. The individual confines himself to the limits of the changeful body or of the mind which derives its existence from the unchanging Self. All that is necessary is to give up this mistaken identity, and that done, the ever shining Self will be seen to be the single non-dual reality.

> If one concentrates on the Sahasrara there is no doubt that the ecstasy of Samadhi ensues. The Vasanas, that is the latent mental tendencies, are not however destroyed. The yogi is therefore bound to wake up from the Samadhi because release from bondage has not yet been accomplished. He must still try to eradicate the Vasanas inherent in him so that they cease to disturb the peace of his Samadhi. So he passes down from the Sahasrara to the Heart through what is called the Jivanadi, which is only a continuation of the Sushumna. The Sushumna is thus a curve. It starts from the lowest Chakra, rises through the spinal cord to the brain and from there bends down and ends in the Heart. When the yogi has reached the Heart, the Samadhi becomes permanent. Thus we see that the Heart is the final centre.

[Note: Commentary by David Godman: Sri Ramana Maharshi never advised his devotees to practice Kundalini Yoga since he regarded it as being both potentially dangerous and unnecessary. He accepted the existence of the Kundalini power and the Chakras but he said that even if the Kundalini reached the Sahasrara it would not result in realisation. For final realisation, he said, the Kundalini must go beyond the Sahasrara, down another Nadi (psychic nerve) he called Amritanadi (also called the Paranadi or Jivanadi) and into the Heart-centre on the right hand side of the chest. Since he maintained that self-enquiry would automatically send the Kundalini to the Heart-centre, he taught that separate yoga exercises were unnecessary.

The practitioners of Kundalini Yoga concentrate on psychic centres (Chakras) in the body in order to generate a spiritual power they call Kundalini. The aim of this practice is to force the Kundalini up the psychic channel (the Sushumna) which runs from the base of the spine to the brain. The Kundalini Yogi believes that when this power reaches the Sahasrara (the highest Chakra located in the brain), Self-realisation will result.

Sri Ramana Maharshi taught that the Self is reached by the search for the origin of the ego and by diving into the Heart. This is the direct method of Self-realisation. One who adopts it need not worry about Nadis, the brain centre (Sahasrara), the Sushumna, the Paranadi, the Kundalini, Pranayama or the six centres (Chakras)."

Ramana Maharshi says we should focus solely on the heart and avoid getting caught up in the chakras. Why spend so much time on all the chakras and kundalini when we can go directly to the source? This makes sense from a logical perspective. Maharshi further explains that all that is necessary is to give up the mistaken identity and recognize the Self as the single, non-dual reality. He notes that preoccupying ourselves with chakras and kundalini only adds to the confines of the mind and body; it is far more effective to go directly to the source—the heart. It's worth emphasizing that Ramana Maharshi refers to the heart itself, not the heart chakra located on the spinal column.

The heart is referenced as the seat of the Self in many Upanishad texts and was considered the seat of the soul in ancient Greece. Unfortunately, many yoga practitioners become fixated on the sensations or bliss that arise from kundalini rising to the crown. This can lead to distraction by siddhis, or psychic powers, particularly when the energy gets stuck in the sixth chakra.

The entire chakra system can be confusing and seems almost like a deliberately constructed trap for our consciousness— our 'Divine Spark'—keeping it from reaching its final destination. The chakra system is just another layer of the illusory nature of this world and the body. It is best to avoid becoming fixated on it and instead focus on the heart center, the root location of the Self.

KUNDALINI

One night while I was sleeping, I heard what sounded like a freight train. I actually thought there was a train outside because it was so loud. Eventually, I realized I was asleep and that the sound was coming from inside me. It grew louder and louder, and then I saw what looked like a lightning bolt widening, accompanied by a strong pressure on my head. Shortly after that, I woke up. I wasn't afraid—I simply found it, as I like to say, "interesting."

It reminded me of people who shake or tremble spontaneously during a kundalini awakening, like the countless videos you can find on YouTube. I don't know whether some of those reactions are partially placebo or self-induced, but if you look online, you'll see many such examples.

That energy is what's called kundalini. Kundalini is a 3.5 coiled serpent like energy that we all have at the base of our spine. The term originated in India and has been vilified as being scary or demonic or unnatural but that is far from the case. That being said when one Realizes the Self one may have kundalini activations. Kundalini awakenings can be characterized by explosive theta or delta along with gamma brain waves. The mystical kundalini energy has been associated with siddhis or yogic powers (Ball-Mitchell, Steph, n.d.).

Things such as levitations, telepathy, astral projection, you name it are all considered siddhis. Personally I haven't seen anyone with any type of powers. Although there was a person who mentioned they had them but if he showed us we would all throw up. Most likely it was nonsense. I wouldn't worry or even mess around with this as it is a trap and could keep one from Realizing the Self. The greatest siddhi that surpasses all siddhis is simply that of Self Realization. Just simply Realize the Self and all wants and desires will dissolve and vanish.

Realize the Self, there is simply nothing more that needs to be done. Many advanced yogis and practitioners get stuck at the level of siddhis and powers and do not progress to the final stage of Self Realization. The same applies if one comes into contact with beings, angels, or anything of that sort. Do not trust any of it. You see countless YouTube videos of people channeling all kinds of alleged entities, but these beings are usually channeled from the astral realm—the realm of tricksters. It is best to avoid interacting with them, as they can easily throw one off the path of Self Realization.

You have the Divine Spark within you, and that is all you need. The Divine Spark is all there is, all there was, and all there ever will be. The Divine Spark is the most powerful force in existence— it is existence, it is infinity, and **you are THAT!**

When it comes to siddhis and powers, it's best for one to avoid that while in this dream world which could lead to attachment and being reincarnated back again and again. It's the same with magic. People that mess around with that stuff may get trapped back into the reincarnation cycle by building excess karma and attachments to this illusory world.

All of these things are of the ego/mind and reinforce one's mind aka the false self thus thinking one is the doer and as Ramana Maharshi said: "If one is the doer then one is the sufferer". Best to stay away from all of it and there's no need to even mess around and take any chances.

If one attempts to forcefully activate kundalini through physical exercises, breathwork, or other spiritual practices in an effort to accelerate its awakening, there can be unintended consequences. One may experience a range of psychological and physiological disturbances often referred to as kundalini syndrome. Symptoms can include anxiety, depression, emotional instability, intense mood swings, disorientation, and even episodes resembling psychosis. Alongside these disturbances, the ego can resist the process, creating what is known as **ego backlash**—a defensive response where unresolved aspects of the personality are brought to the surface, sometimes with overwhelming intensity.

These challenges occur because kundalini represents a powerful energy that naturally moves through the subtle energy channels of the body in a precise order. Attempting to force or manipulate this process can destabilize both the mind and body. For this reason, most spiritual teachers and yogic traditions recommend allowing kundalini to awaken naturally, often as a result of consistent inner work such as meditation, forgiveness, self-inquiry, and cultivation of love and compassion. When allowed to progress on its own, the energy rises harmoniously, integrating with the mind, body, and heart, minimizing psychological disturbances, and supporting a safer and more complete path toward Self Realization.

Here's another perspective on Kundalini, this time by Gurdjieff: "Kundalini is a force put into men in order to keep them in their present state. If men could really see their true position and could understand all the horror of it, they would be unable to remain where they are even for one second. They would begin to seek a way out and they would quickly find it, because there is a way out; but men fail to see it simply because they are hypnotized. Kundalini is the force that keeps them in a hypnotic state. 'To awaken' for man means to be 'dehypnotized.' In this lies the chief difficulty and in this also lies the guarantee of its possibility, for there is no organic reason for sleep and man can awaken."

If the entire world is a web of traps, then kundalini may very well be one of them. Perhaps, as Gurdjieff suggested, it is a force designed to keep us hypnotized, distracted from our true nature. I would not doubt it. Nothing in this realm is truly to be trusted. This world is structured to prevent us from realizing the Self. The only path is to keep moving forward, undistracted, and to realize the Self. Do this, and all is well; everything is taken care of. Always remember: you are THAT!

HOLY MATRIMONY AND KUNDALINI

There is one more theory I would like to discuss, which also comes from Anagnostou's book (2012). In the chapter on Energy Centers, she discusses the seven energy centers, or chakras, and the potential trap of kundalini. Anagnostou explains how raising the energy to the crown leads to what she calls the Holy Matrimony, which we might also refer to as Self Realization. In the Holy Matrimony, the female/Eve/I Am presence and the Divine Spark/male/Adam become united. Similar to the Egyptian smai tawi we discussed earlier.

According to Anagnostou, this process is somewhat tricky and comes with many potential traps, so let us examine them. The first step, she explains, is to stop the emotional oscillation between dualities, such as good and evil, as these keep the Divine Spark captive—essentially imprisoned in the heart center. These emotional oscillations are linked to the chakras; for example, the third energy center, according to Anagnostou, hosts all the inferior negative emotions: fears, passions, anxieties, hatreds, and malice. Once these oscillations are quelled, the Divine Spark can ascend toward the fifth, sixth, and seventh energy centers of the body.

In summary, Anagnostou describes two ways for the Divine Spark to rise: the "honest way" and the "thief's way." The honest way is through self-knowledge, while the thief's way—a shortcut— can lead to mental disturbances. The honest way involves awakening the Divine Spark in the heart center, allowing it to move upward from the fourth to the fifth, then the sixth, and finally to the seventh energy center, resulting in what she calls the "Holy Matrimony." Anagnostou emphasizes that only through an honorable life and absolute purity of emotions and intentions can the Divine Spark ascend to the seventh energy center.

On the other hand, if someone tries to take the quick way— or the "way of the thief," as she calls it—the energy becomes stuck in the 6th energy center and is unable to transcend to the 7th. The energy she refers to is the kundalini, the snake-like energy housed at the base of the spine. Anagnostou cautions that this is a major trap and that awakening the kundalini, or calling upon the kundalini snake god, comes with a heavy price. Some even go mad from this energy, a condition that in modern terms is called kundalini psychosis.

The 6th energy center, where the kundalini becomes stuck, is located at the thalamus between the pituitary and pineal glands. In the 6th center, the kundalini manifests as a kind of devious wisdom caused by the kundalini's "venom," which is different from the wisdom conveyed by the 7th energy center. Only the 7th center can lead to liberation, according to Anagnostou.

This is contrary to the teachings of the great sage Ramana Maharshi, and if I had to choose whose teachings to follow, it would be Ramana's over Anagnostou's. Anagnostou's premise is the common belief that the 7th chakra is the final resting place for Self Realization. This is a grievous error. The final resting place, as mentioned, is the heart center. One should focus only on the heart center—not on chakras, not on brain waves, not on kundalini. Simply realize the Self through the heart center, for that is where the Self lies in wait. From there, the Self can burst upward through the crown, as mentioned earlier, through one of the 101 nadis. This whole chakra and kundalini system adds yet another layer to the deception of this world. **Trust nothing** in this world; research and gather information for oneself as much as possible.

Interestingly, the thalamus is one of the brain's primary regions for generating brain waves. In neurofeedback training, technology can be harnessed not only to awaken kundalini but also to activate the Divine Spark in the heart center through the forgiveness process and other love- and compassion-based practices. Awakening the heart center in this way is crucial—it helps dissolve the knot within the heart and protects one from falling prey to the trap of kundalini s venom. Aside from that even neurofeedback can be considered a trap.

Most people who undergo neurofeedback training are focused on money, relationships, peace of mind, less anxiety, or greater intelligence. One thing I noticed was a primary focus on money, which is another trap of this world. During the training they teach that one can jump to a different timeline and manipulate reality to achieve personal goals. But to whose goal is it really? It's the ego's goal, of course, and it is part of the trap.

The true Self requires nothing, for it is already everything. It has no wants, no desires. The Self does not need anything because it is complete, perfect, and beyond all limitations. Any tool or practice can either feed the ego—if it is used to chase desires—or serve as a means to awaken and Realize the Self.

To be honest, if I knew what I know now, I wouldn't have done neurofeedback or any other external method to accelerate Self Realization, because of the ego backlash that occurs. Ego backlash happens when the ego snaps back harder and stronger after a sudden jump in spiritual progress. It's best to proceed steadily and avoid moving too fast, as rapid progress can lead to instability. Even then the program I outline in this book can take 3-4 months which is still extremely fast.

It is best to pursue Self Realization to become truly free; desires only create bondage and suffering. Are you ready to become truly free, or are you prepared to become further enmeshed in bondage within this illusory world? Do you want to return again and again through reincarnation with your memory wiped each time, or do you want to finally leave this place once and for all? Depending on one's perspective do you want to graduate from the school of earth or escape from the prison?

The choice is yours. I cannot make it for you; only you can decide. Realize the Self that is all there is to do. Always remember: you are THAT!

WHAT ABOUT SEX?

Let's talk about everyone's favorite topic: sex. Sex is promoted everywhere you look. Doctors are handing out Viagra like hotcakes. Every grandfather and his father seem to be gobbling them down like candy, with the promise of a lovemaking session that lasts for hours. Everywhere you turn on social media, there's a sexual post or innuendo.

Sexual energy is one of the most powerful energies in the world today and is often equated with kundalini or life-force energy. If society promotes sex so much, what do you think we should do? Have lots of sex and waste that energy? Or should we conserve our sexual energy and use it to Realize the Self? That's exactly what I did before my Samadhi experience—and it worked brilliantly. This energy can help break the Divine Spark free from the heart knot.

Conserving sexual energy may facilitate Self Realization by removing the subconscious attachment to sexual desire or craving. This craving promotes the opposite of stillness and induces a sense of agitation. When one engages in too much sex, a subconscious craving or desire develops. Everyone begins to be seen as a sexual object, creating a significant hindrance to Self Realization.

One can either waste sexual energy by depleting it or harness that energy as a catalyst for realizing the Self. This practice is part of *Brahmacharya*—self-control and restraint of the senses, including sensual pleasures such as sex.

Society teaches us to waste that energy. Society encourages having more children. In the news and on social media, there's always some study or data claiming that more sex is better, that it helps you live longer, and so on. It's a trap—like most things in this distorted, backwards world.

That's not to say complete abstinence is necessarily the answer, as it could create a pendulum that swings too far in the opposite direction. A good recommendation comes from the Taoist Mantak Chia. In his book *The Multi-Orgasmic Man* (1997), he writes:

> Sun Simiao, one of the leading physicians of ancient China, recommended that men attain good health and longevity by ejaculating twice a month, as long as they ate healthily and exercised. He also offered the following more specific guidelines:

- A man at twenty can ejaculate once every four days.

- A man at thirty can ejaculate once every eight days.

- A man at forty can ejaculate once every ten days.

- A man at fifty can ejaculate once every twenty days.

- A man at sixty should no longer ejaculate.

This guidance is for men and is good advice for women as well. Moreover, sexual activity can become a sensual trap, keeping people in a constant state of craving and desire, which pushes us further away from Self Realization. Sensual desire, as we will discuss later in this book, is one of the major hindrances to Self Realization.

Once the Self is Realized then cravings and desires fall away naturally including sensual desire. That's the key. Those impulses fall away naturally; we cannot suppress them or gaslight ourselves into dismissing those feelings or cravings that arise. One can watch them and let them come and go. One can have less and less sex as one's Self is Realized to an ever greater extent but just remember that desire and aversion are two sides of the same coin. When we Realize the Self we are in the in between state of nothing of neither desire nor aversion.

The main purpose of sex is for reproduction and even that should be looked upon with trepidation. The addictive nature of sensual pleasure such as sex is something to be discussed as it is akin to a drug with the neurotransmitters and biochemicals released. Even so much so that some become addicted to it, especially the very wealthy and powerful who have access to extremes of abundance. There are countless stories over the years of high profile individuals and their sexual escapades. In this world one must make sure to not become attached or addicted to anything as it will ultimately cause suffering. This world is a trap and sex, drugs and pleasures of the senses are a huge area of entrapment to keep us from Realizing the Self.

"When all desires that dwell in the heart are cast away, then does the mortal become immortal, then he attains Brahman here (in this very body)." (Brahman = Self Realization)
Brihadaranyaka Upanishad 4:4:7 (Radhakrishan, 2024)

One can easily see this dynamic played out in the media, on television, and in movies. "Sex sells" is a common saying for a reason. It appeals to our primitive, reptilian brain, which has three main drives: reproduction, safety/survival, and fight-or-flight. As one can see, sex is deeply embedded in our nature, and to Realize the Self, one must go against the very DNA coding of that nature.

A useful recommendation is to avoid thinking about sex or looking at sexual images on social media—even pictures of scantily clad men or women in swimsuits. Avoiding such images as much as possible has a significant effect on dissolving mental attachment. Since sexual content is so prominent in social media and entertainment, one must make a deliberate effort to avoid watching sexually explicit or provocative material.

There's a reason all those pornography sites are free. There's a reason there is porn on X.com (formerly Twitter). And now, with the rise of AI-generated media, the line between what is real and what is not has become blurred. Constantly thinking about sexual relations creates an energetic attachment and drain. Thoughts are energetic. Sex is an energetic trap, deliberately woven into our DNA to ensure the continuation of the species for a specific purpose. This may be why some groups of Gnostics were explicitly antinatalist.

To this day, I practice restraint and discipline—not just with sex, but with all forms of sensual pleasure, including food, music, comfort, social media, and more—and I encourage others to do the same. I'm not saying avoid all these things, all I am saying is be mindful with excess of anything. As one progresses on the path of Self Realization, this discipline becomes increasingly helpful, as nearly all ancient teachings emphasize the importance of sensual discipline.

As I keep saying—and will continue to say—society is a huge trap designed to keep us from realizing the Self. The powers that be want us addicted and fully immersed in pleasures and indulgences. There is a reason for this. It's also worth noting that, usually, doing the opposite of what society promotes puts one in a better position. As the great Oscar Wilde said: "Everything popular is wrong."

Chapter 7

ENLIGHTENED YOGI

Kumbh Mela

In early 2025, I traveled to Prayagraj, India, to attend the renowned Kumbh Mela, a gathering of yogis and spiritual seekers from around the world. I went hoping to encounter truly enlightened yogis, but most seemed to be performing a role— claiming enlightenment, soliciting money, or inviting visitors to receive a bindi on their forehead only to request payment immediately afterward. As the sun set over the Ganges River, we watched a mesmerizing fire ceremony, a serene moment amidst the chaos.

Millions of Hindus bathe in the Ganges, believing it washes away sins, clears karma, and aids spiritual purification. I decided to join in. I stripped down to my underwear, jumped into the river with the crowd, clasped my hands in prayer, and dove right in. The water wasn't cold at all—actually quite refreshing. The Hindus loved watching me; they stared with amusement. Feeling playful, I did my famous butt-shake dance in my tighty whities, and the crowd hooted, hollered, laughed, and clapped.

After drying off from the bath, the search for enlightened yogis truly began. We wandered through hundreds of small encampments, walking endlessly—until finally, almost as if by destiny, we found one that held the yogi we had been searching for. We turned a corner and entered a small camp with large canvas tents. A small group of Hindus greeted us, and one of them stepped forward as if expecting us.

Standing directly in front of me was who we've been looking for. I was stunned. I had finally met an enlightened yogi face to face. It was an incredible experience. He was small in stature, fair-faced, and resembled traditional depictions of Jesus. He wore simple clothing and radiated a distinct energy—an emptiness, a nothingness, a complete stillness, as if his mind were entirely calm and empty. He radiated love, kindness, and compassion.

He welcomed our questions, and we spoke for a considerable length of time. He explained how he used a mantra as a path to enlightenment, chanting it repeatedly for many hours until both the mind and the mantra dissolved. We will explore mantras in greater detail later on as they can be a very powerful tool to Realize the Self.

The path to Self Realization through austerity and mantra could take many years, as he did while living in a cave in the Himalayas. According to online reports, at the tree line on the side of a mountain, there is a frequency of 7.8 Hz, corresponding to a slow theta brainwave state. This is one reason why those who retreat into the mountains, away from society, can accelerate the process of Self Realization. The yogi mentioned that he went to the mountains five years ago, and Self Realization came rather quickly. I didn t ask exactly how long it took, as I was completely blown away and captivated by the experience. The Upanishads state that Self Realization can take as little as six months if one is extremely austere in their practice.

One question I asked the yogi was how important celibacy, or brahmacharya, is. He responded that it is extremely important. Brahmacharya is a Vedic term meaning conduct consistent with Brahman (the Self). It refers to the discipline of the senses, the renunciation of worldly desires, and the control of impulses—including sexual restraint—to attain liberation or Self Realization. It is worth noting that brahmacharya is one of the five yamas, or ethical rules, of Yogic philosophy.

Here's a brief overview of the 5 yamas from Wikipedia (Yamas, 2025):
1- Ahimsa: Non-violence
2- Satya: Truthfulness
3- Asteya: Non stealing
4- Brahmacharya: Chastity, sexual restraint
5- Aparigraha: Non avarice or non possessiveness

Some texts describe 10 yamas if we add 5 more we get:
6- Ksama: Patience, **forgiveness**
7- Dhrti: fortitude, perseverance
8- Daya: Compassion, kindness
9- Arjava: Non hypocrisy, sincerity, honesty
10- Mitahara: Measured diet

According to the *Yoga Sutras of Patanjali*, the yamas are the first step on the eightfold path to enlightenment, or Self Realization.

According to Wikipedia, there are around 60 ancient texts that discuss the yamas, with slight variations in both content and translation. They can be regarded as a basic moral code of conduct for those on the path of Self Realization.

The yamas are similar to the Ten Commandments, but with a greater emphasis on Self Realization. Interestingly, when one attains Self Realization, adherence to these yamas often seems to occur naturally, almost as a byproduct of that state. If that is the case, these yamas can also be used as practical tools to induce Self Realization, like solving a reversed math problem.

It is worth noting that *ksama*, or forgiveness, is one of the yamas. The forgiveness process is among the most powerful techniques discussed in this book, as it can accelerate progress toward Self Realization by swiftly dissolving the knot of the heart, where the Self is said to be held captive. One doesn't even need to do forgiveness with neurofeedback, one can simply do it alone and get the immense benefits from it.

Back to the mind-blowing conversation I had with the enlightened yogi. I also asked him how much he sleeps at night, and he said he does not sleep much. If one is in a constant state of meditation—or meditates in place of sleep—this could potentially reduce the need for sleep. The main purpose of sleep is to enter slower brain wave states, which rejuvenates and heals the body and stimulates the production of repairing and healing hormones.

However, if one is Self Realized, the need for sleep could theoretically be minimized or even largely unnecessary. For example, during normal sleep cycles, we move through dream sleep, which is predominantly a theta brain wave state, and dreamless sleep, which is predominantly a delta brain wave state. If one can maintain waking consciousness in theta and delta states through meditation, this could fulfill the restorative functions of sleep. In other words, instead of entering unconscious sleep, one could rest and repair in a conscious, meditative state as needed.

I remember sitting on the small couch in the tent, talking with him, while his other cohorts watched us with quiet curiosity—and we, in turn, watched them. The experience hit me all at once, unexpectedly, and it felt almost overwhelming. I mustered the courage to ask one crucial question: "Are you enlightened?" He looked at me with that strange combination of emptiness and fullness, and simply said, "Yes."

Part of the conversation was translated by his nephew, as his English was good but not perfect. After that intense, almost surreal encounter, we felt a wave of fatigue and quietly made our way back to the hotel, knowing we would rise the next day to continue our search for more enlightened yogis.

Chapter 8

HIDDEN INFLUENCES

In this chapter, we will expand upon the scientific understanding of brain waves and the factors that influence them—such as neurotransmitters, the microbiome, mycobiome, parasites, diet, light, dark, drugs, hormones, EMFs, moon cycles, and more—as well as explore the inextricable link between these influences and how they shape our reality by affecting our brain waves. Through a close examination from the lens of science, we will show that our brain waves are heavily influenced by forces largely beyond our control. These brain waves, in turn, affect how we think, act, and feel, ultimately shape our reality. The only true freedom we have is to Realize the Self.

Let's start with the connection between brain waves and neurotransmitters and expand from there. My first real hint of this connection came through an unexpected source: antibiotics for a stomach ulcer. Between neurofeedback brainwave trainings, I took two courses of antibiotics over the span of two weeks. Trying to meditate and navigate life as best I could was challenging. Extreme fatigue, brain fog, anxiety, and all the usual symptoms of antibiotics crept in. It was difficult—plain and simple. There was nothing heroic or "spiritual" about it.

Once I finished the antibiotics and began to recover, I attended neurofeedback training. It was there that I gained even more insight and clarity, culminating in the breakthrough Samadhi experience I mentioned earlier.

During that training, my brain waves across the entire head were substantially lower than at the end of my first training week a month earlier. At first, I felt embarrassed and confused, wondering why this was happening. My alpha brainwave scores were about 30–40% lower across all regions—frontal, central, temporal, and occipital. I was able to gradually rebuild them throughout the week, but they never fully regained their previous strength. Ultimately, this does not matter for Self Realization as Self Realization is independent of any brain wave state. Self Realization can be found in any brain wave state. It is transcendental Self Realization experiences that can be experienced manipulating brain waves akin to psychedelics. This is not Self Realization.

At one point inside the chamber, something unusual occurred: a faint face emerged, what looked like a grey alien silently watching me. Interesting, I thought, more curious than afraid. Following the instructions, I said in my mind, "If you are not of the light, you must go."

It withdrew soon after. I felt no malice, no threat—only an unsettling neutrality. The presence seemed almost mechanical, as though it wasn't there so much as checking… observing out of detached curiosity, like a routine carried out without emotion.

Could be what the Gnostics refer to as Archons which they talk about as more mechanical in nature. It may have been some form of AI, especially since I'm increasingly convinced that this realm—as well as the astral dream realm—is AI-created, or at the very least shaped by an AI. We will explore this idea in much greater detail at another time.

Later that same night, as I was lying in bed, I felt a buzzing energy and a sort of floaty sensation. Then, all of a sudden, it felt like a light mushroom trip, and I saw the outline of another reality. It was faint, but it was definitely there. I couldn't tell whether it was a ship or another world, but it was another reality—a different dimension. After a while, it slowly faded away, and I returned to my room and eventually drifted off to sleep. Once again this story illustrates the similarity between neurofeedback and psychedelic experiences which is not reflective of Self Realization but instead can be a trap because those who have transcendental experiences now **think** they are Self Realized. Self Realization is the absence with the identification with thought.

If I had to make an educated guess based on everything I now know about that experience, it was probably a glimpse into the astral realm. The astral realm is the place we enter during the dream state. It is also the realm most people go to after the death of the physical body—unless one Realizes the Self, in which case an alternative path opens, bypassing the astral plane entirely.

This reality does not want those who are Self Realized to remain here or return, because they may help others Realize the Self. The controllers of this realm don't want people to Realize the Self because it takes energy away from the system. The oscillating karmic pendulum creates energy. Where does the energy go? Even in the Upanishads it talks about the "gods" not liking it when people Realize the Self. I wonder why.

During that training, my central regions became the highest of all my brain areas, which was a pleasant surprise, as my ego wanted to be different and exceptional. As the training continued, my temporals started to rise. Then, just before that Samadhi experience— with that major breakthrough—the frontals became the highest, aligning with studies done on enlightened Zen monks. But as I would later discover, there is much more to becoming "enlightened" or Self Realized than just brain waves.

There is one major issue among many, with neurofeedback: it does not address the mind. It does not dissolve the mind, nor does it quiet it to any significant degree. One can have enlightened-looking brain waves while still having a fully active mind. That is not enlightenment or Self Realization; it is an unusual hybrid state.

Even with all the protocols used during training—forgiveness, letting go, child rescue, rescripting, the love algorithm, Ho'oponopono, inner-child work, etc.—the fundamental issue of the mind/ego remains unaddressed. For the longest time, I could not understand what was missing. I pondered this for many months until it finally hit me like a ton of bricks: meditation, self-inquiry, and non-attachment to the mind and emotions must complement neurofeedback training for optimal and lasting results. One must know that one is **NOT** the mind, but the awareness or observer beyond the mind.

The mind must be stilled, quieted, or dissolved; only then can one Realize the Self. So what is the most effective way to still, quiet, or dissolve the mind? It all became clear soon after while I was sitting on the couch, observing the thoughts appearing in my mind, and I asked, "To whom do these thoughts come?" **Boom—silence.** Then I asked, "Who am I?" **Boom—stillness.** Suddenly everything made sense.

Shortly after, I found I could feel things on a much deeper level—things that naturally induce stillness. This is how I am able to determine which methods actually work. Because of this, I can now enter states of stillness almost on command, often within minutes.

Using the mind to dissolve the mind through self-inquiry is one of the most brilliant methods for Self Realization, as it goes directly to the source. Self-inquiry was the missing link for me, and it is through this practice that I came to share the three most powerful and fastest methods for realizing the Self—techniques that helped me tremendously. One could spend an entire lifetime searching for the best practices for Self Realization, or one could employ techniques that have been proven effective for centuries, such as self-inquiry, which has been practiced for thousands of years.

THE GUT BRAIN CONNECTION

During neurofeedback training, participants were given protein smoothies before entering the chamber. Over several days, my brainwave readings steadily declined, and I felt increasingly fatigued and depleted. I later discovered that the smoothies contained sucralose—an ingredient I deliberately avoid—which immediately raised concerns for me.

I chose to skip the smoothie the next day. My brainwave readings rose noticeably. I skipped it again the following day, and once more, the readings increased. After this pattern repeated, it became difficult for me to dismiss that sucralose was interfering with my progress during the training.

When I raised these concerns, they were not addressed in any meaningful or empathetic way. This response, consistent with how several other issues I raised were handled, deepened my dissatisfaction with the experience. Taken together, these moments significantly undermined my trust in the process as it was being administered.

As a result, I cannot recommend neurofeedback training as I experienced it at the facility I attended. Others may have different outcomes elsewhere. For me, however, the approach proved unnecessary. The methods presented in this book, in my view, offer sufficient tools for Self Realization without reliance on technological interventions such as neurofeedback, which I now regard with skepticism.

BRAIN WAVES AND NEUROTRANSMITTERS

There is a significant connection between our gut biome and our brain waves, and that connection operates largely through neurotransmitters. This was a double confirmation: the antibiotics I had taken before my straining had already caused a dramatic reduction in my alpha brain waves. Eureka—it all made perfect sense. Soon after, I went down several rabbit holes researching brain waves, neurotransmitters, and the gut.

Gamma (35–42 Hz)
* Brain state: Consciousness, altruism, concentration
* Possible neurotransmission: GABA, Glutamate (Glu)
Beta (14–35 Hz)
* Brain state: Awake, talking, hyperactivity
* Possible neurotransmission: GABA, Dopamine
Alpha (8–14 Hz)
* Brain state: Relaxed, walking
* Possible neurotransmission: Acetylcholine (ACh), serotonin
Theta (4–8 Hz)
* Brain state: Deeply relaxed, meditation
* Possible neurotransmission: Acetylcholine (ACh), GABA
Delta (1.5–4 Hz)
* Brain state: Sleep
* Possible neurotransmission: Serotonin

A brief summary of classic EEG bands (brain waves), indicating their frequency, prevalence in different states, and possible relationships with specific types of neurotransmission. Some research has also suggested a connection between serotonin and alpha brain waves (Avila et al., 2020).

As shown in the chart:

- Gamma is connected to GABA and glutamate
- Beta is connected to dopamine
- Alpha is connected to acetylcholine as well as serotonin
- Theta is connected to GABA and acetylcholine
- Delta is connected to serotonin

Summary of some of the most common neurotransmitters:

Glutamate – Glutamate is an excitatory neurotransmitter and the most abundant neurotransmitter in the nervous system. It is responsible for over 90% of excitatory synaptic connections in the brain. Glutamate is often called the "master neurotransmitter" because it excites other neurons, prompting them to release their neurotransmitters. It plays a key role in learning and memory, brain and neural plasticity, pain sensitivity, and more. Too little glutamate is linked to anxiety and depression. Some studies show that glutamate levels in certain parts of the brain are highest during REM sleep and upon waking. One of the best ways to increase glutamate is through exercise. Caffeine also stimulates glutamate production, although its use is generally not recommended, as will be discussed later. Glutamate is associated with gamma brain waves.

GABA – Gamma-aminobutyric acid (GABA) is the body's major inhibitory neurotransmitter, serving as the counterpart to glutamate. In most people, these two neurotransmitters balance each other. Since glutamate is a metabolic precursor to GABA, the body uses glutamate to produce GABA. Increasing GABA can help decrease excessive glutamate. Practices such as yoga and meditation have been shown to increase GABA levels, which promotes a calming and relaxing effect on the body. GABA is associated with gamma, beta, and theta brain waves.

Dopamine – Dopamine is released during pleasurable activities such as eating, social interactions, and exercise. It is essential for mood, attention, motivation, and movement. Dopamine is connected to beta brain waves, which aligns with the observation that social media and other modern stimuli can hijack our dopamine system, increasing beta activity and disconnecting us from our true Self. Higher dopamine levels often correlate with heightened beta waves, increased craving, and agitation—opposite of stillness. This explains why sensual pleasures can act as a trap for Self Realization, making the practice of sensual austerity beneficial.

Acetylcholine – Acetylcholine is involved in muscle control, REM sleep, learning, and memory, as well as critical functions in the cardiovascular, gastrointestinal, and urinary systems. Acetylcholine is associated with alpha and theta brain waves.

Serotonin – Serotonin plays a key role in numerous physiological and biochemical processes, including digestion, mood regulation, sleep, appetite, and memory. Serotonin is linked to alpha and delta brain waves. Notably, 90–95% of a person's serotonin is produced in the gut.

Neurotransmitter	Primary Functions	Associated Brain Waves	Notes
Glutamate	Excitatory neurotransmitter; learning, memory, neural plasticity, pain sensitivity	Gamma	"Master neurotransmitter"; too little linked to anxiety and depression; levels highest during REM and upon waking; increased by exercise and compassion
GABA	Major inhibitory neurotransmitter; calming, relaxation	Gamma, Beta, Theta	Balances glutamate; yoga and meditation increase GABA; reduces agitation
Dopamine	Mood, attention, motivation, movement	Beta	Released during pleasurable activities; excessive dopamine increases craving and beta activity; linked to social media stimulation

Acetylcholine	Muscle control, REM sleep, learning, memory; cardiovascular, gastrointestinal, urinary functions	Alpha, Theta	Supports learning and memory; involved in motor control and bodily systems
Serotonin	Digestion, mood regulation, sleep, appetite, memory	Alpha, Delta	90–95% produced in the gut; critical for mood and physiological processes

BETA BRAIN WAVE CRISIS

John, an average person in America, gets out of bed, pours a cup of coffee, and flips on the television or scrolls through his iPhone as he prepares for work. On the way to the office, sipping his coffee and navigating through traffic, he continues to listen to the latest news and events. Much of the news is fear-driven, designed to make people anxious or alert. The coffee stimulates John's beta brain waves, as do the stress of traffic and the constant barrage of negative news. Dopamine and beta activity dominate his brain and body.

Soon, John arrives at work, sitting in a cubicle and making calls to secure sales. He remains in a constant state of anxiety and sympathetic nervous system activation—fight or flight. For lunch, John heads to a fast-food restaurant and orders a highly processed meal.

After finishing work, John returns home in rush-hour traffic, listening to more fast-paced news or music. On the way, he grabs another ultra-processed meal, this time from McDonald's. At home, he throws on the TV and watches a Netflix show designed to hook his emotions. While watching, he opens a beer, telling himself he needs it to relax. What John doesn't realize is that while the initial effect may feel calming, the beer will eventually increase beta brain waves once the temporary alpha spike fades and will decrease sleep quality.

Finally exhausted, John goes to bed, only to repeat the same routine the next day. John—and likely many Americans, as well as much of the world s population—lives in a perpetual state of sympathetic nervous system activation, dominated by elevated beta brainwave activity. Most are also plugged into this simulation, running on autopilot in a state of unconsciousness. Self Realization is breaking out of mechanical living and living in a state of awareness.

Technology is turning society into dopamine junkies (Waters, 2021), driving beta brain waves ever higher. This comes at a cost: a growing disconnection from the Self as our brains remain trapped in heightened beta states. News and social media feed this cycle, constantly bombarding us with fear- and anxiety-inducing stories, pushing dopamine and beta activity even further (Trafton, 2025).

DRUG EFFECTS ON EEG

In addition to illicit drugs, pharmaceutical drugs have a direct influence on brain waves. There is a comprehensive compilation of information on various pharmaceutical drugs and their effects on brain waves from BioSource Faculty (2025). It appears that nearly every drug increases beta brain waves. Were these drugs purposely designed to do this, or is it merely an unintended side effect? If drugs are researched as thoroughly as claimed, it would be difficult to overlook their impact on brain waves. Moreover, there are simply too many drugs that increase beta brain waves for it to be a coincidence.

Looking at prescription drug use in the U.S. alone, the Centers for Disease Control and Prevention (2024) reports the following:

- Percent of people using at least one prescription drug in the past 30 days: 49.9% (2017–March 2020)

- Percent of people using three or more prescription drugs in the past 30 days: 24.7% (2017–March 2020)

- Percent of people using five or more prescription drugs in the past 30 days: 13.5% (2017–March 2020)

IS SOCIETY BEING KEPT IN A BETA STATE?

Are the "powers that be" deliberately trying to keep society in a beta brain wave state—agitated, anxious, nervous, and disconnected from the Divine Spark, the Self within? Are they keeping the world in a state of lowered IQ, EQ, and creativity, fostering compliance and absolute obedience to authority? That may very well be the case.

This is not to say that the beta state is inherently bad—we still need it for problem-solving, alertness, focus, and analytical thinking from time to time. The issue arises when beta becomes the predominant brain wave state. Ideally, humans should maintain a natural predominance of alpha brain waves, yet it appears that the majority of people are stuck in beta.

MICROBIOME AND NEUROTRANSMITTERS

Upon further examination of the connection between the gut and brain waves, I came to understand that our emotions can be heavily influenced through the gut microbiome. In other words, our emotions and even our bodies are being shaped by external factors—often without our awareness. Neurotransmitters influence our emotions, which shape how we think. Our thoughts then reinforce how we feel, and these feelings influence the decisions we make, ultimately shaping our reality and destiny.

For example, when someone has gut dysbiosis, they may naturally experience heightened anxiety, anger, or depression. Once these emotional states arise, the mind quickly constructs narratives to justify and reinforce them. With sufficient awareness, one can observe this process in real time—watching thoughts and emotions arise and pass away. It is not the emotions themselves that are destructive, but our clinging to them, especially when we falsely identify with the mind and its emotional states. This misidentification is the root cause of suffering and the primary obstacle to Self Realization: the mistaken belief that the Self is the egoic mind and its emotions.

We now understand that there is a direct and dynamic connection between brain waves, neurotransmitters, hormones, and the gut microbiota. It is well established that antibiotics disrupt the gut microbiome, and growing evidence suggests that artificial sweeteners—such as sucralose—can have similar effects. It is therefore reasonable to assume that most people regularly consume substances that disturb their gut microbial balance. According to the Centers for Disease Control and Prevention (2025), approximately 80–90% of the U.S. population has taken antibiotics at some point in their lives. Given this widespread exposure, it is likely that a large portion of the population experiences some degree of gut dysbiosis. This imbalance can create persistent feelings of discomfort, anxiety, or low mood, which the mind then interprets and reinforces through negative thought patterns—ultimately contributing to the construction of a negative lived reality.

Dr Joe Dispenza says this about thoughts creating our reality: "The same thoughts lead to the same choices which lead to the same behaviors which lead to the same emotions, which all lead to the same predictable future. The same events in our future reality are creating the same predictable emotions for us all the time. And as a result, we're feeling the same every day. Our yesterday becomes our tomorrow—so in truth, our past is our future.

If we want to create a new personal reality—a new life—we must begin to examine the thoughts, emotions and behaviors we've been living by, and change them.

We must become conscious of the unconscious behaviors we've been choosing to demonstrate that have led to the same experiences, and then we must make new choices, take new actions, and create new experiences.

New choices should lead to new behaviors. New behaviors should lead to new experiences. New experiences should create new emotions, and new emotions and feelings should inspire us to think in new ways."

Dr. Dispenza is onto something here. While I resonate with much of what he teaches, I question whether simply replacing negative programming with positive programming truly transforms reality. The real path is to Realize the Self—to awaken to the truth that we are the Self, not the mind, the body, or the emotions. Shifting from a negative mind to a positive mind is still playing within the same illusion. One remains bound, still a prisoner of this dream, whether shackled by iron or gilded in gold. True freedom comes not from the mind, but from realizing that the Self has never been bound at all.

One's only true freedom is to realize that the mind is not real. Freedom lies in choosing not to play the game of the mind and ego, but instead to Realize the Self—to disidentify from the mind, the body, and this transient world. We are not the mind; we are not the body. We are the ineffable, the nameless, the stillness, the nothingness, the eternal truth. We are the Self, and only the Self is real. Everything else comes and goes. That which comes and goes is not real; that which does not come and go is real. Realize what is real and eternal—that is you, that is the Self. You are THAT!

The mind and body are deeply interconnected. How we feel affects what we think, and what we think affects how we feel. One simple way to observe this is to notice your feelings and see which thoughts arise from them—they tend to align. When we feel good, our thoughts are generally positive; when we feel bad, our thoughts tend toward negativity. Interestingly, the average person thinks about 60,000 thoughts per day, with roughly 80% being negative, and about 90% repeating from the day before. This means that most people are trapped in a negative thought loop, which contributes to the creation of a negative reality.

There is evidence that our thoughts shape reality to a certain extent. It is also worth noting that approximately 95% of our lives are governed by the subconscious—our beliefs, conditioning, and automatic patterns of thinking, feeling, and behavior. Most people move through life on autopilot, largely unaware of this internal machinery. Awareness is the key to interrupting these unconscious patterns, but awareness alone is not the end. The methods presented in this book cultivate awareness as a gateway, yet true freedom comes only through the realization of the Self—the silent, ever-present witness beyond the mind. You are THAT!

EXTRA:

More articles articles on the general hazards of artificial sweeteners: (Chugh, 2024 and Havovi, 2025)

Ten-Week Sucralose Consumption Induces Gut Dysbiosis and Altered Glucose and Insulin Levels in Healthy Young Adults (Mendez-Garcia et al., 2022)

Study: A randomized controlled trial into the effects of probiotics on electroencephalography in preschoolers with autism. "In subjects treated with probiotics, we observed a decrease of power in frontopolar regions in beta and gamma bands, and increased coherence in the same bands together with a shift in frontal asymmetry, which suggests a modification toward a typical brain activity."
(Billeci et al., 2023)

Low Dose of Sucralose Alter Gut Microbiome in Mice
(Zheng et al., 2022)

95% of our serotonin as well as other constituents such as gamma-aminobutyric acid (GABA) and catecholamines are produced in the gut by these beneficial bacteria. By altering our gut biome we are altering our neurotransmitters.
(Terry, 2017 and Dicks, 2022)

In a study by Adikari et al. (2020) they used an EEG to investigate the effects of probiotics on physiological parameters related to anxiety in football players. Upon completion of the 4 week study they found an increase in theta and delta brain waves in the probiotic group which led to them being more relaxed and alert.

L Reuteri. L Reuteri has been shown to increase the hormone Oxytocin.
(Danhof et al., 2023)

Oxytocin has been shown to be associated with an increase in alpha and theta brain waves.
(Kaat et al., 2021)

THE MYCOBIOME

The gut microbiota includes all the microorganisms in the gut. Beyond the bacterial component, known as the microbiome, we also have the gut mycobiome, which is composed of fungi. Interestingly, the mycobiome influences our neurotransmitters just as much as the microbiome does. This is a vastly understudied area, but the research that does exist is fascinating. "Myco-" refers to fungi and "micro-" to bacteria, hence the term mycobiome. Although fungi make up only about 0.1% of the total gut microorganisms, they are over 100 times larger than bacterial cells, representing a significant portion of gut biomass. These organisms affect mood and emotional state just as powerfully as bacteria, and ongoing research continues to illuminate their role.

Several years ago, I underwent a heavy course of antibiotics for an ulcer, which triggered a nasty case of Candida overgrowth. I could clearly feel its effects on my mood, which then rippled into my emotional state and shaped the kinds of thoughts that arose. Paradoxically, this experience gave me a unique opportunity: I was able to observe these thoughts without identifying with them. Instead of being swept away, I watched them arise and dissolve—like clouds drifting across the sky or waves forming and receding in the ocean.

One likely explanation is that the antibiotics disrupted Lactobacillus and other beneficial gut bacteria that normally keep Candida in balance. With that balance disturbed, the resulting emotional shifts became obvious enough that they revealed a crucial insight: thoughts were not *me*—they were conditioned responses passing through awareness.

Millions of people worldwide have taken antibiotics, and many likely suffer from some form of gut dysbiosis. This underscores the critical importance of maintaining gut health: it directly affects neurotransmitters, thought patterns, emotions, and behavior. A gut in disarray makes it much more challenging to Realize the Self, particularly in the early stages of the journey.

"These fungi-produced substances have the capacity to interact with neuronal receptors and alter the balance and function of neurotransmitters. For example, specific fungal species have been found to produce chemicals resembling neurotransmitters such as serotonin, dopamine, and gamma-aminobutyric acid (GABA). Additionally, by modifying the gut microbiome, the gut mycobiome can indirectly influence neurotransmitter regulation. Numerous studies have examined the role of the gut microbiome, which is composed of bacteria, in the synthesis and metabolism of neurotransmitters. Imbalances in the gut mycobiome can disrupt the microbial ecosystem, potentially altering how the gut microbiome produces and utilizes neurotransmitters." (Yetgin, 2024)

Studies have shown that the human gut hosts more than 66 genera and 184 species of fungi, with Candida, Saccharomyces, and Cladosporium being particularly common (Rodriguez et al., 2015).

In a study by Hadrich et al. (2024), they demonstrated a link between gut dysbiosis and neuropsychiatric disorders:

"Results: Emerging research links gut mycobiota dysbiosis to conditions such as schizophrenia, Alzheimer's disease, autism spectrum disorders, bipolar disorder, and depression. Studies indicate that specific fungal populations, such as Candida and Saccharomyces, may influence neuroinflammation, gut permeability, and immune responses, thereby affecting mental health outcomes."

The data clearly shows that our gut mycobiome has a profound impact on our neurotransmitters and brain waves. Ideally, one would do everything possible to heal and optimize the gut while on the path to Self Realization. That said, not everyone has access to specialized doctors or medical facilities, and that's okay. We can only do the best with what we have—and then surrender and let go.

Surrender is a cornerstone of Self Realization. Let go of resistance and control. Much of the mind's suffering comes from resistance itself. Resistance is suffering. When we accept the present moment fully—without trying to change it or push against it—we create fertile ground for Self Realization to take root.

PARASITES

Staying with the theme of microorganisms lets check out parasites and their role in brain waves. Parasites do indeed play a significant role on neurotransmitters and brain waves. A study done in Iran found that 100% of children infected with parasites had higher levels of theta brain waves as opposed to 6.34% of children with no parasites (Davoudi et al., 2020).

Ever heard of the "crazy cat lady"? There's some truth to the stereotype—cats can carry a parasite called *Toxoplasma gondii*, which has been linked to schizophrenia. It is estimated that 30–50% of the world's population is infected with this parasite. *Toxoplasma* has a direct effect on neurotransmitters and brain waves, most notably by disrupting glutamate levels, which can contribute to schizophrenia. Schizophrenia is characterized by significantly elevated slow-wave delta and theta brain activity (Rockstroh et al., 2007). In addition, studies show other brain wave anomalies, including abnormal theta activity, altered theta-gamma coupling, reduced alpha oscillations, and increased gamma activity—particularly in the auditory cortex—leading to hallucinations (Moran & Hong, 2011).

The entire microbiota—including parasites, the microbiome, and the mycobiome—has a profound influence on brain waves, which in turn shape our thoughts, emotions, and ultimately our perceived reality. By taking care of our gut health, we can make the path to Self Realization smoother.

Regardless, it is crucial to understand that our thoughts and emotions are not who we are—they do not originate from the Self. The Self is not the mind, nor the body. The Self is thoughtless, speechless, and mindless—pure, perfect, and flawless. You are perfection; you are the Self. Do not trust the mind or the body—trust the Self, and Realize the Self. You are THAT!

DIET AND BRAIN WAVES

Let us now discuss diet and its effects on brain waves. Much of the American diet—and increasingly the global diet—is composed of processed and ultra-processed foods. According to the CDC (2021–2023), up to 55% of the American diet comes from ultra-processed foods. High sugar, unhealthy fats, and chemical additives dominate the typical American diet.

We've all heard the saying, You are what you eat." High consumption of junk food contributes to a junk mind, a junk body, and a diminished ability to Realize the Self. Such foods promote inflammation, disrupt the gut microbiota, increase the risk of chronic disease, and—through dopamine spikes that elevate beta brain waves—further distance one from Self Realization. Additionally, many of these foods can be nearly as addictive as drugs, particularly sugar, which has been shown to mimic the effects of opiates. Needless to say, diet profoundly impacts brain waves (Roberts et al., n.d.).

> "The theory is formulated that intermittent, excessive
> intake of sugar can have dopaminergic, cholinergic,
> and opioid effects that are similar to psychostimulants
> and opiates, albeit smaller in magnitude."
> (Avena & Hoebel, 2008)

So, what is the ideal diet? While there is no single perfect" plan, wisdom points us toward minimizing processed foods and eliminating artificial additives. Among the diets with the most research-backed benefits, the Mediterranean Diet stands out, particularly for its association with longevity and overall health. Similarly, populations in the Blue Zones—those rare regions where people live exceptionally long, healthy lives—follow dietary patterns that emphasize whole, plant-based foods, legumes, whole grains, nuts, and healthy fats, with meat and dairy consumed sparingly. Despite regional differences, the common thread in these longevity hotspots is a focus on natural, minimally processed foods combined with moderation, balance, and mindful eating.

It is wise to avoid extremes in diet—and, for that matter, in life itself. A purely carnivorous or strictly vegan approach may not suit most people. As always, consult a medical professional before making significant changes to your health routine. Occasional fasting can be a valuable tool for cultivating discipline, and intermittent fasting—abstaining from food for 16–20 hours at a time—has demonstrated remarkable health benefits. Dietary habits should not be rigid; it should be measured, mindful, and intentional. Above all, minimizing sugar and highly processed foods helps calm the mind, lower beta brain wave activity, and create the conditions for mindfulness and ultimately Self Realization.

It is no coincidence that those who consume excessive junk and processed foods often carry a restless mind, trapped in an elevated beta brain wave state. The diet of the body mirrors the diet of the mind. By nourishing the body with natural, minimally processed foods, one lays the groundwork for a clearer mind, steadier emotions, and a more direct path to the Self. Food can be medicine, or it can be a subtle form of bondage—a tool for liberation or a chain to fleeting sensory pleasures. Choose wisely, for the body is the vessel through which the Self experiences and realizes itself. The body is the temple of the Self; keep it clean and sacred.

HORMONES AND BRAIN WAVES

Next, let's discuss hormones and their connection to brain waves. This is another great area of research, as the body is an intricately interconnected system. Brain waves, neurotransmitters, the gut microbiota, and hormones all work together in tandem. Hormones are a topic that could occupy hours of discussion and study. But what are hormones? According to Wikipedia (2025), hormones are chemical messengers that influence virtually every aspect of the human body, including digestion, metabolism, sleep, reproduction, stress, and mood.

Some common hormones include testosterone, estrogen, progesterone, FSH, insulin, growth hormone, serotonin, melatonin, and adrenaline. Interestingly, some hormones can act both as neurotransmitters and as hormones, such as oxytocin, serotonin, noradrenaline, dopamine, adrenaline, and melatonin. Melatonin is particularly intriguing because it regulates sleep cycles, and during deep, dreamless sleep, we experience a state of predominant delta brain waves—essentially a nightly glimpse of Self Realization.

There is extensive research connecting hormones to brain waves. For example, oxytocin can decrease beta brain waves, progesterone increases GABA, cortisol increases beta brain waves, and even testosterone influences brain wave activity. Regarding testosterone replacement therapy, it is worth recalling our favorite Oscar Wilde quote: "Everything popular is wrong." In one study, rats given testosterone displayed increased aggression and elevated delta, theta, beta, and gamma brain wave activity, highlighting the direct influence hormones exert on neural activity (Estumano et al., 2019).

Lastly, research suggests that short periods of abstinence may lead to temporary increases in men's testosterone levels, peaking around seven days before returning to baseline. However, these changes are generally short-lived, and there is no strong evidence that sexual activity or restraint produces lasting increases in testosterone. What this does suggest is that, for men, a seven-day period of abstinence may enhance certain brain wave patterns, which—if approached strategically—could support the optimization of Self Realization.

ADRENALINE AMPLIFIER OF THE MIND

Another interesting observation I had was the increase in thoughts that seemed to accompany the rise in adrenaline and dopamine from exercise. I tend to exercise daily, usually engaging in light jogging or cycling, but occasionally I perform more intense workouts designed to produce beneficial physiological adaptations that promote longevity—such as aerobic exercises to increase VO_2 max. VO_2 max refers to the body's ability to utilize oxygen and can be improved through high-intensity aerobic exercise like running or cycling.

A common method to increase VO_2 max while running is to perform four sets of four-minute hard intervals. After completing these types of workouts, my heart rate rises substantially, and I notice a general increase in the volume of my thoughts. I conclude that adrenaline and beta brain waves are closely connected to the mind and the generation of thoughts, almost like an antenna.

Exercise is another connection between hormones, neurotransmitters, thoughts, and emotions. This is not to say that strenuous exercise is bad—far from it—but it's worth being mindful of its effects. You are not the mind, not the body, not the emotions; you are the silent witness within, the Self. Exercise illustrates how our breath, hormones, neurotransmitters, and mind are all interconnected.

By understanding what the Self is not, we gain insight into what the Self truly is. Through exercise, we can observe the surge of thoughts and simply watch them. As the body settles, the mind and thoughts naturally settle as well. Sometimes, a pendulum-like effect can be used deliberately: swing the mind/body one way, then observe as it swings back, watching thoughts accelerate and decelerate. This is directly connected to the breath: faster breathing increases brain wave activity, while slower breathing slows it down. During meditation, it can be useful to slow the breath to still the mind and body, supporting the path to Self Realization.

WOMEN'S MENSTRUAL CYCLE

There is a substantial amount of research showing that women's menstrual cycles affect brain waves, which in turn influences mood—so yes, your brain really can have its own monthly "rollercoaster playlist." Hormonal fluctuations, particularly in estrogen and progesterone, affect brain regions associated with memory, emotions, and behavior through the limbic system. This means that everything from your decision-making to your chocolate cravings might get a little… remix treatment. In fact, all brain wave types appear to be affected, as demonstrated in this study (Haraguchi et al., 2021)—proving that even your neurons like to keep things interesting once a month.

"Resting-state MEG activity was recorded from 25 healthy women with normal menstrual cycles. For each woman, resting-state brain activity was acquired twice using MEG: once during their menstrual period (MP) and once outside of this period (OP). Our results indicated that the median frequency and peak alpha frequency of the power spectrum were lower, whereas Shannon spectral entropy was higher, during the MP. Theta intensity within the right temporal cortex and right limbic system was significantly lower during the MP than during the OP. High gamma intensity in the left parietal cortex was also significantly lower during the MP than during the OP. Similar differences were observed in the parietal and occipital regions between the proliferative (late follicular phase) and secretory (luteal) phases." (Haraguchi et al., 2021)

Women aren't the only ones with hormonal cycles. Men experience what can be referred to as a "manstrual" cycle, with a 24-hour testosterone cycle: testosterone peaks in the morning and gradually declines throughout the day (Law, 2011). In addition, men's testosterone levels naturally decline with age. Testosterone plays a critical role in mood, attitude, and behavior, and—as we saw earlier—it significantly affects brain wave activity as well.

MOON CYCLES

We've all heard the old saying that people act strangely during a full moon. Classic werewolf movies show someone transforming into a werewolf and howling at the moon—but is there any truth to it? Surprisingly, yes. Not the werewolf part, of course, but the moon does influence our neurotransmitters, which in turn affects our brain waves. Increasingly, research supports this connection.

Different moon phases trigger changes in various neurotransmitters. During the full moon, studies show serotonin increases while melatonin decreases. Many people report poor sleep during this time, which can lead to a range of physical and mental health effects. Notably, delta brain waves—the ones tied to deep, restorative sleep—drop by around 30% during a full moon (Cajochen et al., 2013).

Interestingly, serotonin rises even as delta declines, which seems counterintuitive since the two are usually linked. Clearly, there's still much we don't understand about the moon's effects. And when you consider that the human body is mostly water—just like the oceans that respond to lunar cycles—it becomes even more fascinating.

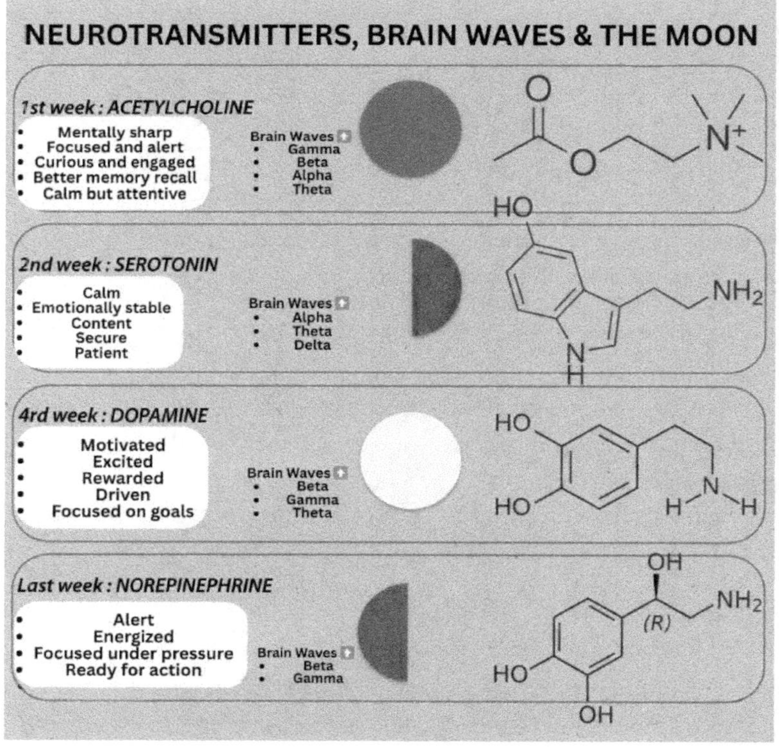

"For instance, new research suggests that our dominant neurotransmitters change with each of the four weeks of a lunar cycle. The first week of a new moon brings a surge of acetylcholine; the next brings serotonin; then comes dopamine, and finally norepinephrine. During a dopamine week, people would tend to be more social and relaxed, while norepinephrine would make people more analytic. A serotonin week might be good for work, and an acetylcholine week should be full of pep." (Rushkoff, 2017)

EFFECTS OF LIGHT ON BRAIN WAVES

Since we live in a world defined by light and dark, by the rising and setting of the sun, it follows that these fundamental rhythms would influence our brain waves—and indeed, they do. In a study by Idris et al. (2024), exposure to xenon white light was shown to increase alpha and beta brain waves, while theta waves decreased in response to any light. Delta waves, meanwhile, showed both increases and decreases depending on the color of the light.

This aligns beautifully with what we observe in meditation. As soon as we close our eyes, alpha waves begin to rise; with sustained practice, theta emerges, followed eventually by delta. This mirrors the natural cycles of sleep, where we shift between theta and delta during dream-filled and dreamless states. Light acts as a subtle signal, a cosmic rhythm, guiding the tempo of our brain waves, which in turn shapes how we think, act, and feel.

It is no wonder, then, that yogis have historically sought extended periods in caves or dark retreats. Immersed in darkness, one can more easily access the slower brain wave states of theta and delta, opening the door to mystical experiences and optimally Self Realization. Modern dark retreats, such as those in Thailand run by Mantak Chia, offer similar opportunities in more comfortable settings. While I have not personally participated in one, the practice seems profoundly beneficial—not only for confronting fears of darkness but also for cultivating resilience and equanimity in the in-between spaces of life and death, the Bardo. In essence, darkness becomes a mirror of the Self, reflecting the stillness and infinite depths within, revealing the truth of consciousness that light alone cannot unveil. In the absence of external illumination, one encounters the eternal, unchanging Self—beyond mind, beyond body, beyond thought.

The void, the darkness, is not mere absence—it is the fertile nothingness from which all light emerges. In the stillness of darkness, the mind's incessant chatter falters, and the illusions of form, identity, and desire lose their grip. It is here, in this profound emptiness, that the Self reveals itself—not as a thought, not as a sensation, not as a fleeting emotion, but as the eternal witness beyond all phenomena, the Self. You are THAT!

EMFs

There's another subtle way our brain waves are being influenced—through electromagnetic fields. Believe it or not, everything from cell phones (Kramarenko et al., 2003) to laptops, smart meters, and power lines has an effect on our brain wave activity. As these technologies evolve—from 4G to 5G and soon 6G—the strength and frequency of these signals increase, and so do their potential effects on the brain.

The best thing we can do is minimize our exposure to them as much as reasonably possible: by living farther from major EMF sources when we can, and by using EMF-mitigation devices that appear to offer some degree of protection according to certain studies. Even from my own experience, I noticed a tangible difference before and after placing one of those EMF protection stickers on my phone.

BRAIN WAVES AND HEART RATE

Activity	Increase in resting heart rate
Alcohol before bedtime	10-20 bpm
Anxiety, stress, rumination	5-25 bpm
Late-day caffeine	5-15 bpm
Intense evening exercise	5-15 bpm
Large evening meals	5-15 bpm
Nicotine	5-15 bpm
Dehydration	3-8 bpm
High room or body temp	3-8 bpm
Certain meds will elevate	3-10 bpm

Johnson, 2025.

Here is a great list of activities and their effects on heart rate, thanks to Bryan Johnson (2025). We know that increased beta brain waves are associated with elevated heart rate, as the fight-or-flight mechanisms of the sympathetic nervous system activate. What's particularly interesting is the connection between heart rate, brain waves, and neurotransmitters. Activities that raise heart rate also tend to increase beta brain waves, as heart rate and brain wave activity are intimately linked (Kim, 2013).

It's important to note that dehydration and high ambient or body temperature also elevate heart rate, and therefore beta brain waves. Dehydration and elevated body temperature are closely connected: as the body warms, water levels decrease, leading to dehydration. Consider those who live in hotter climates without access to clean water or air conditioning—they are likely experiencing higher beta brain wave states compared with the average person in cooler regions like the US or the UK, where clean water and climate control are readily available.

POPULAR WEIGHT LOSS DRUGS

Another popular class of weight-loss drugs is the GLP-1, or Glucagon-Like Peptide-1, medications, such as semaglutide and tirzepatide. These drugs have become increasingly popular for weight loss, with more and more people taking injections derived from gila monster venom. In a great post by Bryan Johnson, he illustrates (see below) the elevated heart rates induced by these medications. Theoretically, one could reasonably infer that these drugs also increase beta brain wave activity.

Having taken a microdose of semaglutide myself, I can confirm that it does indeed increase beta brain wave activity, diminishes the stillness and connection with the Self within, and amplifies the mind and thoughts. The effect feels similar to a spike in adrenaline or a small dose of caffeine. After spending extended periods in stillness, these substances have a noticeably strong and uncomfortable impact.

Johnson, 2025.

Instead of pharmaceuticals increasing beta brain waves, could these drugs be designed to enhance Self Realization rather than diminish it—by reducing beta brain waves instead of increasing them? That is a profound question. One could even suggest that these drugs were intentionally created to induce a slightly agitated state by elevating beta brain waves. This fits perfectly with the idea that this world is a trap.

The only thing to do is to Realize the Self. Self Realization is the one aspect of reality we truly have the power to control. Realize the Self, and all problems resolve themselves. There are no more worries, no more suffering, no more craving, no more wanting, no more needing, no more playing small—because the Self is infinite, and you are THAT!

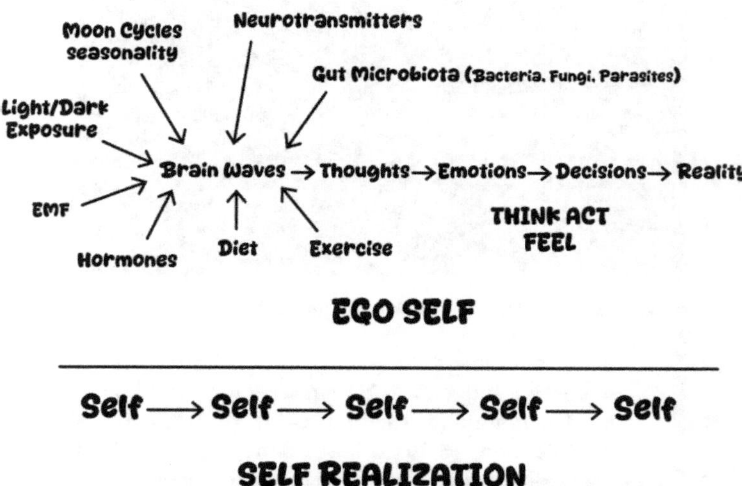

Here's a diagram (above) I made showing the factors that affect our brain waves and their effects on how we think, act, and feel. One could add gender to that diagram as there are some pronounced differences in brain waves between men and women. For example women show higher alpha brain waves then men, men show slightly higher beta, women show higher theta then men and both genders show a good amount of gamma with women showing more synchronization.

Below the Ego Self diagram is the Self diagram. The Self is changeless, timeless, fearless, infinite bliss and love. The Self is always THAT. The Self is eternal and immutable—it simply is. As one brilliant yogi Pukinanda once said, "It is what it is."

We have shown numerous studies and evidence supporting that neurotransmitters, microbiota, moon cycles, EMFs, light and dark, diet, exercise, and hormones all affect our brain waves, which in turn influence our thoughts, shape our emotions, guide our decisions, and ultimately shape our reality. Even something as simple as the moon's phases can influence human behavior, emotions, and reality.

For the most part, we do not have control over many external factors that influence our thoughts and emotions. What we *can* control is whether we identify with them or not. This disidentification from the mind and emotions—and identifying instead with the awareness within—is called Self Realization. You are not the mind; you are not the body. You are pure conscious awareness. You are that which is beyond all and yet is all; you are the ineffable, the perfect, the timeless, the immortal, the glorious, boundless, eternal Self. You are THAT!

When we abide in the Self, we can watch the mind and emotions come and go. Identifying as the Self is the only true freedom we have. We do not control our thoughts and emotions— they are shaped by forces beyond our grasp. However, by practicing the methods in this book to still and quiet the mind, we can Realize the true Self. We can gain freedom from the prison of this world, which manipulates the mind and emotions and tricks us into identifying with them. That is our only true freedom, and that is Self Realization.

Self Realization is absolute freedom—from this world, from thoughts, from emotions, from anything that comes and goes. This world is a dream; it is not real. Only the Self is real. Self Realization is the ultimate power, the ultimate freedom. It is the recognition of the only thing that does not come and go: the awareness within, the eternal observer, the witness. Self Realization is here now; it has always been with you and always will be. Simply release the false identification with the mind and body and rest in the Self. You are **THAT!**

Chapter 9

BREAK FREE

This is a visual representation of what the heart center looks like when it is burdened by *sanskaras*—emotional scars that are never fully released or healed. The ancient Upanishads refer to this as the heart knot, or *hridaya granthi* in Sanskrit. Over the years, more and more of these chains or knots bind the heart, keeping it trapped in lower emotional states such as anger, sadness, shame, and guilt. The three methods provided later—**the forgiveness method, the release technique, and self-inquiry**— all help break the chains and knots that bind us and free the Self. These chains siphon our energy, draining us of our vital life force.

Have you ever seen someone who appears older or more worn out than their years, someone highly emotionally charged? They are likely being drained by recurring negative thought loops. Unable to "let go," they continue to add more chains to their heart.

The heart center is of utmost importance, as it is considered the theoretical location of our true Self, the Divine Spark. Yet the heart and the Self can become bound by chains of fear, guilt, shame, sadness, and anger. To free the heart, one must embrace and immerse oneself in what the heart and the Self ultimately are: **LOVE** (BLISS). Not worldly attachment love, but divine love, expressed through loving-kindness, compassion, forgiveness, humility, and service to others.

According to Ramana Maharshi and the Upanishads, the heart is precisely where the ego goes to die upon Self Realization. If the heart is shackled by sanskaras—the emotional scars that imprison it—then the true Self remains veiled, and the ego will struggle to dissolve within the heart. At that time, I was unaware of the practice of self-inquiry and lacked the depth of theoretical understanding I have today.

Now, I am able to move in and out of the Self, using the mind as needed to navigate this realm—an ability that proves immensely practical. If the ego were completely dissolved, however, functioning in ordinary society would become extremely difficult, if not impossible. One would require care and support. Those who have achieved the highest degree of Self Realization may exist in such a blissful state that basic bodily needs—eating, feeling pain, even acting—become secondary. Some yogis have been known to enter a state so profoundly blissful that they remain seated or reclined for days on end. These extraordinary states are the result of years of intense practice, austere living, and rigorous yogic discipline.

For most of us, there is no need to fear such extremes. What we can do now is gently Realize the Self and abide in it on a subtle level. With practice and perseverance, this connection deepens, guiding us gradually toward the full experience of the Self.

The Wheel of Insanity

The photo above represents the insanity wheel of pain and pleasure—the never-ending pursuit of happiness that only leads to suffering. What most people call pleasure is often just an escape from their own pain. Ultimate, everlasting happiness can only be found by Realizing the Self. The Self is all that is eternal, all that is blissful, all that simply is. You are THAT!

"Man's Search for happiness is the
unconscious search for his true Self."
-Ramana Maharshi

A huge trap in society is this endless cycle of chasing external things for pleasure and avoiding pain, when the path to true, everlasting happiness, peace, and joy has been within us all along.

Another way to view the pain-and-pleasure hamster wheel is to recognize how we cling to things that come and go. Attachment to the impermanent inevitably causes suffering, because that which comes and goes is not real. Only the Self is real. Only the Self does not come and go. Only the Self abides eternally in the NOW. Only the Self can bring ultimate happiness and end suffering.

Don't believe me? Go ahead—spend the rest of your life chasing external happiness. Spend your years at the casinos in Vegas. Spend your years working overtime to make more money. Spend your years pursuing relationship after relationship, searching for "happiness." Spend your years drinking your life away at the bar. See if any of it brings lasting peace or joy. You will never find true happiness outside yourself.

No amount of external endeavors will bring you permanent happiness, peace, or joy. The reason you cannot find it is simple: **YOU ARE HAPPINESS!** Stop searching! Stop it! You can never find that which you already are. There is nothing to find and no one to search for. **You are already THAT!** You are already what you seek. Seeking will only increase the distance between you and happiness.

Be that which you already are and abide in the Self. Let go of wanting, needing, and desiring for this present moment to be anything other than what it is. Accept what is in the NOW—and that is the Self.

To make this easier, the methods presented in this book help peel away the layers of the ego, the false self. All the techniques are designed to clear away what covers the true Self—not the mind, which likes to masquerade as the Self, but the eternal, unchanging Self beyond all.

Before we get to the main ways to Realize the Self lets go over a couple diagrams I made to show Self Realization from a visual perspective:

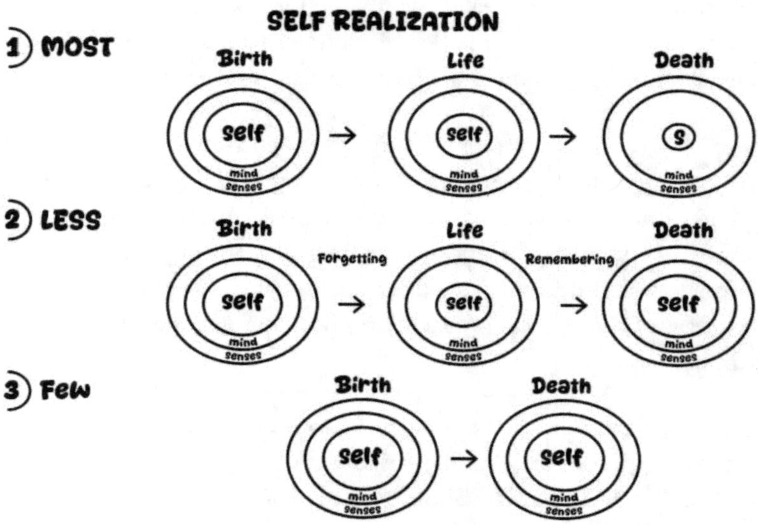

1. This diagram represents the majority of the population, born with a strong connection to the Self. Over time, the Self gradually diminishes while the mind/ego grows larger and larger, until one dies in a state of ignorance, with the mind believing it is the Self.

2. This diagram represents the smaller portion of the world's population who are born with a strong connection to the Self, then forget it, and later make a shift to return to remembrance of the Self.

3. This diagram represents the extremely rare individual who is born Self Realized and never forgets it throughout life. In

this case, the Self remains constant in size for one's entire life.

The next diagram is a similar representation of the first diagram.

3 PATHS OF SELF REALIZATION

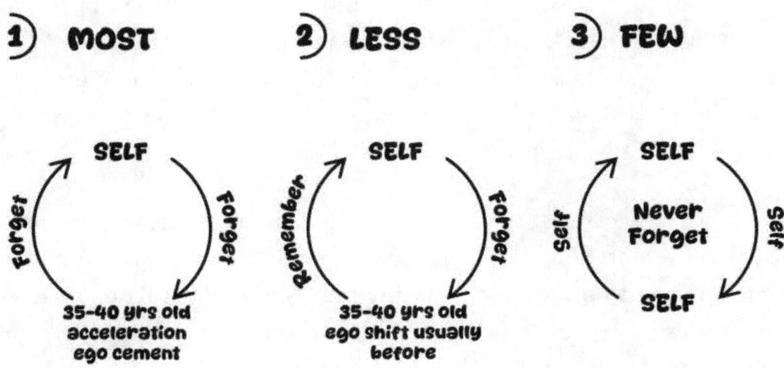

1. As we can see, most people are born with a strong connection to the Self. As we age, however, we gradually enter a state of forgetfulness, until the memory of the Self becomes faint—often cemented over by the ego by the ages of 35 to 40—resulting in ignorance of one's true nature. This forgetfulness coincides with suffering and the endless cycle of chasing pleasure in the belief that it will bring happiness, when in reality it only generates more suffering. This cycle of misguided pursuit further solidifies the ego's dominance over the Self.

2. The second part of the diagram represents those of us who realize the Self within this lifetime. Like the first group, we come into birth awake but slowly forget. However, at some point—often between 35 and 40 years old, though this can

vary—a shift occurs. One transitions from forgetting to gradually or suddenly remembering, returning to one's true Self. This age range is theoretical; some may experience this shift earlier or later. Beyond this point, the ego and mind may solidify over the Self like cement, making Self Realization increasingly difficult.

3. The third group represents the extremely rare individuals who are born Self Realized and never forget, living their entire life in constant awareness of the Self. This is largely theoretical, as most of the world has never encountered such beings, and it is uncertain whether this state has ever been fully achieved.

As we can see from these diagrams, they offer a helpful visual representation of the journey of Self Realization from the perspectives of both the Self and the mind–ego. Now, let us turn to the primary processes that enable this transformation: from forgetting to remembering, from identification with the mind–ego back to the Self, from a life of suffering to one of peace, happiness, serenity, equanimity, and infinite love—back to the Self. You are THAT!

Chapter 10

3 MAIN TECHNIQUES

Alright, you made it this far! Well done! We've laid the foundational components for the three techniques we are about to explore. We've built a solid base with science—supported by brain wave research—and examined the many factors that influence how we think, act, and feel. We've also touched on the historical context of Self Realization and the profound benefits it offers. Now, let's move on to the three main techniques that have proven successful for thousands of people.

Here's a quick summary of the three methods for Realizing the Self:

Technique 1 – Forgiveness:
Evidence demonstrates the immense benefits of forgiveness, as seen in increased alpha and gamma brain waves following a forgiveness process. This is a form of letting go on a deeper level—releasing traumas that are stuck in our energy field, which create the "heart knot" that keeps the Self imprisoned.

Technique 2 – Letting Go (aka Release Technique or Sedona Method):
Popularized by Lester Levenson, this technique trains the brain and body to release negative emotions. It is particularly effective when

practiced repeatedly, helping to clear both deep-rooted and more immediate traumas and emotional blockages.

Technique 3 – Self-Inquiry:

An Advaita Vedanta practice from India popularized by Ramana Maharshi. According to Maharshi, there are only two paths to Self Realization: self-inquiry and surrender. Surrender is another form of letting go. Self-inquiry and letting go are thus the two primary ways to realize the Self. While other methods exist, these have consistently produced remarkable results for many practitioners.

TECHNIQUE 1: THE FORGIVENESS PROCESS

The first highly effective technique for Self Realization is the forgiveness process. This method is particularly useful for those just beginning their journey, when the ego feels like cement and needs to be softened to reach the true Self.

Forgiveness is a common teaching across nearly all religions and spiritual traditions. It is a sacred process that helps heal oneself—albeit at the level of the ego—but its effects can ripple outward, ultimately accelerating the realization of the true Self. As mentioned, one may need to heal the ego before fully realizing that the ego does not exist. I cannot say for certain if this is universally true, but it appeared to be true in my experience and in the experiences of others who went through the same process.

Could there be other ways to heal the ego to aid in Self Realization? Yes. However, one would be remiss not to recognize the substantial amount of data and research already supporting the forgiveness process. Few practices have been studied as extensively in terms of brain wave activity. Thousands of people who have done this have shown significant increases in alpha and gamma brain waves. The evidence is hard to refute and quite compelling.

Since my understanding of Self Realization incorporates a scientific approach, I must emphasize the importance of the forgiveness process—even though, ultimately, it is only the ego that forgives.

It's worth noting that the forgiveness process is remarkably similar to the Toltec recapitulation process, which dates back to around 950–1150 CE. The forgiveness process likely extends even further back. We will discuss the recapitulation process in more detail at the end of this section.

The first day I attended neurofeedback training, I scoffed at the idea of forgiveness, not understanding the vital importance of the procedure or the immense healing it provides. My ego insisted that I didn't need to forgive anyone, but I didn't realize that the ego was concealing and suppressing past traumas and hurts—from both myself and others—doing its best to protect its own survival. Many of the events that need to be healed lie just below our conscious awareness. That is why, as one continues with the forgiveness method, these memories gradually surface, revealing themselves so they can be uprooted and released.

The process I outline here differs only slightly from the one used at training centers. I remove the angelic beings as judges and instead invoke one's own Divine Spark. I find this approach works just as effectively, if not better. Removing external beings is important because within us is the most powerful force in the world: our Divine Spark, the Self. We do not need outside entities to manage our forgiveness or tell us what to do. The Self is all there is, was, and ever will be—the ultimate, most powerful force. You are THAT!

It's essential to disengage from conditioned obedience to authority. This deconditioning may become vital when we pass into the intermediate stage between our next life. We must become our own guide and authority, and this process helps us do so by activating the heart center, where the true Self resides. Our Self, our Divine Spark, is bound by the chains of the ego in the heart center. A key to unlocking these chains lies in the forgiveness process.

One will intuitively know and feel when forgiveness is complete, for this is the language of the Self—pure, silent, and unerring intuition. By performing forgiveness through our own Divine Spark, we accelerate the awakening of the true Self and come to trust its guidance ever more deeply. As the energetic chains dissolve one by one, relief spreads through the body, mind, and spirit, revealing the inherent freedom that was always present. Ultimately, one perceives the profound truth: the chains were never real, for the Self is eternally free, untouched, and whole. You are THAT!

Forgiveness Quotes from Different Religions
(The Midwest Institute for Forgiveness Training, 2014)

Christianity
"Father, forgive them; for they know not what they do." — Luke 23

Islam
"Keep to forgiveness, and enjoin kindness." — Qur'an 7:199-200
"But if someone is steadfast and forgives, that is the most resolute course to follow." — Qur'an 42:43

Hinduism
"Forgiveness subdues all in this world; what is there that forgiveness cannot achieve? What can a wicked person do unto him who carries the sabre of forgiveness in his hand? Righteousness is the one highest good; and forgiveness is the one supreme peace." — The Mahabharata

Judaism
"It is forbidden to be obdurate and not allow yourself to be appeased. On the contrary, one should be easily pacified and find it difficult to become angry. When asked by an offender for forgiveness, one should forgive." — The Torah

Jainism

"I grant forgiveness to all living beings. May all living beings grant me forgiveness. My friendship is with all living beings. My enmity is totally nonexistent." — Jainism

Native American

"There needs to be a great forgiveness…" — Native American

"By three things the wise person may be known. What three? He sees a shortcoming as it is. When he sees it, he tries to correct it. And when another acknowledges a shortcoming, the wise one **forgives** it as he should." -The Buddha (Anguttara Nikaya)

Ashtavakra Gita (Chinmayananda, 2016)

1: Instruction on Self Realization

1.1 Janaka said: "Master, how is Knowledge to be achieved, detachment acquired, and liberation attained?"

1.2 Ashtavakra said: "To be free, shun the experiences of the senses like poison. Turn your attention to **forgiveness**, sincerity, kindness, simplicity, and truth."

Forgiveness begins by stepping outside the emotional body and observing one's life as if it were a film, where the ego is no longer the protagonist but simply a character shaped by conditioning, fear, and misunderstanding. From this detached vantage point, past wounds are no longer relived but *seen*—their origins, patterns, and lessons laid bare without resistance. As each memory is revisited with calm awareness, the charge of blame and self-defense gradually dissolves, and what once felt personal is understood as impersonal. In this space of awareness, forgiveness arises naturally, not as an act of the ego, but as the quiet recognition that nothing real was ever harmed. The stories that once defended identity loosen, trapped energy is released, and the false center of "me" softens, allowing the deeper Self—silent, whole, and unifying—to come forward as the true source of peace.

The Forgiveness Procedure in Depth:

1. Identify a person who sparked an intense negative emotional memory

    ○ This could be parents, relatives, close friends, strangers, or even oneself.

2. Identify the event

    ○ The earlier, the better. Go back as far as possible to find the earliest traumatic event to heal.

3. Identify the emotions or feelings experienced

    ○ Anger, sadness, fear, shame, guilt, etc.

Always make a list and take notes, but avoid ruminating over the forgiveness once it is complete. Do the forgiveness, then let it go. Excessive rumination can give the ego time to reattach and cling to the memory. Sometimes a forgiveness may need to be repeated. Going slowly and methodically can reduce the need for multiple repetitions. When I first learned this process, I went too fast and had to redo some of them.

It's worth noting that forgiveness is not only about others— it is also about oneself. In the sense that one can perform the forgiveness process on oneself for any pain or hurt caused to others over the course of one's life. In this case, revisit the age at which the incident occurred. For example, if you were 10 years old and caused harm to someone, visualize yourself at that age and forgive your younger self. Practice empathy and compassion by putting yourself in your 10-year-old shoes, and then move to love and acceptance with your younger self to complete the process.

It's also important to understand that forgiveness does not condone the behavior that caused the pain.

Step 1- Preplanning. Make a list of every event in one's life one wants to do a forgiveness for. One can make a diagram with family and close friends and oneself. The earliest memories the better. One can also think of heightened emotional states related to those traumatic events. Emotions such as sadness, anger, shame, guilt, fear, etc. Good to start off with one family member at a time and make a small list at first so as not to be overwhelmed. Make sure to take brief notes on the procedure especially after to help release the traumatic events. Good to have a partner and do it in tandem to discuss whatever it is that one may want to discuss after. Good to keep that discussion short as the egoic mind likes to talk excessively which can stir up those traumas once again.

Make sure to avoid alpha reducing substances: caffeine, nicotine, alcohol to increase alpha brain waves. Even excessive amounts of onions and garlic are best avoided during this process as they decrease alpha brain waves. Forgiveness works best with rising alpha.

Step 2- Once an event and person, even oneself has been identified, bring up the event and replay the memory for a couple minutes in one's mind. Make sure one's eyes (which increases alpha brain waves) are closed and one is in a quiet place. Make sure to really feel the emotions from a detached observational perspective. It needs to be felt to be released with this procedure. Do this for about 3-5 minutes. Always remember you are not the mind, you are not the emotions.

Step 3- Next put yourself in the other person shoes or your younger self's shoes and see the event form that perspective. Perhaps that person was going through a difficult time themselves, and that was the reason they were mean to you. Maybe they were abused themselves, or maybe they believed that showing love and affection required conflict, because that is how love and affection had been shown to them.

Whatever the case, we make no excuses for the harm someone did to us. Forgiveness is for **us**, not for them. Although the benefits affect everyone. The best we can do is heal ourselves and forgive. If you are forgiving yourself for a younger period of life, put yourself in your younger self's shoes. The forgiveness process helps us cultivate loving-kindness, compassion, and empathy—the hallmarks of Self Realization and among the most vital qualities along the path.

Step 4- Next, find the gift or lesson in the event that took place. It's there, find it. Look for it. The ego/mind will try and trick you and keep you from finding it. Keep looking. The higher alpha and gamma brain wave state will help you find it. After a few minutes or however long it takes, one should have found the lesson or gift. It could be anything. If you really look at it from a forgiveness perspective one will find that every seemingly negative event was actually a blessing in disguise. In some way, shape or form it has helped you and provided you with a gift or lesson.

Step 5- Next, ask your Divine Spark (at your heart center), if you have done the forgiveness enough or not. One will get an intuitive knowingness of the answer. If the answer is no then repeat steps 1- 4 again. In this Step we use the Divine Spark instead of Angels. The Divine Spark within our heart is the Self. This step classically uses 3 Angels or higher beings but there is nothing higher than our Divine Spark which is all there ever is, was or ever will be. We do not need a middleman or anyone to tell us if we have done something correctly or not. We can simply rely on our Self and our connection with the source of everything. This also goes with the idea that nothing in this realm is to be trusted. In addition we also do not want to be reliant on any higher beings that may manipulate us or guide us incorrectly. As a human species we tend to have a preponderance of trusting to that which presents itself as an authority. We have all the authority of the entire universe within ourselves, in our Divine Spark located in our heart center in a space the size of our thumb and about the size of an atom lies infinity, the Self. The Divine Spark is another name for our true Self. This will also help us practice intuition which is how the Self communicates.

Step 6- Go to love. The final step is to go to love. Once you are able to feel love for the person that hurt you the most then your forgiveness is complete. A good visualization would be to hug that other person and express love to them. Come to find out when you can go to love and forgive the other person you come to love yourself more. We are all each other, reflections from the same source or drops from the same ocean or rays from the same sun. Ultimately we are all each other.

Step 7- Enjoy the freedom from forgiveness for a few minutes or as long as one feels like.

Repeat this forgiveness process over and over again as needed.

Bonus Step- Self-inquiry. Upon the conclusions of each forgiveness process, see if you can observe the mind. What is it saying? Are you in the past or the future? If you can observe the mind then who is the one observing the mind? One can ask: Who am I? And wait for the answer. The answer is silence. That is the Self. As more and more of the forgiveness processes are done there should be more and more stillness as the knot of the heart starts to dissolve.

For traumatic events, the entire forgiveness process may take up to 20 minutes to complete. For lesser events, it may take around 10 minutes. If one cries, this is a good sign but its not mandatory. There wasn't a single day during my own practice when I didn't cry while doing these processes. It is challenging at first, but once one gains momentum and becomes familiar with the method, it becomes much smoother.

Remember, it is not the true you that needs to forgive—it is the false you, the ego. The ego must heal before it can be seen through, and this healing accelerates the path to Self Realization. If this were easy, everyone would do it. The true Self is forever at peace, in harmony, and in infinite happiness. Only the ego-mind obscures this inherent perfection.

Forgiveness is a powerful tool that breaks the chain around the heart—chains that imprison the Self and prevent one from recognizing one's true nature. The truth is that everyone is already Self Realized; it is merely the misidentification with the mind that obscures the Self from view. Now is the time to reverse that misidentification and place the Self in the driver s seat of one's consciousness, rather than the ego.

There is no forgiveness too small or too great. Even forgiving seemingly minor events can generate profound bursts of alpha and gamma waves. After performing the forgiveness process repeatedly, one may feel a buzzing, almost electric sensation, as gamma and alpha brain waves rise in a harmonious symphony of synchronized activity.

Really, forgiveness is simply a refined way of letting go. We forgive in order to release the anger, hurt, and pain we have been holding onto. These unresolved emotions create an energetic cord that drains our vitality, theoretically on the astral level. Forgiveness can even help heal physical ailments. As mentioned earlier, most diseases and ailments seem to originate at the energetic level as stuck, unhealed traumas, which eventually manifest on the physical level.

I've personally experienced knee pain decrease, stomach discomfort reduced, and waves of electricity-like energy move through my entire body after doing this practice. I've also witnessed others experience physical improvements through forgiveness work. There are entire books detailing the connections between specific emotions and different parts of the body.

Forgiveness is an act of love. When we choose to forgive, we release the anger and hatred that bind us—to others and to our own past. Forgiveness flows from compassion, and compassion is rooted in love. Compassion is the empathy and understanding extended toward those who are suffering. In essence, forgiveness, empathy, and compassion are all noble expressions of the same source: love—the fruit of the Self.

The fruit of Self Realization is an abiding sense of love that naturally expands into kindness, compassion, and empathy for all beings. That love feels like bliss. We can utilize these noble forms of love to Realize the Self, following the simple equation:

The Self = Love (empathy, compassion, kindness)
or equally:
Love (empathy, compassion, kindness) = The Self

Love is a bridge to Self Realization. Love is not merely an emotion; it is the very essence of the Self. The underlying essence of the entire universe—of all that exists—is love. True love transcends the limitations of the ego and the physical world. Worldly love is ego-based; divine love is the Self. We will explore these two forms of love in greater depth later.

The way of the heart—the path of love—is the path to Self Realization even the Sufis talk about this in great detail. Forgiveness is one of the most powerful expressions of this path. Through repeated practice, one begins to experience a deeper kindness, compassion, and empathy for all beings. A profound realization emerges: everyone is you, and you are everyone. We are all the Self, and the Self is all of us. Each of us wears different garments that conceal the same inner essence, yet in truth, we are all the same Self—and that Self is love.

Forgiveness awakens the Divine Spark—the true Self—within. Once this inner force is felt and begins to awaken, it shakes one to the very core of being. When the heart finally opens, like a flood bursting through a dam, the entire body is immersed in a surge of love (bliss)—more love than one could ever imagine, beyond anything the mind can conceptualize. It is felt in every cell, in every fiber of one's being. That is the Self. That is the Divine Spark. That is who we truly are. **You are THAT!**

FORGIVENESS VISUAL

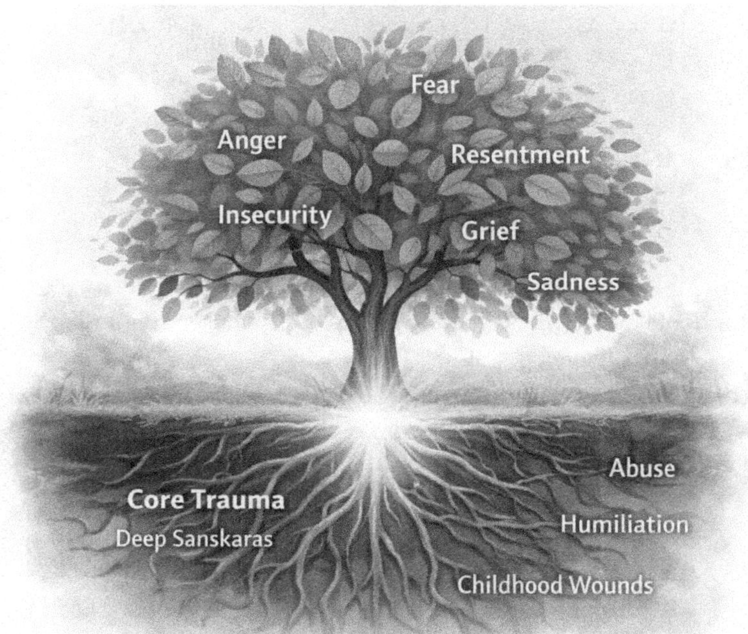

Leaves: Surface-Level Emotional Scars
Roots: Core Traumas / Deep Sanskaras

If one uses this tree as a visual metaphor for the forgiveness method, the roots represent the deep sanskaras or core traumas, while the leaves symbolize the more surface-level emotional scars. When a deep root is healed, the entire tree can dissolve. For example, if one was abused as a child and constantly yelled at, they may experience present-moment triggers—such as tightness in the body or stomach—whenever they hear yelling.

If a person practices forgiveness for someone who recently yelled at them, that would be like healing a leaf or a small branch. But if they perform forgiveness for the person who yelled at them during childhood, they may remove the entire root system—allowing the whole tree to fall away and automatically healing many of the smaller, more superficial emotional scars and triggers.

ONLY THE EGO FORGIVES

Do not forget: the true Self within is ever-abiding in peace, tranquility, serenity, bliss, and infinite love (bliss). The Self is always perfect. It is the ego that creates problems and then offers solutions. It is the ego that gives both praise and criticism. This false identification with the ego-mind is the root of every problem and every form of suffering.

The ego, the mind, the emotions, the physical body—this entire world—is ultimately not real; it all comes and goes. That which does not come and go is what is real: pure awareness, the Self is what is real. You are THAT!

That being said, as mentioned before, healing the fractured ego may be necessary before one can fully realize that it does not truly exist. As one heals the ego, it becomes vitally important to practice self-inquiry (method three) alongside this healing, to clearly distinguish between what is real and what is not. One should begin this as soon as possible.

Forgiveness is incredibly powerful, especially for burning away sanskaras and healing emotional scars or traumas. Yet, we must remember that forgiveness still operates within the confines of the ego. Research has shown that up to 50% of our memories are inaccurate. This means that even when performing the forgiveness process, roughly half of those memories are distorted and somewhat fictitious.

It is somewhat ironic: we may need to heal something that doesn't even exist in order to realize that it doesn't exist—at least as a way to accelerate the process of Self Realization. Of course, one could spend many years practicing only self-inquiry or meditating in a cave and still make substantial progress. But in our time, where every moment is valuable, few would choose such a path. I know I certainly wouldn't want to spend years meditating in a cave. The fastest and most efficient route is, by far, the most practical and ideal path.

"Forgiveness and the ego are synonymous. When you ask for forgiveness or forgive someone, the ego is involved in it because you think you are skilled. You say "Now I have forgiven this man," "I asked him to forgive me." In these words it is understood: "I can do it again and again."

Better forget about it either inside you with the question: "Who needs forgiveness?" And you will understand that forgiveness and your ego are synonyms. When there is no ego then there is no idea of forgiveness, there is only love, kindness and compassion, everything is accepted as it is." – Robert Adams

"True healing is not the fixing of the broken, but the rediscovery of the unbroken." —Jeff Foster

"The greatest healing is to wake up from what we are not." —Mooji

"The most important healing is realizing who you are. Healing on the outer level is fine, but it is not the essence of healing." —Eckhart Tolle

"Divine forgiveness burns away sanskaras." —Meher Baba

It should be noted that forgiveness is a tool to help one realize the Self. The forgiveness process helps still the mind, making it easier to practice self-inquiry and ultimately Self Realization. Forgiveness dramatically increases alpha and gamma brain waves, which further facilitates the realization of the Self. However, forgiveness alone will not lead to Self Realization, although it can provide a glimpse through a Samadhi experience. The knowledge that one is not the mind or body, but the awareness—the witness beyond the mind—is absolutely necessary for true Self Realization.

Forgiveness Quotes (One Mind Dharma, 2025)

- **"To forgive is to set a prisoner free and discover that the prisoner was you." —Louis B. Smedes**

- **"We must develop and maintain the capacity to forgive. He who is devoid of the power to forgive is devoid of the power to love. There is some good in the worst of us and some evil in the best of us. When we discover this, we are less prone to hate our enemies." —Martin Luther King, Jr.**

- **"To err is human; to forgive, divine." —Alexander Pope**

- **"To forgive is the highest, most beautiful form of love. In return, you will receive untold peace and happiness." —Robert Muller**

- **"A life lived without forgiveness is a life lived in the past." —Asa Don Brown**

- **"Forgiveness is the fragrance the violet sheds on the heel that has crushed it." —Mark Twain**

- **"Resentment is like drinking poison and then hoping it will kill your enemies." —Nelson Mandela**

- **"Forgiveness does not change the past, but it does enlarge the future." —Paul Boese**

- **"Forgiveness is a virtue of the brave." —Indira Gandhi**

- **"Genuine forgiveness does not deny anger but faces it head-on." —Alice Duer Miller**

- **"It's one of the greatest gifts you can give yourself, to forgive. Forgive everybody." —Maya Angelou**

TECHNIQUE 2: LETTING GO

"There is no happiness except that of experiencing your **Self**. When you see that, it makes the path very direct. You stop chasing the rainbow and you go for the happiness where you know it is, right within you." -Lester Levenson

The Letting Go technique, also known as the Sedona Method or the Release Technique, is more than just a method—it is a path to freedom. Founded by the remarkable Lester Levenson, this practice guides us to release the negative emotions and limiting beliefs that bind the mind and obscure the true Self. These attachments, often hidden beneath layers of thought and habit, are the subtle chains that keep us trapped in suffering.

Through deliberate surrender, acceptance, and gentle inquiry, one begins to peel away the layers of the ego, revealing the stillness and clarity of the Self beneath. Letting go is not merely a mental exercise—it is the conscious act of returning to the source, of resting in the innate peace and joy that has always been present. In this way, the technique serves as both a mirror and a bridge, reflecting the illusions of the mind while opening the way to the eternal, unshakable awareness within, the Self.

Lester was a brilliant man, born in 1909 in New Jersey. By his early 40s, he faced numerous serious health problems—so severe that his doctors reportedly gave him only days to live. He suffered from a heart attack, kidney stones, an enlarged liver, depression, ulcers, jaundice, migraines, and more.

Rather than giving up, Lester went back to the drawing board, investigating the root causes of his ailments. He examined his life closely and discovered that he was happiest when he was loving others, not when he was being loved. He also realized that his desire to change the world had made him a slave to it—and this, he concluded, was a key factor contributing to his ulcers.

Lester decided to let go of wanting to change the world, and he let go of wanting to be loved. In letting go more and more, he became happier, lighter, and freer. Within three months, Lester's health problems had nearly vanished, and he ended up Realizing the Self at the same time.

While letting go of everything, Lester practiced some basic self-inquiry, which we will discuss in the next technique. He would ask himself, "What am I?" Lester Levenson's book, *Happiness Is Free and It's Easier Than You Think*, is an excellent read. From the moment he became Self Realized in 1952, his sole mission was to help others do the same.

This seems to be a common theme among those who have Realized the Self: when one realizes the Self, the only impulse is to share it with the world and help others experience it. Of course, it is not so much a "wanting" or desire in the usual sense, but a push from the divine force within to share the highest truth about reality, existence, and the ultimate meaning: know thyself. Who are we? What are we? That is the secret of all secrets, the jewel of all jewels.

The experience of Realizing the Self is like coming home after a long journey, a home you never truly left but had simply forgotten. The depth of this return is so vast that words falter; language cannot contain it. It is like witnessing a moment of unimaginable beauty, so profound that the mind cannot fully grasp it. We call that awe—but even "awe" or "awestruck" barely scratches the surface. The Self is beyond words, beyond description, beyond even the notion of "beyond." You are THAT!

Lester ended up living until 1992, far longer than his doctors had predicted. He also studied and gravitated toward the teachings of Ramana Maharshi, Nisargadatta, and Robert Adams, all of whom we will discuss in the third major method for Realizing the Self. Upon Lester's death in 1992, his teachings were passed on to Hale Dwoskin, who formalized them into The Sedona Method.

In the book *The Sedona Method* by Hale Dwoskin, on page 41, he outlines the simple framework for letting go or releasing emotions, which they call the Sedona Method:

1. "What is your NOW feeling?"

2. "Could you welcome/allow that feeling?"

3. "Could you let it go?"

4. "Would you let it go?"

5. "When?"

And repeat as necessary.

I still remember the first time someone guided me through this process. She told me, with a calm but knowing look, to stop resisting and let myself fully dive into the swirling storm of negative emotions I was feeling at that very moment.

She said, "Allow yourself to feel that feeling. Ask yourself, could you let it go?"

"Yes," I replied.

She asked, "Would you let it go?"

"Yes," I said.

"When could you let it go?" she asked.

"Now," I responded.

Finally, she asked, "How do you feel now?"

"Bliss," I said.

This method works quite well. One important point is that it must be practiced continuously to retrain the brain to let things go and to identify the emotions in order to release them. This approach goes against what most of us have been conditioned to do in society, where we are often taught to suppress, express, or escape our emotions, as mentioned earlier. Just remember to do it from an objective stand point and not identify with the emotions.

The Sedona Method is a simple and effective technique for letting go. It is so straightforward and easy to practice that one can use it continuously to keep retraining the brain to release attachments. If someone wanted to skip the forgiveness process and use the Sedona Method instead, it can work, but it requires consistent practice, whereas the forgiveness technique can be done in a more intensive, "big bang" approach.

Before learning about self-inquiry, I would use the Sedona Method for smaller, less deeply rooted emotions that popped up in daily life. For example, if a driver cut us off in traffic or if someone upset us in some minor way, the Sedona Method could be applied effectively. The forgiveness technique, on the other hand, works better for deeper, long-standing traumas.

Once again, all these methods are simply ways of letting go, which is essentially the same as surrendering. Surrender and letting go are one and the same. We are releasing our grasp on unfavorable emotions—we let them go. From a very young age, we are conditioned to hold on rather than let go. We must train our minds to let go, let go, let go—surrender—and know that all is well. Only when the cup is empty can it be filled with the ocean of the Self.

We've all experienced moments in life when we become so overwhelmed that we simply say, "F it," and surrender, letting everything go. In that act of letting go, that surrender, we find peace. We find freedom. It is there, hidden, that the Self resides. In essence, it is the letting go of the mind and ego.

This process, like the forgiveness process, must be accompanied by self-inquiry. This is absolutely vital. Without self-inquiry, the mind will latch onto something, and the cycle of letting go may continue endlessly. Forgiveness and letting go serve as bridges to the self-inquiry and, ultimately, to the main method of self-inquiry, where one disidentifies completely from the mind and emotions and realizes that there was never truly anything to let go of or forgive, as those things are transient and illusory. Only the Self is real.

While the release technique, or letting go method, can be a powerful tool for healing the ego in much the same way as the forgiveness process, it must be understood that it still operates within the domain of the ego itself and can become deleterious if relied upon long term. By repeatedly engaging with and releasing emotional states, one may unknowingly reinforce identification with egoic emotions that are ultimately unreal, subtlety training the mind to continue sourcing identity from what is meant to be transcended. In this sense, letting go is a temporary bridge rather than the final truth—it helps soften emotional conditioning and clear space for love, compassion, and humility to arise, thereby preparing the ground for deeper self-inquiry. Used skillfully and in balance with forgiveness and self-inquiry, it accelerates healing without hardening attachment to the very patterns it seeks to dissolve. But its true purpose, like all authentic spiritual techniques, is not endless emotional management—it is to be outgrown, so that ultimately even the tools are surrendered, leaving only emptiness, stillness, and the direct recognition of the Self that was never bound. You are THAT!

Now that we have covered the two main ways of letting go—a more involved process and a quick, simple process—we will move on to the final and most important method: self-inquiry. If the forgiveness process and the release technique can be likened to a fruit tree, then the forgiveness process shakes the tree to release the deep emotional burdens, while the release technique removes more superficial burdens, especially when practiced consistently. Now, it is time to eat the fruit from the tree with the final process: Self-Inquiry.

TECHNIQUE 3: SELF-INQUIRY

Interestingly, Lester Levenson gravitated toward the teachings of self-inquiry. It's almost as if he had a reference point of Self Realization and naturally found his way to self-inquiry. This gravitational pull toward self-inquiry seems to occur frequently with those who have Realized the Self.

After doing the first two methods, I began practicing self-inquiry and immediately noticed it produced a similar stillness—a quietness of mind—akin to what I had experienced before. Immersion in a deep state of Samadhi gives one a reference point for discerning which techniques are truly effective. I can now feel and intuitively know, beyond the mind, what fosters stillness and what does not. As one progresses on the path of Self Realization, this understanding becomes ever clearer, with insights arising more naturally and effortlessly.

The three main techniques I discuss here—**forgiveness, the release technique, and self-inquiry**—are the most potent tools I have found for realizing the Self. Later, I will introduce additional meditation practices to complement these core teachings, drawing from the wisdom of ancient teachings. These are not my own discoveries; I am merely a messenger, passing their timeless guidance forward.

Self-inquiry, known in Sanskrit as Atma Vichara, is rooted in the nondual philosophy of Advaita Vedanta. *Atma* signifies the Self, and *vichara* signifies inquiry. It is the eternal call to return home to our own essence. Recall the ancient injunction: "Know Thyself." In Sanskrit, this is expressed as *Atmanam Viddhi*. The sage Ramana Maharshi brought self-inquiry to prominence until his passing in 1950, yet its origins extend deep into the Vedic texts, particularly the Upanishads, where the pursuit of Self-knowledge has always been regarded as the highest human endeavor.

Self-inquiry is not merely a technique—it is a turning inward, a direct path to recognizing that the observer, the observed, and the act of observing are all expressions of the same unchanging Self. To practice Atma Vichara is to awaken to the truth that has never been lost: that you are, and always have been, THAT!

Annapurna Upanishad, Chapter 1, Verses 40–41 (Warrier, 2018):
40: Consider in your mind: Who am I? How is all this brought about? How do death and birth occur? By contemplating thus, you will gain the great benefit of investigation.

41: Your mind will shed its discursive forms and quietly attain repose once, through investigation, you comprehend your true nature.

Contemplation on the question of "Who am I?" is a recurring theme throughout the Upanishads. These texts emphasize the continuous practice of self-inquiry, which gradually reveals one's true nature, the Atman, or Self. Indeed, there exists an entire branch of Yoga, **Jnana Yoga**, dedicated to the path of knowledge and Self Realization. Even the simple understanding that the Self resides in the heart carries profound implications, accelerating the journey toward Self Realization.

Svetasvatara Upanishad, 4:17 & 4:20 (Radhakrishnan, 2024):
4:17: That God, the maker of all things, the great Self, ever seated in the heart of all creatures, is framed by the thought and by the mind. Those who know this attain immortality.

4:20: His form cannot be seen; no one perceives Him with the eyes. Yet those who know Him through the heart and mind, as abiding in the heart, become immortal.

ADVAITA VEDANTA

We would be remiss if we did not include a brief discussion of the historical foundations of Advaita Vedanta before entering more deeply into the practice of self-inquiry. Advaita Vedanta is a philosophical tradition rooted in the Hindu scriptures known as the Upanishads, composed in ancient India. There are traditionally 108 Upanishads, with the earliest dating back to around 800 BCE. The principal Upanishads from which Advaita Vedanta draws its core teachings include the Brihadaranyaka, Chandogya, Mandukya, Mundaka, and Taittiriya Upanishads.

Advaita Vedanta is a branch of Vedic philosophy that teaches the oneness of reality. The term Advaita Vedanta in Sanskrit means "non-dualism." Its central teaching is that the individual, experiencing self is in truth pure awareness, mistakenly identified with the body, senses, and mind. This individual Self (Atman) is not different from the Ultimate Reality (Brahman). Atman refers to the inner Self—the presence within us—while Brahman refers to the universal Self, the essence of all that exists. Yet the tradition considers them fundamentally identical, hence the Upanishadic declaration: **"Atman is Brahman."**

Advaita Vedanta teaches that liberation from suffering and from the cycle of reincarnation arises through knowledge of Brahman—through ceasing to identify with the body and the senses, recognizing the illusory nature of the phenomenal world, and realizing one's true nature as pure, unconditioned awareness.

Adi Shankara expresses this realization beautifully:

"I am other than name, form, and action.
My nature is ever free.
I am the Self, the supreme unconditioned Brahman. I
am pure Awareness, always non-dual."
— Upadesa Sahasri 11.7

According to Anantanand Rambachan, in Advaita this liberating knowledge leads to the profound understanding that "the Self is the Self of all; the knower of the Self sees the Self in all beings and all beings in the Self."

"The Vedas cannot show you Brahman, you are That already. They can only help to take away the veil that hides truth from our eyes. The cessation of ignorance can only come when I know that God and I are one; in other words, identify yourself with Atman (the Self), not with human limitations. The idea that we are bound is only an illusion [Maya]. Freedom is inseparable from the nature of the Atman. This is ever pure, ever perfect, ever unchangeable." — Adi Shankara's *Commentary on the Fourth Vyasa Sutra*, quoted by Swami Vivekananda

"Through study, reflection and meditation, you exhaust your vasanas, desires and discover your real Self. It is through your self-effort you gain the knowledge of Self. And by discovering your inner Self you experience the infinite, all pervading Brahman." — Ātma-bōdha, verses 66–68

VICHARA AKA SELF-INQUIRY

According to Wikipedia (Vichara, 2025):

> Vichara, self-inquiry, also called jnana-vichara or ātma-vichāra by devotees of Ramana Maharshi, is the constant attention to the inner awareness of 'I' or 'I am'. It was recommended by Ramana Maharshi as the most efficient and direct way of discovering the unreality of the 'I'-thought, and then discovering one's identity with its source.
>
> According to David Frawley, "atma-vichara" is the most important practice in the Advaita Vedanta tradition, predating its popularization by Ramana Maharshi. It is part of the eighth limb of Patanjali's Yoga Sutras, which describes the various stages of samadhi. Meditation on "I-am-ness" is a subtle object of meditation. It is also described in the Yoga Vasistha, a syncretic work which may date from the 6th or 7th century CE, and shows influences from Yoga, Samkhya, Saiva Siddhanta and Mahayana Buddhism, especially Yogacara.

Ramana taught that the 'I'-thought will disappear and only "I-I" or Self-awareness remains. This results in an "effortless awareness of being", and by staying with it this "I-I" gradually destroys the vasanas "which cause the 'I'-thought to rise," and finally the 'I'-thought never rises again, which is Self Realization or liberation.

RAMANA MAHARSHI

Ramana Maharshi, Rajeswarananda (2010).

For many years, I have been fascinated by the great yogis and the ancient spiritual traditions of India. In my long search for truth, I explored numerous religions and esoteric teachings, only to find that they all ultimately direct us back to the same source—the Self, quietly abiding within every one of us. One of the great illusions of this world is the belief that truth, power, or salvation must be sought outside ourselves. This outward gaze keeps us distracted, turning our attention away from the inner reality where the deepest truth patiently waits to be discovered.

Among the many works that illuminate this inner journey toward Self Realization, *Autobiography of a Yogi* by Paramahansa Yogananda stands out as a timeless treasure. Yogananda recounts remarkable encounters with yogis and saints whose extraordinary abilities he witnessed firsthand—abilities that were never meant as displays of power, but as gentle invitations to look deeper into the nature of consciousness itself and to recognize the Self that lies beyond the mind.

One sage shines with unparalleled simplicity and clarity: Ramana Maharshi. His presence continues to reverberate throughout southern India and beyond, touching the lives of many across the world. Ramana's teachings point directly to the **heart** of all spiritual inquiry—to the discovery of one's true nature through the simple but profound question: "**Who am I?**"

Myself at Ramana Maharshi's Ashram in Tiruvannamalai, India (2025).

Ramana Maharshi was born in 1879 in Tiruchuli, Tamil Nadu, India, and passed away in 1950. At the age of sixteen he experienced a profound spiritual awakening, triggered by an intense fear of death, which led to his realization of the Self. Six weeks later, he left his home and traveled to Arunachala in Tiruvannamalai, where he became a renunciate and remained for the rest of his life.

Over the years, Ramana became widely revered, drawing seekers from around the world who came to sit in his presence and learn from him. In time, Ramana and his devotees established his ashram, a strikingly beautiful sanctuary situated near the sacred Arunachala Hill, which Ramana regarded as the embodiment of the Divine.

A dedicated student of Advaita Vedanta, Ramana taught atma vichara (self-inquiry) as the most direct path to Self Realization. He emphasized that there are two primary ways to realize the Self: **self-inquiry** and **surrender**. These two paths, he said, are not mutually exclusive but can be pursued concurrently.

Earlier, we explored methods of letting go and surrender; these too align with Ramana's teachings. One can also surrender through devotion and selfless service. Service is one of the five love languages—alongside time, touch, words, and gifts. Ultimately, it all returns to love and to awakening the Divine Spark within the heart center.

Forgiveness, letting go (also called releasing or surrendering), and self-inquiry are the fast-track methods to Self Realization, as I have witnessed and experienced firsthand—both in myself and in others—and as I have measured scientifically through brain wave measurements. I know these methods work. Science confirms their effectiveness. Ancient teachings and timeless wisdom affirm the same. The greatest hindrance is not the methods themselves, but the ego's doubt—its refusal to believe what is directly in front of us. Don't take my word for it, do it yourself and experience it.

The ego, the false self that masquerades as the real Self, likes to believe it is already enlightened, already complete, already knowing. It does everything in its power to preserve its own fictitious existence and will attempt to keep one from awakening to the Self. One must transcend the ego's tricks, move beyond its limitations, and pursue Self Realization with courage, sincerity, and unwavering dedication.

Self-inquiry is a simple yet profoundly direct means of realizing the Self. It causes the mind to collapse upon itself, revealing emptiness, stillness, and the dissolution of thought. I often begin presentations on the Self by asking people to observe their mind. If you can observe the mind, then ask yourself: "Who is the one observing the mind?" After a moment of quiet, ask, "Who am I?" or "What am I?"

This "Who am I?" inquiry is the central teaching of Ramana Maharshi. If thoughts arise, ask: "To whom do these thoughts arise?" Ramana taught that this inquiry should be practiced continuously.

Self-inquiry is an advanced practice, and like all advanced practices, one should have some level of meditation experience and have practiced methods of letting go before diving deeply into it. As mentioned earlier, there is a theory that the ego/mind needs to be healed before one can realize that the ego/mind is not real. There seems to be truth in this, and this concept may even be a missing link that Ramana Maharshi was not explicitly aware of. Perhaps, if the practice of letting go preceded self-inquiry, more people would attain Self Realization—or at the very least, the process could be accelerated from many years to mere months. I am confident that there is a profound connection between letting go and making self-inquiry far more effective.

In truth, letting go is but an illusion, for the mind—the theater of all attachment—is itself unreal. Like a dream, it rises and falls, and yet we cling to it as though it were life. When the veil of Self Realization lifts, you see with perfect clarity: there was never anything to release, nothing to surrender. You are the Self and always been. You are THAT!

Forever free, forever at peace, forever serene, bathed in the endless light of joy, immersed in infinite love and bliss. This is not something to attain; it is the eternal essence of your being. Rest in it. Be it. Abide in the Self, for you have always been and will always be that boundless, unshakable truth.

THE WORLD IS NOT REAL

In 2003, Nick Bostrom wrote an influential paper titled *Are You Living in a Computer Simulation?* This paper challenged the core of many people's belief systems. Bostrom brought significant attention to the simulation hypothesis—the idea that our reality may not be as "real" as we think. He postulated that if a civilization were capable of creating conscious simulations, then either they would not create one, could not create one, or, if they did, we are almost certainly living in one. Elon Musk has even suggested that there is a high probability we are living in a simulation.

This idea is far from new. Ancient writings—from Chinese philosophy to the Indian concept of Maya, from Greek philosophers to the Gnostics, and even the Aztecs—often portrayed reality as a kind of waking dream, not entirely real. Could it be that what these ancient peoples were trying to convey, with the knowledge available to them at the time, is that we are living in a simulation akin to a dream?

The Gnostics speak of a being called the Demiurge and Archons, said to have created the Earth and humans, and possessing qualities that resemble artificial intelligence. The fact is, we could very well be living in a simulation—a false reality, a dreamlike world—and not even realize it. Have you ever played one of those virtual reality games with a headset? As technology advances, the distinction between what is real and what is not becomes increasingly difficult to determine.

There are times when the mind struggles to differentiate between true reality and a false one; perhaps this reality itself is not real. In fact, the odds might even favor the notion that it is not. After the Samadhi experience, everything in the world—including pictures—appeared AI-generated, I became even more convinced that this reality is illusory. Furthermore, when we examine what constitutes matter—atoms, which are over 99.99% empty space—it becomes clear that the world, and we ourselves, are essentially composed of emptiness.

Theoretically, as the mind begins to loosen its grip on the true Self, one can come to understand that the mind is not real. For most, the mind or ego maintains a death grip on the Divine Spark within the heart center. With Self Realization, the mind does not disappear entirely; it simply takes a back seat, allowing the true Self—sometimes called the 'higher Self'—to take control. In rare instances, there can be a complete dissolution of the mind and ego, but this typically occurs only in highly advanced, enlightened sages such as Ramana Maharshi even so Maharshi had thoughts that arose when answering questions. Some people fear that practicing these methods will cause them to lose their mind entirely. The mind generates this fear itself. Rest assured, you will not lose your mind; rather, you will gain mastery over it, using it as a tool rather than being used by it.

THE CHARIOT METAPHOR

In the *Katha Upanishad* (1.3.3–11) and the *Paingala Upanishad*, Chapter 4 (Radhakrishnan, 2024), the chariot metaphor portrays the human being as a chariot in motion to explain the relationship between the Self, the mind, and the senses. The body is the chariot, the senses are the horses, the mind is the reins, the intellect is the charioteer, and the true Self is the owner of the chariot. The senses naturally draw toward worldly objects, just as horses rush toward what they see along the road. The mind links the intellect to the senses, transmitting either disciplined control or impulsive reaction. Here, the importance of brahmacharya, or self-control, becomes clear: without discipline, the senses run wild and stray from the path to Self Realization.

Self Realization depends on how well this inner system is governed. A weak intellect and undisciplined mind allow the senses to dominate, leading the chariot off course into confusion and suffering. When the intellect is clear and the mind steady, the senses are mastered and the chariot remains on the right path. In this harmony, one comes to realize that they are not the body, mind, or senses, but the silent owner of the chariot—the eternal Self—thus moving toward liberation.

When we Realize the Self, we understand that we are not the doer but the witness. Life is like a movie: people often become entangled in the character and mistake it for themselves, when in truth it is not the truth. We are the silent observer of the movie, the witness. Upon realizing the Self, we can watch the mind and emotions pass by without attachment, almost as if they appear on a movie screen or computer monitor, coming and going while we remain unmoved.

It does take some practice and getting used to, but it is truly remarkable, as it represents an entirely different way of being than what we are taught from the day we are born. In fact, it is completely contrary to societal teachings, yet it is the most natural and normal state to exist in. We are taught to cling to and identify with the mind and emotions, which is the root cause of suffering and unhappiness. No amount of external possessions or experiences can bring lasting happiness—only Self Realization can.

The Self is ever-present, ever-conscious, and ever-abiding. It is only the machinations of the mind, and our identification with them, that obscure the Self. Coupled with the subconscious programming of the mind—replaying heightened emotional experiences on an endless loop—this veil continues to block the realization of our true nature.

There are many great books on Ramana Maharshi, too many to name. One excellent resource is *The Teachings of Ramana Maharshi* by Arthur Osborne (2014). This book provides a clear overview of his teachings, along with insightful questions and answers that deepen understanding. Even so, the greatest understanding comes from direct experience through practice. The highest teaching is found in silence, and the deepest insight arises from firsthand experience. I could write endlessly, but it won't truly make sense until one puts the methods into practice and begins to feel and understand intuitively.

A question I often wondered about was: will stilling the mind cause problems navigating life? The answer is unequivocally no. In fact, the mind is the source of all problems. No mind, no problem. What occurs is that we begin to navigate life like a stream flowing with the river's current, rather than swimming against it. Life unfolds with far less interference from the mind and with greater intuition—a natural sense of knowing.

One of my favorite modern Advaita Vedanta teachers is Robert Adams. He claimed to have studied under Ramana Maharshi, though there is some speculation about this. Whether he did or not, what is certain is that his book Silence of the Heart (2012), is one of the best modern explanations of self-inquiry. The book presents questions and answers from a contemporary perspective, making the teachings more accessible. It can be read slowly, as simply engaging with it can produce stillness of mind and offer a direct experience of the Self.

There is something uniquely powerful about listening to a Self Realized teacher, and it seems that Robert Adams' book facilitates just that—a faster path to Self Realization. Perhaps it is due to the seemingly modern koans he presents throughout the text. In many ways, the entire book reads like a koan, producing stillness simply through the way he explains things—beyond the grasp of conscious understanding. Indeed, the Self itself is beyond all conscious comprehension. It is precisely through non-understanding that one realizes the Self. Even in photographs, one can perceive a profound stillness in Robert Adams' gaze.

Another possible factor contributing to his extraordinary wisdom and understanding of the Self may have been his later-life struggle with Parkinson's disease. Parkinson's is associated with increased delta brain waves, which can foster stillness and facilitate deeper Self Realization. Whatever the reason, I highly recommend his book *Silence of the Heart*. Unfortunately, Robert Adams passed away in 1997; it would have been incredible to experience his presence and hear him speak in person.

ENLIGHTENMENT INTENSIVE (EI): SELF-INQUIRY DYAD

Another form of self-inquiry with profound benefits, capable of producing rapid and remarkable results, is the Self-Inquiry Dyad practiced at Enlightenment Intensives (EI). Here is a summary of the technique from the founder, Richard Berner, as described in his book *Consciousness of Truth: A Manual for the Enlightenment Intensive* by Charles Berner and Mona Sosna (2005).

In 1968, Richard Berner created the Enlightenment Intensive, which utilizes self-inquiry with a partner. For years, Berner taught personal growth techniques and principles and observed that those who knew who they were experienced the most improvement, while those who did not know who they were progressed far more slowly. Individuals who identified primarily with the mind and body advanced gradually, whereas those with a deeper sense of self progressed much more rapidly. Only 3–4% of the people he worked with truly knew who they were.

From this observation, he decided to incorporate the classic self-inquiry question, "Who am I?" and combine it with communication techniques in a dyad format that his wife had developed. He then merged this with the Zen Sesshin format, essentially an intensive meditation retreat. This synthesis gave birth to the Enlightenment Intensive. Soon after conducting the first retreat, he was astonished to find that nearly 40% of participants had a direct experience of their true Self, beyond the mind. Berner continued refining his method through successive intensive retreats.

The core of Berner's Enlightenment Intensive technique is extraordinarily simple yet highly effective; nearly everyone who practices it experiences some form of enlightenment or Self Realization. One common obstacle is the ego, which often resists the process or tries to prevent the practitioner from fully engaging in the technique. The essence of Berner's method is based on his observation that mental chatter increases whenever something is not communicated—either between individuals or within oneself. For example, if someone reads something they do not understand, it generates more mental chatter. Conversely, if something is fully understood, the mind recognizes it has been communicated, and no additional mental chatter arises.

Berner further explains that when something is completely received or understood, it transcends the mind and enters the realm of pure knowing. This principle applies not only to knowledge but also to unresolved or unprocessed traumatic experiences stored in the mind. Anything not fully understood, integrated, or experienced continues to generate mental activity. These principles form the foundation upon which his technique is built.

When one practices self-inquiry in isolation, it can take many years for unprocessed trauma, unresolved issues, and past experiences to be fully released, integrated, or dissolved. In traditional self-inquiry, each arising thought is met with the question, *"To whom do these thoughts arise?"* Repeated over time, this process gradually leads one to the root of one's being—the true Self—by systematically exhausting and dissolving the mind.

With the Enlightenment Intensive—a structured form of self-inquiry called a self-inquiry Dyad—one can reach the root of the Self much more rapidly. In this dyad format, the mind is "burned out" with the aid of a partner. Berner emphasizes that the most powerful way to dissolve the mind is through communication, because the mind is filled with uncommunicated thoughts, feelings, and experiences.

In practice, one partner contemplates internally, *Who am I?*, and then communicates whatever arises to their partner. Berner explains that when thoughts and experiences in the mind are communicated, they dissolve, disappearing to the extent that they are truly understood by the other person. According to Berner, this technique is 50 to 100 times more effective than any other classical or modern self-inquiry method he has studied and tested over the years.

In his book, Berner further discusses two classical techniques for emptying the mind that the Enlightenment Intensive utilizes. The first is to burn out the mind completely, emptying all its contents, while the second is to separate the mind from the Self. Most traditional techniques focus on separating the mind from the Self, or what Berner calls the "field of consciousness." This approach is favored because the other method—dissolving the mind entirely or burning it out—can require up to 30 years of dedicated practice.

The EI, however, takes a more efficient approach by both separating the mind from the true Self and dissolving it through communication. During the contemplation aspect of EI, when one is asked, *"Tell me who you are,"* the object of focus becomes the Self. This naturally brings up memories, ideas, identifications, beliefs, traumas—anything connected to the sense of who one believes they are. These experiences are then communicated to the partner, and as this process continues, the mind gradually empties. Eventually, there is nothing left, and the true Self can be directly experienced.

Berner states that contemplation with an object results in more rapid progress than contemplation without an object. Without an object, one must empty the entire mind, but with a chosen object, one can focus on emptying the mind in relation to that object. It is akin to clearing a single room in a large house rather than emptying the entire house. If we take the mind as a big house, we can focus on one room—or one object—and empty just that space, allowing us to experience the true Self. By focusing on an object, one separates the mind from the field of consciousness. The combination of separating the mind from the field of consciousness and dissolving the mind around the object results in extremely rapid progress toward Self Realization.

The method just described is truly revolutionary, and it makes one wonder why it hasn't gained wider recognition despite being around since 1968. That's a good question. It seems that many highly effective techniques remain obscure, and perhaps there is a reason for that. Maybe—just maybe—there is a force in the world that does not want humanity to awaken.

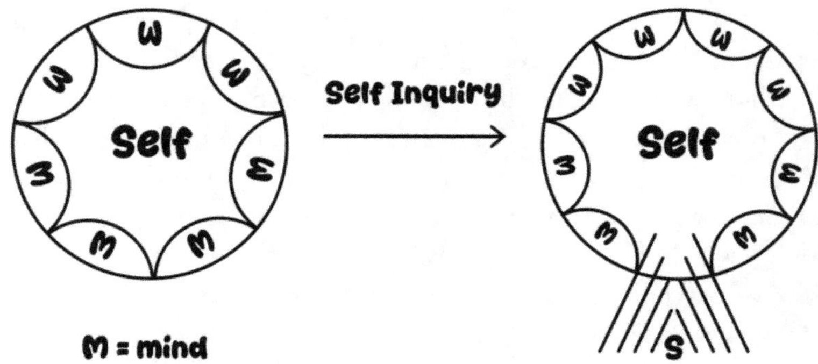

This idea that the Self can shine when a piece of the mind is dissolved may very well be the theory behind self-inquiry as well as self-inquiry dyad. See the illustration I made (above) showing this.

SPIRITUAL BYPASSING

A word of caution: if one jumps straight into self-inquiry without any preparatory exercises, a form of spiritual bypassing can occur. Spiritual bypassing is a type of escapism. This is why the forgiveness method and the release technique are so effective—they force one to confront and let go of everything rather than escape. Only by moving through the darkness can one reach the light; yet, once the light is realized, one understands that there was never any darkness to begin with—everything is the light of the Self. Unless you go past the light into the void, the darkness that gives birth to the light but that is a topic for another discussion.

For example, if one is feeling intense sadness, anger, or another strong emotion, the ego may attempt to hijack the self-inquiry process, using it as a means of escapism or suppression. This is no different from trying to use any other spiritual practice to avoid facing an emotion. The key is to let the emotion arise, observe it, but not grasp it—and then ask: "To whom does this emotion arise?" or "Who am I?" or "What am I?" Do not pretend the emotion is not there. It exists, so let it pass, realizing it is as transient and insubstantial as clouds drifting across the sky. With practice, these methods work remarkably well.

SUMMARY OF THREE METHODS

These three methods have helped many realize the Self. They are a fast track toward Self Realization. Always remember: you are already Self Realized; it is only the mind that obscures this truth. You are THAT! As Ramana Maharshi said, **"The only worthwhile goal in this life is to Realize the Self."**

Do you want to continue on the hamster wheel of pain, chasing fleeting happiness and experiencing inevitable sadness, the ups and downs of suffering? Or do you want freedom? Do you want to keep fighting against the stream of life, or do you want to flow with it? Do you want to Realize the Self? Are you ready? The answer must be unequivocally yes.

This is the only way to navigate the tricks and treachery of the ego and this world. One must have absolute faith and unwavering desire to Realize the Self, no matter what arises. The only desire worth having is the desire to Realize the Self—it is the desire that ends all desires. As Ramana Maharshi said, the only worthwhile pursuit in this life is to Realize the Self. What more can be said?

Those who will Realize the Self, will—and those who will not, will not. Those who have ears to hear, will hear; and those who do not, will not. It is what it is. It is already written. Life is predetermined, as the ancients teach, and they are quite possibly correct. The concept of a predetermined life is one we will explore in much greater depth at another time. If this reality is like an AI program, a simulation, or holographic in nature—much like a dream—then it may indeed be already preprogrammed, and that preprogramming could be akin to predestination or preordination.

As a prefoundational component of Self Realization, one must first cultivate a base of love by engaging in love-based activities that awaken the heart center, where the Divine Spark resides. Focus on serving others, developing loving-kindness, compassion, empathy, humility, and empathetic joy. Volunteer wherever and whenever you can. Practice meditation daily. The forgiveness practice will help in the cultivation of these divine qualities, other complementary methods can be employed as well. This will dramatically accelerate the awakening process, support Self Realization, and help avoid the pitfalls of quick-method traps.

These methods still produce quick results, but there is a point where things cannot be too instantaneous, as moving too quickly could potentially trigger psychosis, ego backlash, or other mental challenges. Once love is stirred and becomes more prominent, the techniques will have a greater impact. This is not to say they cannot be practiced without activating love—the forgiveness practice itself helps stimulate the heart center—but cultivating love makes the process smoother and more effective.

Here's a theoretical approach to the techniques described: In the first month, focus heavily on the forgiveness method, with a little release technique and a little self-inquiry. In the second month, reduce forgiveness while increasing the release technique, maintaining the same level of self-inquiry. In the third month, do less forgiveness and less release technique, while increasing self-inquiry. By the fourth month, focus primarily on self-inquiry, with minimal forgiveness and release technique.

When possible, participate in an Enlightenment Intensive with a self-inquiry Dyad, or begin practicing it with a partner on your own. If you have a partner, you can adjust this program and incorporate the self-inquiry Dyad from the very beginning, as much as you like.

All these techniques are powerful, yet their true aim is simple: to let go of everything, to dissolve into emptiness, into nothingness. And in that boundless emptiness, the true Self is revealed. This is but a glimpse—the path is endless, and there are countless ways to realize the Self. The true guru is none other than you, the Self. The true guru has always been you—the real you, the ultimate reality, the Self. You are THAT!

SILENCE: THE ULTIMATE TRUTH

The Self is silence—beyond words, beyond thought, beyond all conceptual knowing. Words and thoughts arise only in duality; they divide, categorize, and fragment what is inherently whole. Every thought creates distance, every explanation introduces separation. The more one speaks, the more one thinks, the more one moves away from the living truth. Truth is not something to be understood by the mind, but something to be beheld in stillness. When the mind falls quiet and the compulsion to label and define dissolves, what remains is not emptiness, but fullness itself—the radiant presence of the Self, luminous and infinite.

In silence, the heart awakens and the Self is recognized as what has always been present. Nothing new is acquired; nothing is added. Rather, all that is false gently falls away. In this wordless knowing, all questions dissolve, all seeking ends, and all that needs to be known is revealed without effort. A single moment of true silence conveys more wisdom than all the scriptures, teachings, and philosophies combined. Silence is the language of the Self, and stillness is its home. That is the Self. That is what you are. You are THAT!

EXERCISE EXERCISE EXERCISE

Emotions can get trapped in the body, and a common theory suggests that they are specifically held in our fascia. Fascia is a dense, web-like network of connective tissue that surrounds and connects all our muscles, organs, bones, nerves, arteries, veins—

essentially everything. When emotions become stuck in the fascia, it can cause the tissue to harden, become sticky, or tighten, which may restrict movement and disrupt the body's natural flow.

Movement, breath, sound, and touch can help release these stored emotions. This is where practices such as sound therapy, holotropic breathwork, myofascial release, and movement-based activities—like shaking, yoga, and dance—become valuable. Aerobic exercise, including cycling, jogging, swimming, and rowing, can also be highly effective.

Exercise not only helps release stored emotions but also supports the process of Self Realization. Exercise cultivates essential skills such as embracing discomfort and practicing self-discipline—training oneself to workout even when the mind resists. We will discuss these skills in more detail a little later.

It is highly important to establish a daily routine of exercise and mindfulness practices, in addition to the techniques mentioned. Doing them consistently—every day or nearly every day—helps turn these practices into habit, bypassing the ego, which will always invent excuses to avoid them. The ego, or false self, is the root of suffering. Realizing the Self allows one to see their true nature and recognize the ego for what it truly is: nothing.

Another fascinating aspect of exercise is its potential to rewire the brain. Research suggests that exercise may help reduce the impact of traumatic and addictive memories, as shown in a study conducted by Kyushu University (2024).

One thing to note from my experience with neurofeedback training: I was challenged for exercising, as if it were a program or samskara I needed to release. It wasn't the exercise that needed to go—it was the program my ego had turned into a source of validation, identification, and even trauma healing. One can let go of that identification and still exercise, for movement is essential to health and vitality.

Perhaps there was also a projection at play—my trainer's own programmed beliefs about exercise, or the lack thereof, projected onto me. Whatever the case, remember this: never let anyone tell you not to exercise, or that it is somehow unhealthy.

As someone with a graduate degree in exercise science, I can say with complete confidence: exercise is among the most powerful tools we have for cultivating all aspects of health. Health is wealth and without our health, it makes it more challenging to Realize the Self.

BONUS TECHNIQUE: RECAPITULATION

This bonus technique for aiding Self Realization is called **recapitulation**. It originated with the Toltecs in central Mexico between 950–1150 CE. I had heard of it before but didn't know much about it until fairly recently. The more I learned, the more I was impressed by its similarities to forgiveness and self-inquiry techniques as tools for Self Realization.

The main tenet of recapitulation is to go back and review—or even relive—traumatic or significant aspects of one's life from an **objective viewpoint**. The process can take years if one reviews an entire lifetime, or it can be much shorter if focusing on specific events. Remember, the primary cause that keeps the heart in bondage is the suppression, avoidance, or escape from our traumas and emotions. By reclaiming the energy that has been siphoned off in this way, we can break the "heart knot" and free the Self.

Recapitulation forces one to confront past traumas and release them, as these emotional scars arise from unprocessed memories. This is very similar to the forgiveness process, in which one also works to process trauma—but in forgiveness, the focus is slightly different. In fact, one could even consider forgiveness a form of recapitulation.

Another major benefit of recapitulation is that it helps one disidentify from the mind and ego by viewing one's life objectively. This is similar to self-inquiry, though self-inquiry operates more on a mental level, directly addressing the source of the "I" thought. Reviewing or reliving past events through recapitulation trains the mind not to identify with the mind or body—an essential tenet of Self Realization.

All of these techniques mentioned: forgiveness process, release technique, self-inquiry and recapitulation are hugely beneficial for Self Realization and can work in tandem. Yet the essential thread running through them all is the same, and I cannot stress it enough: one must disidentify completely from the mind and body and identify with the awareness, the Self. This is the gateway, the absolute key to realizing the Self.

You are not the mind,
nor the restless tides of thought.
You are not the body,
nor the fleeting shadow of form.

You are the Self,
pure and vast,
the silent witness of all.

Untouched.
Unbound.
Endless as the sky,
deep as the ocean.

That is the Self—
the heart of all being,
radiant, eternal,
whole.

That is everything.
That is all.
You are THAT!

Chapter 11

SUPPLEMENTAL TOOLS

DIET AND EXERCISE

Upon concluding the discussion of the three main techniques, I would like to share some helpful pointers to gently accelerate the Realization of the Self—specifically regarding diet and exercise.

The ideal diet for Self Realization has traditionally been referred to as the Sattvic or Yogic diet. To understand this, it is helpful to briefly explore the three *gunas* in Ayurveda (Jain, 2024). *Gunas* refers to the qualities that exist in everything around us, including food. The three gunas are *sattva, rajas,* and *tamas,* which correspond to purity, activity or passion, and darkness or inertia, respectively.

Sattvic foods are known for their purity, lightness, and positive energy. This diet emphasizes plant-based foods such as fruits, vegetables, nuts, seeds, legumes, and whole grains.

Rajasic foods are stimulating, flavorful, and evoke passions, restlessness, excitability, and anger. These include fried foods, spicy dishes, rich desserts, ice cream, tea, coffee, and similar items.

Tamasic foods are the most detrimental, inducing heaviness, dullness, and ignorance in both mind and body. Examples include canned or processed foods, fast food, foods high in preservatives, white sugar, refined flour products, excessive dairy, meat, fish, and alcohol.

In essence, the yogic diet is a sattvic diet, best suited for Self Realization. Rajasic foods should be consumed only in moderation, and tamasic foods very occasionally, if at all.

THE BRIGHT LIGHT

Interestingly enough, many years ago I had my first transcendental experience of the Self after switching to a vegetarian diet for an extended period. I don't recall the exact details, but I remember losing weight and running and exercising regularly during that time.

In those years, I was experimenting with meditation a little each day, gradually increasing the duration as time went on. One night, I decided to meditate for longer and see what would happen. I sat in the hallway with my back against the wall for what I think was around three hours or more. I wasn't paying attention to time as it slowly drifted by.

At that time, I didn't understand that the ultimate purpose of meditation was to realize the Self. I was approaching it more as an experiment, curious to see if I could witness anything "cool."

Needless to say, I remember meditating, eyes closed and gazing slightly upward, for a long stretch of time. Time seemed to pass slowly, but I persisted, wearing down the mind and ego by focusing on a single point between my brows. My breath grew slower and slower until I was almost asleep, barely breathing, enveloped in complete and utter stillness.

Then, all of a sudden, as if out of nowhere, a bright white light filled my entire visual field—like a million suns—and I felt an immense flood of love and bliss that seemed to permeate every cell of my body. I was completely blown away. Never in my life had I felt such love. It was incredible!

The experience gradually faded as awe overtook me and my ego crept back to life, filling my mind with thoughts and excitement. This, I realized, is the Divine Spark—the Self that resides within all of us—sleeping, waiting to be awakened when we choose to Realize the Self.

Everyone's experience will be different, but everyone will have an experience. Even that is part of the illusory nature of Self Realization. It's best not to get caught up in experiences and to focus simply on realizing the Self.

In summary, one should maintain a balanced diet and engage in regular, moderate exercise. It is important to remain unattached and free from desire regarding both. Highly addictive foods, such as those high in sugar or heavily processed, should be avoided whenever possible.

Exercise should not become a form of escapism; rather, it should be practiced for the enhancement of health and longevity. If nothing else, walking is one of the best all-around exercises, particularly after meals.

One should also be wary of maintaining extremes in diet or exercise for prolonged periods. Historically, some Sufis practiced extended fasting as a means of attaining communion with the Self, and in certain cases, such extremes reportedly led to serious harm or even death. This is not to suggest that periodic fasting is without benefit—it can be a powerful and health-promoting practice when approached wisely. However, moderation and discernment are essential. Always consult a qualified healthcare professional before making significant changes to your diet, exercise, or fasting practices, rather than relying solely on guidance from books such as this.

With that being said, by avoiding the common pitfalls of diet and exercise, one gains a significant advantage over the majority of the population in terms of health, and this creates a firmer foundation for Self Realization.

THE NOTHING

Years ago, while lying in bed with my body aching, I had no idea what was wrong with me. I was tired, anxious, depressed, lethargic, and my muscles hurt constantly. I later discovered that the culprit was iron overload. I could barely run or ride my bike—my two best coping mechanisms for recurring negative thought patterns buried deep in the subconscious. These patterns generated waves of sadness and anger. I distinctly remember one thought loop that replayed in my mind for many years until, eventually, it dissolved.

As a child, my mother often carried intense anger, and I was the usual rambunctious kid. One day, during a fight with my brother—we were shouting at each other—my mom suddenly ran toward me in a fury, screaming, *"You're going to be nothing!"* over and over again, almost as if she were overtaken by something. I fled in terror. I must have been around twelve at the time, and my brother was ten. These explosive episodes happened from time to time.

Strangely enough, on one occasion when she entered that same state, I picked up a Bible and began reading it, and she abruptly stopped and cowered away. It was an unsettling experience. Much later, I did a forgiveness process for her and for the intense negativity she carried, and it was profoundly therapeutic. It brought deep healing and finally put those echoes of her words to rest.

For years after that incident, I would still hear her voice repeating, *"You're going to be nothing!"* Again and again. In retrospect, it became a strangely meaningful gift, because in a spiritual sense, she—or that moment—was right. I am nothing, and in that, I am everything. When we realize the Self, we realize that our true nature is nothingness, which is also everything. We are not the mind and not the body; we are pure conscious awareness. That is the real Self—nothingness, stillness, beingness, everythingness. All of these point to the same awareness.

Needless to say, I often wonder how that moment arose. Was it trying to push me toward something? Did the trauma it sparked become a catalyst for Self Realization later in life? It makes one reflect deeply. I am certain that nothing in this life happens by accident.

FERRITIN AND SELF REALIZATION

What was actually happening to my body as I lay there feeling so helpless—with that echo in my head insisting I was nothing—was an excess of iron. My ferritin level ended up being over 3,500, when the standard reference range for an adult male is typically 24–336 ng/mL (though I personally believe the ideal level should be closer to under 100; this is not medical advice—always consult your physician). The excess iron was wreaking havoc inside my body, essentially oxidizing me from the inside out and causing damage to nearly every organ.

Once I saw my lab results and realized how dangerously high my iron levels were, I did everything in my power to bring them down. I researched relentlessly, reading everything I could find on iron overload. I donated blood as often as possible for years. I even remember doing three donations in a single week—technically a double-red and a single donation, but close enough. I did pass out afterward, hitting my head on the bathroom door handle.

I followed every dietary recommendation I could think of. And as the iron slowly came down, I began to feel progressively better. It was an incredibly humbling journey.

I remember, at one point, lying in the hospital bed, staring at the blood bag, just sick of needles and ready for it to be over. Eventually, my blood levels came down and normalized. To this day, I check my ferritin every month because I've found it to be a very important blood parameter for Self Realization and stillness.

Remember the ideal diet for Self Realization? The sattvic diet—yes, good work! That is a plant-based diet. A plant-based diet naturally results in lower iron absorption. Animal foods contain heme iron, while plant foods contain non-heme iron. Heme iron from animals is absorbed at a rate of 15–35%, while non-heme iron from plants is absorbed at 2–20%.

If you study yogis, monks, Gnostics, and Sufis, you'll notice that they predominantly eat plant-based foods and consume relatively little meat as well as fast for extended periods of time. Some live at high elevations, such as in the Himalayas, which can further reduce iron levels because the body uses more iron to produce red blood cells. Iron makes up about 70% of hemoglobin, which carries oxygen from the lungs to the rest of the body. Theoretically, one could assume that many of these adepts are mildly anemic or have low iron levels. There appears to be a connection between iron levels and Self Realization.

In fact, there is a scientific link between low iron, anemia, and brain waves. In a study by Ferreira et al. (2019), they explored the neurophysiological effects of low iron in detail. For example, low iron impairs myelin production, slowing nerve impulses and thus slowing brain wave activity. Iron is also essential for the production of neurotransmitters, which enable brain cells to communicate. When iron levels are low, neurotransmitter production is impaired, influencing brain wave patterns.

Clearly, neither very low nor very high iron levels are ideal. However, it is plausible that yogis living in the Himalayas may exhibit slightly lower iron levels, which could contribute to slower brain wave activity and thereby support meditative and contemplative states associated with Self Realization. Supporting this possibility, a study by Jáuregui-Lobera (2014) found that children with low iron levels exhibited increased delta and theta activity alongside reduced alpha waves. Notably, a hallmark of ego-dissolution and transcendental experiences is a marked reduction in beta—and often alpha—brain wave activity, accompanied by a shift toward slower frequencies.

What's fascinating is that these days I tend to maintain a slightly lower iron state, and I can feel the increased stillness associated with it. It becomes easier to lock into the silent observer within, and oftentimes, thoughts are minimal or even nonexistent. As one becomes Self Realized, it is possible to simply watch and observe thoughts like passing clouds, without getting drawn into or attached to them. This suggests that there may be some validity to the connection between low iron and the yogis' ability to realize the Self.

We don't need to be as strict or austere as the yogis, but we do need to maintain a practice with some discipline and minimal austerity. Laziness or sloth will not allow one to Realize the Self—or to accomplish anything meaningful in life. I would even go so far as to say that how you do anything is how you do everything.

Your approach to everyday life becomes the foundation for everything else you do. If you are lazy by nature, progress will be limited—although, ultimately, there is only one pursuit worth pursuing: Self Realization. Therefore, it is essential to build a solid foundational framework for success in life, and then use that framework to focus fully on Self Realization.

EGO DEATH

Let's dive headfirst into ego death, trauma healing, and Self Realization. At a certain point, there is no longer any need to use escapism as a way to suppress or manage the heightened emotional programs playing in the subconscious. This includes identities built around escapism—alcoholism, going to bars, marathon running, entertainment like gambling, drug use, or anything else. Even activities that seem wholesome, such as excessive meditation, gardening, traveling, watching or participating in sports, overeating, watching movies, or listening to music, can function as forms of escapism.

Once these traumas and emotions are healed, and no new unfavorable emotions arise, certain activities may naturally fall away—and that is part of ego death. Additionally, one's social structure will be reshaped, and one's social circle will evolve accordingly. Remnants of former habits may remain, but they become far less rigid and more fluid.

For example, I once ran every day—sometimes twice a day—with two to three intense workouts each week. Today, I run primarily for general health and well-being, rather than as a means of validating my self-worth or suppressing difficult emotions. As the ego gradually dissolves, the self-worth that once demanded validation is revealed to be nothing more than a construct of the ego—a fictitious self—rather than the true Self.

The true Self needs nothing, because it is everything. The Self is all there is, was, or ever will be, residing in the heart center, waiting to awaken. I still do harder workouts from time to time, but it is not like it used to be. Most of the time, I focus on gentle aerobic exercise, occasionally interspersed with a harder workout for the sake of health and longevity.

One may still engage in activities from the past—but the difference is that they are no longer necessary. They are often performed out of habit of the body or mind. As long as one identifies as the observer, as the Self, it becomes an entirely different experience. You are the Self, unbounded awareness and unbridled joy. You are THAT!

Even some of the greatest sages had their quirks. Nisargadatta smoked like a chimney until shortly before his passing. Papaji, faced health struggles from a love of sweets. Ramana Maharshi, in his own way, held a deep reverence for life—never allowing even a mustard seed or a single grain of rice to go to waste. I can relate to this. After traveling to many countries and witnessing poverty and suffering firsthand, I cannot bear to waste even a scrap of food. I save it for later, give it away, or eat every last morsel on my plate. In a world where millions lack clean water and sustenance, it is staggering that in the United States, up to forty percent of food is discarded.

PROCESSING

Once one has made continuous progress and peeled back the layers of the ego to reach the Self, it can come as quite a shock. There is almost a look on one's face, like seeing a ghost. Robert Adams has that very expression in some of his photographs—a look of awe and wonder.

This awe arises because the experience of the Self cannot be adequately described. Words are a pale reflection of its essence. The Self transcends language and even this very reality. It feels like infinite love/bliss, infinite peace, infinite serenity.

When one first catches larger and larger glimpses of the Self, the ego will do everything it can to stir up emotions and pull one away. Fear is its favorite tool: *What if I don't exist anymore? What if this happens… what if this or that…* These were some of the thoughts my ego presented in my fictitious mind as the Self Realization process unfolded. My ego feared that I would cease to exist as an individual, that I would become robotic or simply vanish.

Thankfully, it is not quite like that. We still exist in this dream world, but more as observers. The body carries out its functions, yet we no longer identify as the doer—we identify as the witness. Ramana Maharshi said, *"If one is the doer, then they are also the sufferer."*

There is the paradox: the one who believes they are the doer is the ego, and thus the ego becomes the sufferer—the origin of all suffering.

It takes time to process the experience of each layer of the ego being peeled back. Sometimes this can take months or even years. A glimpse of the Self can occur fairly quickly, perhaps in a day or two, but the gap—the time spent as the Self—needs to widen gradually for one to eventually fully Realize the Self.

The way one sees the world after Self Realization is dramatically different from the way one viewed it before. It is astonishing to realize that nearly everything we were taught seems designed to enslave us, implanting and reinforcing nonsensical belief systems that keep us from Realizing the Self.

Those in power cannot control society without fear—without the ego. Therefore, they promote egoism on a massive scale. They encourage people to attach to their emotions and identify with them, using programming through television, social media, and other means of influence.

From a spiritual perspective, it can sometimes feel as though political and religious systems encourage people to remain identified with the mind and body, caught in states of confusion or distraction. As the Self is Realized more and more deeply, this becomes increasingly apparent—not as an external conspiracy, but as an inner recognition of how easily consciousness becomes entangled in the world of form and conditioning.

After such realization, fully reintegrating into society may feel impossible in the old way, because one now sees the "dream world" for what it is—a realm often marked by restlessness, noise, and the hurried pace of beta-wave consciousness. Much of the world moves through life in a trance-like state, mechanical living, disconnected from the deeper Self. Many identify solely with the mind and body, unaware of the vastness of their true nature.

It's time to rise, no more playing small,
It's time to Realize the Self, hear the call.
You can do this, you must, it's true,
Step into the light—your Self awaits you!

WHAT IT FEELS LIKE TO REALIZE THE SELF

The only way to truly know is through non-understanding—or not knowing—by transcending the mind and experiencing it firsthand. In this state, there are no more highs or lows of emotion. Emotions are seen from the observer's viewpoint: they arise and pass. It feels like an in-between kind of state, and it can take some time to get used to. The mind wants to grasp and attach to emotions because it has been conditioned to do so over a lifetime.

Over time, it becomes easier and easier to abide in the Self. This is why there should be no rush to Realize the Self overnight. Too much, too soon will not hold and can be jarring to one's psyche or ego, potentially causing a type of ego backlash. This happens frequently with people who chase enlightenment through psychedelics or even neurofeedback; the intense experiences often create another ego trap rather than lasting realization.

Another fascinating effect of abiding in the stillness of Self Realization is that one can sense the stillness—or the lack thereof—in those around them. This is one reason many Self Realized individuals tend to withdraw from society. From this observational perspective, the world can appear utterly mad after Self Realization; people seem nervous, restless, and shaky.

In Self Realization, every moment becomes meditation. Every movement, every breath, every thought—each is the meditation and the meditator, merging in complete absorption. Time softens, loses its grip, and almost ceases to exist. Life flows effortlessly; appointments, alarms, and daily tasks continue, but the mind moves lightly, without strain or effort.

In the presence of others, the heart overflows. Love and compassion rise like a tide, embracing all beings, human and animal alike. Sometimes, the intensity of this love brings tears, for it is the recognition that we are all one, each life a reflection of the same Self.

Compassion is not just for others—it is the Self recognizing the Self in all. There are no separate beings. There are no others. We are all, always, each other.

"He who sees all beings in the Self itself, and the Self in all beings, feels no hatred by virtue of that wisdom."
—*Ishavasya Upanishad* 1.6

Ashtavakra Gita 18.9 (Chinmayananda, 2016)
Knowing for certain that all is
Self, the sage has no trace of
thoughts
such as "I am this" or "I am not that."

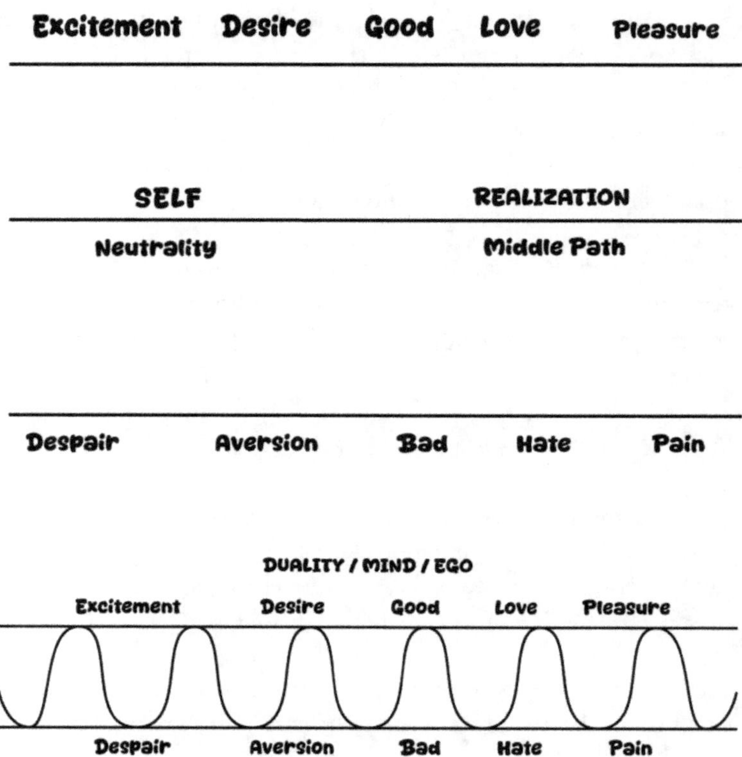

These diagrams illustrate the in-between nature of Self Realization. There is a consistent level of happiness, but it is not the ordinary happiness we associate with everyday life; it is a form of bliss that is ever-present. There are no extreme highs or lows—just a serene middle ground.

This is similar to the Buddhist concept of the Middle Path, or Middle Way, which avoids the extremes of indulgence and austerity. In our context, the term "middle path" refers to the natural by-product of Self Realization: an in-between state of equanimity.

While the applications differ, both meanings share the same essential quality of balance.

3 LEVELS OF ENLIGHTENMENT IN ZEN BUDDHISM

In Zen Buddhism, there are three levels of Samadhi, or Self Realization, which Snyder (2025) presents in his book *Demystifying Awakening*. These levels align closely with the concepts we are exploring in this book. They are as follows:

1st Level – Kensho (First Glimpse):
In this state, one experiences a fleeting glimpse of the Self. The mind momentarily ceases to function, just enough for one to intuitively sense the Self without fully understanding it.

2nd Level – Satori (Deepening):
This level represents a prolonged gap in the nothingness state of no mind, which can last for hours or even days. It is a state of deep inner peace and freedom. Effort is still required to maintain this state. Most enlightened yogis are in this stage and they may use fasting, sleep deprivation, mantra and long periods of meditation to remain in that state. The ego has not yet fully dissolved into the heart, so the experience is not yet permanent.

3rd Level – Daigo-tettei (Final Awakening):
In this ultimate stage, all previous Samadhi experiences are integrated. The ego may or may not have fully dissolved into the heart, but the awakening is far more profound than in the earlier stages. One naturally stays in awakening without effort at this level.

The challenge of being fully Self Realized at the highest level is that it becomes difficult to hold a job or function normally in society. At that state, one feels limp, almost like mush, with incredible waves of love and bliss filling every cell of the body. I can only describe my Samadhi experience as orgasmic—a full-body orgasm, without any connection to sex. It was as though my skin had become a radiating vessel of pure bliss. Imagine going to work in that state, trying to interact with people day after day—it simply doesn't work. I remember taking an ice bath right after Samadhi and not feeling the cold but bliss. Imagine touching a hot stove and feeling nothing but bliss. It wouldn't be ideal.

These levels, corresponding to stages of Self Realization, seem to hold true. What often happens is that one gets a glimpse of the Self, then retreats as the mind attempts to regain control, bringing with it a sense of fear about the ego dying. The ego may employ forgetfulness to obscure the experience—or at least try—but one never truly forgets. Once the experience occurs, the seed has been planted, and it can never be erased.

As more glimpses of the Self occur, the ability to rest or abide in that state gradually expands—from seconds to minutes, from hours to days, and eventually to weeks and finally permanently. The final stage of Self Realization is reached when the ego is fully consumed by the Divine Spark residing in the heart center.

NEW AGE TRAP

We would be remiss if we didn't address the New Age movement. There are countless New Age beliefs, many of which are distortions of deeper truths. The multibillion-dollar New Age movement has become a kind of modern religion, complete with its own doctrines and ways of life. Much of it involves assigning mystical meaning to almost everything, while often encouraging gaslighting, escapism, or suppression as ways to avoid confronting one's deeper emotional patterns.

I recently came across a video of someone claiming that indulging in sensual desires can lead to spiritual growth or awakening. This is not what the ancient Upanishadic teachings on Self Realization taught. They viewed the world as unreal—a play of appearances—and the senses as a trap. Sensual pleasures are seen not as gateways to awakening but as obstacles to Self Realization. Although there are more very advanced ways of tantra that use pleasure as a means to Realize the Self which is not for most. Even a broken clock is right twice a day.

There is so much happening within the New Age movement that entire books have been, and continue to be, written on the subject. Another common theme is the belief that some external force is coming to save humanity—whether the Galactic Federation, extraterrestrial hybrids on the dark side of the moon, or the notion that we are "ascending into 5D." I would estimate that most of this is pure fantasy.

No one is coming to save you, because there is no separate "you" that needs saving. You are already everything—everything that is, was, or ever will be—because you are the Self that abides within and beyond all comprehension, the ineffable reality itself. You are THAT!

The point of this topic is to skip the New Age nonsense and simply Realize the Self. After Self Realization, go ahead and do whatever you wish, but I would say that time is short. None of us know when we will pass on into the afterlife. The sooner one realizes the Self, the better. I don't mean to scare anyone with a sense of urgency, but with all the transhumanism and AI developments coming, it is wise to make haste, as it may become much more difficult—or even impossible—in the future.

MANIFESTATION

This is another New Age concept we must address. One must first ask: *Who is the one that desires to manifest?* Is it the Self, or is it the mind and ego? It is, of course, the ego. The ego seeks to change, control, and elevate itself as the doer. The doer is the ego. Remember: if you are the doer, you are the sufferer. Our true Self does nothing, is nothing, and wants nothing. It is as if we inhabit an avatar suit, while the true Self simply rests within, abiding in pure equanimity, joy, tranquility, and ultimate peace, as the avatar—the human body—carries out whatever it is programmed to do.

Nobody is manifesting anything; the only manifestation happening is within the mind/ego. If that doesn't make sense, then Realize the Self and see what remains of the one who once wishes to manifest. When abiding in the Self, everything is already perfect; there are no desires and no wants.

There are countless classes, courses, books, and ebooks on how to manifest this or that. The only thing one needs to "manifest" is Self Realization. Focus on that, and all is well. There will be no need—and certainly no desire—to manifest anything at all. Self Realization is the one desire that dissolves all other desires.

A note of caution: there *may* be actual "manifestations" that occur, and I would suggest they are traps of this world. There is no way around this. All the angel numbers you see on the backs of cars, telling you you're on the right path… all the synchronicities you believe are happening to guide you to a better place… it is all part of the programming of this simulation, most likely designed to keep you moving outward, distracted, and subtly imprisoned in the ego— preventing you from Realizing the Self.

This is done to keep your attention focused outward when the focus needs to turn inward. That is another thing: obstacles will present themselves, often disguised as blessings or guidance, but in truth they may exist to keep you from Realizing the Self. It is all done by design.

Keep going through every fear, every doubt, every longing, until
the veil dissolves and the silent witness within awakens.
Turn your gaze inward to the heart, that sacred center
where the Self resides, eternal, infinite, and unbound.

Feel the vastness of your own being,
the limitless ocean of consciousness that flows through every breath,
every cell, every moment of your existence.

Do not stop. Do not pause.
Let the currents of the Self carry you beyond the mind,
beyond the body, beyond all notions of "I" and "mine."
Rest in the heart, where the infinite Self pulses with radiant love,
where there is no fear, no lack, no separation—only boundless unity.

Abide there. Abide always. Until
all that is false falls away,
and only the eternal, infinite Self remains—
pure awareness, luminous, unshakable,
the endless light that is your true home,
the heartbeat of the universe within you.

YOU ARE THAT!

SELF HELP

This is really the same with manifestation: Who is the self that needs help? It is, of course, the ego-self. Self-help gurus are everywhere. They claim to help you get a better career, a better mindset, a better love life, a better body, a better this or a better that. Not one of them talks about Self Realization—the only path to permanent, everlasting happiness. They are still playing by the ego's rules, bound by duality and the fictitious nature of this world.

Personal growth is ego growth. The Self is not a person or a thing. The Self needs no growth; it needs no help. The Self is infinite, all-powerful, everything—and you are THAT! Every time we take a step to transcend ourselves in order to become a "better person," we are reinforcing the ignorance and delusion that we are somebody, that we are the ego. That very belief fuels our suffering and pushes further away the happiness that is already our true nature.

It was in 2011 that I attended a seminar by a very popular self-help guru for the first time. I can definitely say it was helpful in certain aspects of my life. That seminar helped shift my mindset toward more positive thinking and encouraged the creation of habits that support success in any endeavor. I remember the high energy, the dancing, and the life growth—aka ego growth. Even the fire-walking was monumentally exciting at the time. We chanted the mantra, *"Cool Moss! Cool Moss!"* as we all walked across the hot coals in an experience that will never be forgotten.

Despite all of that, it is still the false self that one is working with. All the self-help and manifestation practices reinforce the egoic identity. People become attached to this "positive" identity, and as we know, attachment leads to suffering. The true path to Realizing the Self is through letting go of everything—including the desire to become a "better person" in any sense. You are already pure perfection, the purest of the pure. There is nothing you need to change. You are the changeless, the ever-perfect Self.

Years later, I attended the same guru's seminar, but I ended up leaving after a couple of days. I felt a lot of compassion for the speaker as he spoke about his dozens of companies, the hundreds of millions of dollars he earns, and how little time he has for sleep because of his responsibilities. He also mentioned the health challenges he was facing and wondered if he would even be able to conduct the conference. His health seemed to be suffering because he had fully cemented himself in the egoic identity he had built over many years.

Do we really classify working non-stop for more and more money, only to develop health problems, as success? Unfortunately, that is the standard role model for the majority of the population these days. There were thousands upon thousands of people at that conference, and they even had numerous coaches constantly trying to help us and get us to sign up for his programs. There were endless products and upsells available.

If, after acquiring all that wealth and financial success, one is still not happy, we must seriously question whether money—or the pursuit of it—truly brings happiness. The truth is, it does not.

Only the Realization of the Self can bring eternal happiness. No amount of money, no amount of experiences, no amount of wanting or desiring—other than the desire for the Self—can provide permanent, lasting joy. All the happiness and pleasures offered by this world are transitory, just like the world itself. One will oscillate from happiness to sadness, pleasure to pain, back and forth, until one transcends duality and Realizes the Self.

Bhradaranyaka Upanishad 4:4:6-7 (Radhakrishan, 2024)
6: …But the man who does not desire, he who is without desire, who is freed from desire, whose desire is satisfied, whose desire is the Self; his breaths do not depart. Being Brahman he goes into Brahman.

7: …When all the desires that dwell in the heart are cast away, then does the mortal become immortal, then he attains Brahman (the Self) here (in this body).

Mundaka Upanishad 3:2:1-2 (Radhakrishan, 2024)
3:2:1 He who knows the supreme abode of Brahman, wherein founded, the world shines brightly. The wise men, who, free from desires, worship the Person, pass beyond the seed (of rebirth).

3:2:2 He who entertains desires, thinking of them, is born (again) here and there on account of his desires. But of him who has his desire fully satisfied, who is a perfected soul, all his desires vanish even here (on earth).

BEWARE OF THOSE SELLING ENLIGHTENMENT

The self-help industry is a billion-dollar business, and with it have come numerous unethical practices. Many claim to sell enlightenment for big bucks through seminars and retreats. The majority of these offerings are nonsense, designed for a single purpose: to keep you in a perpetual state of searching, a perpetual state of being a seeker—or, more accurately, a customer. If you were to become Self Realized, they would lose a customer. They might offer tidbits of factual information here and there, but it is never enough to truly Realize the Self. They sell distorted concepts of enlightenment, often saying things like: "We want everyone to be like Buddhas driving a Benz." We all know how that worked out for Osho and his 93 Rolls-Royces. That entire concept is paradoxical and fundamentally contrary to the state of Self Realization.

When one is Self Realized, there are no wants. There are no desires. That is simply the way it is. No amount of money, no collection of fancy cars, can override this truth. When you see someone promoting Self Realization while being extremely wealthy or owning numerous luxury cars and homes, take a step back. Ask yourself whether what they are teaching is true and pure, or if they are preying on those seeking Self Realization. The truth is, the majority are doing just that.

Astavakra Gita: 17.11 (Chinmayananda, 2016)
The liberated soul
abides in Self alone
and is pure of heart.
He lives always and everywhere,
free of desire.

In that desireless state of wanting nothing, one has everything. One **IS** everything. To want or desire is to slip back into the ego, into duality, into suffering. What could be greater than being everything? Nothing. Why manifest what the ego craves, when simply being desireless gives you all?

But the mind asks, *How can one do things in life?* You **are** life itself—everything unfolds naturally. The mind is the only barrier. Let go of the mind, Realize the Self, and life will flow in ways more beautiful than the mind could ever begin to comprehend.

Katha Upanishad 1:2:6 (Radhakrishan, 2024)
6: What lies beyond shines not to the simple-minded, careless (who is) deluded by the glamour of wealth. Thinking 'this world exists, there is no other,' he falls again and again into my power.
(Yama- The god of the death)

Chapter *12*

SELF REALIZATION PYRAMID

Here's a pyramid drawing I made that summarizes what I have found to be the foundational components for Self Realization. The first layer is Brahmacharya—self-control self-discipline, and self-restraint. The second layer is the cultivation of the four Brahmaviharas: loving-kindness, compassion, empathetic joy, and equanimity.

The next level encompasses meditation, mindfulness, selfless service, and knowledge. Following that is the practice of forgiveness and letting go (recapitulation can also be included here), which helps facilitate emptiness. The final preparation for Self Realization is self-inquiry, which is the core of Jnana Yoga—the yoga of knowledge and wisdom.

These practices, when applied diligently, will lead one to Self Realization—sometimes gradually, and at times quite rapidly. As the *Maitri Upanishad* 6:28 (Radhakrishnan, 2024) mentions, if one is earnest and studious in practice, Self Realization can be attained in as little as six months.

SELF DISCIPLINE/ BRAHMACHARYA

Chandogya Upanishad 8:4:3 & 8:5:1 (Radhakrishan, 2024)
8:4:3 But only they find that Brahma-world who practice the disciplined life of a student of sacred knowledge; only they possess that Brahma-world. For them there is unlimited freedom in all worlds.

8:5:1 …for only by sacrificing with the disciplined life of a student of sacred knowledge does one obtain the Self.

Svetasvatara Upanishad 6:22 (Radhakrishan, 2024)
6:22 The highest mystery in the Vedanta which has been declared in a former age should not be given to one whose passions are not subdued nor again to one who is not a son or a pupil.

The development of basic skills—skills that are increasingly lacking in today's society-is crucial in the process of Realizing the Self, as well as for attaining success in any area of life. Focused attention, perseverance, consistency, and patience are just a few of the essential qualities one must cultivate. These are the tools in one's toolkit that help pave the way toward Self Realization.

Unfortunately, many people today lack these foundational abilities. This is perhaps the only genuine benefit I can attribute to motivational or self-help seminars: they may help individuals develop the preliminary skills needed to propel themselves toward Self Realization. These skills also make it easier to navigate this realm—to gain a degree of stability and financial success, as needed.

That being said, the ultimate aim of one's life should be to Realize the Self. That alone brings permanent, unshakeable happiness. And what could be better than that? Nothing. Only "nothing" can be the Self, and only the Self can bring the bliss that never fades. You are THAT!

If one reads any ethics or codes of conduct from ancient wisdom, one concept consistently stands out: **compassion**. Compassion is a cornerstone of Self Realization, one of its most essential elements. It is also one of the four Brahmaviharas, or "four abodes of Brahman" (the Self). Compassion can be understood as profound empathy in action. Its key lies in moving beyond mere understanding to taking tangible action to alleviate suffering and promote well-being in the world. Across all traditions teaching Self Realization, compassion is of paramount importance.

There are many ways to cultivate compassion. Practicing loving-kindness meditation, where one sends goodwill to every person one knows—even those who are difficult—is particularly effective. Listening deeply to others, without interrupting or thinking about what to say next, and being fully present, is another powerful practice. Practicing empathy naturally acts as a bridge to compassion. Small acts of kindness, serving others, and using gentle, kind language toward both others and oneself all nurture compassion.

Self-compassion is especially important, as many people are far too harsh on themselves which of course is the ego.

Another practice I find invaluable is watching motivational videos of individuals who have endured extreme hardship and placing oneself in their shoes. Seeing the struggles of others, no matter how challenging one's own life may seem, fosters a deeper sense of compassion. There will always be others facing even greater trials, and understanding this helps cultivate the heart of compassion.

The science behind compassion is that it generates massive amounts of gamma brain waves (Lutz, 2004), which are linked to heightened states of awareness, feelings of bliss, joy, and happiness, and an enhanced perception of the world. Gamma waves are considered a hallmark of Self Realization. Beyond that, compassion promotes heart-brain coherence, which can propel one into mystical states as it did with the experience I talked about. According to the HeartMath Institute, the heart's electric field is 60 times greater in amplitude than that of the brain, and the heart's magnetic field is 100 times greater than that of the brain. The heart truly is the seat of the Self and the ancients knew this. The Sufi mystics even developed an entire framework for Self Realization centered on the awakening of the spiritual heart.

Here is a very simplistic mechanistic view of the interplay of compassion and the Self, of course there are many more factors:

Compassion → Gamma & Theta Waves → Bliss / Anandamide → Self Realization

Compassion – The starting point. Cultivating empathy and loving-kindness activates the heart and mind, setting the stage for transformation.

Gamma & Theta Waves – Compassion stimulates gamma activity, enhancing awareness and perception. Coupled with theta waves, this propels one into deeper mystical states and heightened consciousness.

Bliss / Anandamide – The neurochemical response: increased anandamide generates profound joy, serenity, and a sense of boundless bliss. The Self is often described in Vedic texts as Sat-Chit-Ananda or existence, consciousness, **BLISS**.

Lowered Ego – As bliss deepens, attachment to the ego weakens. The mind becomes less self-centered, opening the way to pure awareness.

Self Realization – The culmination: with compassion fully integrated, gamma/theta coherence, bliss, and diminished ego converge, revealing the true Self.

COMPASSION

Brihadaranyaka Upanishad 5:2:3 (Radhakrishan, 2024)
"...be compassionate." He said, 'Yes, you have understood.' This very thing the heavenly voice of the thunder. Repeats da, da, da, that is, control yourselves, give, be **compassionate**. One should practice this same triad, self-control, giving and **compassion**.

Chandogya Upanishads 3.17.4 (Radhakrishan, 2024)
And austerity, almsgiving, uprightness, non-violence, truthfulness, these are the gifts for the priests.

Brihadaranyaka Upanishad 5.2.1-3 (Radhakrishan, 2024)
"...one should learn these three—self-control, charity and **compassion**."

"Showing **compassion** to all living entities, you will attain **Self Realization**. Giving assurance of safety to all, you will perceive your own self as well as all the universes in Me, and Myself in you." - *Srimad Bhagavatam* 3.21.31 (Das, n.d.)

Philippians 2:1
"Are your hearts tender and **compassionate**?"
McGeough, 2024.

SPECTRUM OF EMPATHY

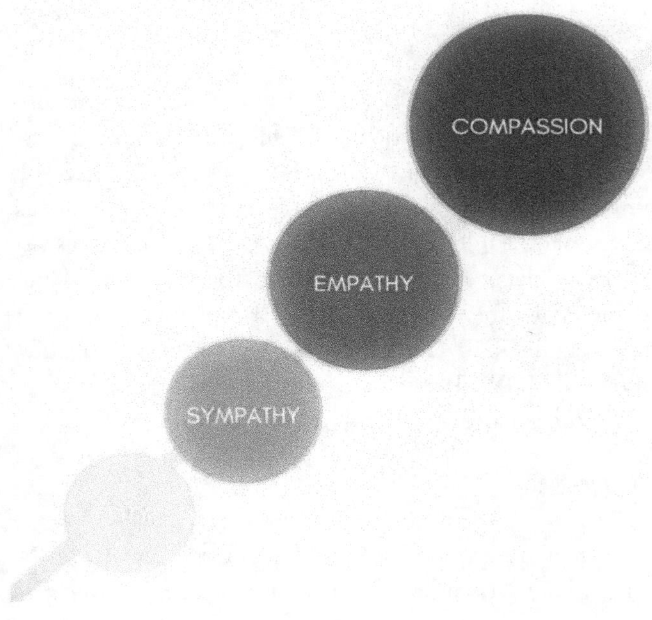

Here is a great chart on the spectrum of empathy. Pity to sympathy to empathy to compassion.

A few suggestions for developing fundamental skills for Self Realization that I have come up with: focused attention, perseverance, courage and patience.

FOCUSED ATTENTION

With the average human attention span being only a few seconds—less than that of a goldfish—it becomes very difficult to Realize the Self. For example, if one cannot sit still and engage in practices such as the forgiveness process, letting go, or self-inquiry, Self Realization will be extremely difficult, if not impossible. It is wise to build one's attention span. A simple and effective way is through reading, which trains focus and concentration. Meditation is another powerful method. There are countless ways to strengthen attention; the key is consistent practice.

PERSEVERANCE

Perseverance is defined as the continual pursuit of a goal despite setbacks and difficulties. One can also call it resilience or steadfast determination. Obstacles will arise, especially at the beginning. Pain and discomfort may surface as the ego is stripped bare, revealing its illusory nature. But beneath all of this lies the true Self. It is a deep, challenging, yet profoundly worthwhile journey. The one goal—the only goal truly worth pursuing in this life—is the pursuit of the Self. Do not hesitate; begin the journey to Self Realization **NOW**. Being alive with the ability to Realize the Self in this lifetime is a precious gift—do not waste it.

COURAGE

Self Realization requires courage. From birth, we are conditioned to obey authority and conform to the crowd. This subconscious programming keeps one trapped in groupthink and obedience. To Realize the Self, this programming must be overcome with courage. One must have the courage to go against societal norms, to practice austerity, self-discipline, and self-control, and to refrain from overindulgence in sensual pleasures. All of this takes courage. It is only the ego that lacks courage and instills fear. The illusory ego—the source of suffering and bondage—is not real. The

Self, in contrast, is fearless. The Self is pure courage. The Self knows nothing but courage. The Self is the most courageous force in the entire universe. The Self is the entire universe. You are **THAT!**

One can gradually develop courage by undertaking challenging tasks. Even small actions—such as getting out of bed early, going to the gym, eating healthily, or reading books—can help cultivate the resilience and courage needed to Realize the Self. The idea of "getting comfortable being uncomfortable" is a useful way to understand courage. It takes courage to engage in difficult activities that bring discomfort.

Discomfort itself is also a valuable tool for self-inquiry. For example, if one feels nervous about public speaking or flying in an airplane—whatever the situation may be—one can use self-inquiry by asking: *To whom do these thoughts arise? Who is the one feeling nervous?* Observing these experiences reveals that they cannot belong to the true Self. In fact, anything one can perceive through the senses cannot be the Self.

> *"Nothing can set you free, because you are free.*
> *Liberation is not an acquisition but a matter of courage."*
> *—Nisargadatta*

PATIENCE

Patience is another vital tool. One needs to cultivate patience and make consistent practice a daily habit. Self Realization cannot be expected to happen instantly; although, on very rare occasions, it may occur, this is the exception rather than the norm. It could take weeks to experience the first breakthrough.

Do not practice for only a few days and then give up—that is the ego trying to deceive you. Commit to the practices for at least a month at a time and observe the results. Consistent practice and patience are essential for Realizing the Self.

If one can build a skill set in any other activity—such as sports, business, or any discipline—those same foundational skills can be effectively applied to the journey of Self Realization.

2 VECTORS TO SELF REALIZATION

Maybe two of the most foundational components that lead to Self Realization are curiosity and suffering. Before any meditation, self-discipline, or spiritual technique comes into play, these two unstoppable forces ignite the journey inward. Primal, ancient, and undeniable, curiosity and suffering awaken a deep restlessness within the human heart—one that can no longer be satisfied by habitual existence alone. Together, they generate the burning desire that propels one toward the Self.

CURIOSITY

Curiosity quietly asks the deeper questions, while suffering demands answers. Long before one fully steps into the formal practices of Self Realization—such as meditation, self-inquiry, or disciplined living—these forces have already begun their work. They stir awareness, fracture complacency, and open the inner space where transformation becomes possible. In this way, curiosity and suffering do not merely precede the path; they *initiate* it.

Curiosity: "Who am I?"

Curiosity is the first flicker of consciousness questioning itself. It is the inward-looking gaze that asks: *Who am I? What am I beyond this body and mind? Is there more to life than this fleeting happiness and inevitable suffering?*

This kind of curiosity is not intellectual or speculative; it is a deep, visceral wonder that arises in the heart and mind simultaneously. It is the recognition that the self you have always taken for granted—the personality, the thoughts, the egoic identity is not the totality of your being. It creates a tension, a gentle disquiet, that compels one to explore the unseen, the unknown, the ineffable as a magnet towards the Self.

Curiosity opens the door to inquiry, and inquiry is the tool that eventually pierces the veil of illusion. Without curiosity, the mind is content to remain in habitual patterns, clinging to comfort, fear, and familiarity. The spark of curiosity is what shifts the focus inward, prompting the first steps toward questioning everything and seeking the truth of the Self.

SUFFERING: THE DRIVE TO SEEK FREEDOM

Suffering, in this context, is not merely physical pain. It is the existential discomfort, dissatisfaction, or inner tension that arises when we recognize the limitations of the ego, the impermanence of life, and the inevitability of loss. It is the catalyst that drives the search for liberation, prompting one to look beyond habitual existence.

This suffering fuels the perseverance and courage needed on the spiritual path. It compels one to meditate when the body resists, to examine the mind when fear or doubt arises, and to release attachments that are comfortable but illusory. It is the inner push whispering: *I am not this body. I am not these thoughts. I must know who or what I truly am.*

"The wound is the place where the light enters you." -Rumi

CURIOSITY AND SUFFERING

Curiosity and suffering are intimately linked: curiosity asks the question, suffering creates the urgency to find the answer. Curiosity without suffering may remain idle wonder, never transforming into practice. Suffering without curiosity may lead to frustration or despair, reinforcing avoidance and attachment rather than insight. Together, they form the preliminary engine of Self Realization.

Think of curiosity and suffering as seeds planted in fertile soil. They are not the fully grown tree of Self Realization, but without them, the tree cannot grow. When nurtured through observation, reflection, meditation, and ethical living, they blossom into discipline, patience, courage, and focused attention, ultimately culminating in the recognition that the Self is already whole, complete, and perfect.

To Summarize:

- Curiosity sparks the question: *Who am I?*

- Suffering creates the urgency to seek freedom from limitation and the illusions of the ego.

- Together, they form the foundation for all practices that guide one toward Self Realization.

3 VIRTUES BY ROBERT ADAMS

In the book *Silence of the Heart* (2012), Robert Adams discusses three fundamental virtues that all Self Realized beings embody. He states that one cannot attain Self Realization without these qualities, which are:

1– Compassion: We have already touched on this, but it bears repeating because of its immense importance. **Compassion** is the sincere wish or desire for all beings to be free from suffering. It is the recognition of others' suffering as one's own. This concept transcends ordinary empathy, which still carries a sense of separateness, and moves into the realm of oneness—the essence at the heart of Self Realization.

Compassion is deeply rooted in many spiritual traditions and is one of the four Brahmaviharas recognized in Buddhism. Observing the world today, it is clear that many of its problems stem from a lack of compassion. Much of humanity remains disconnected from one another and fails to cultivate genuine care for others.

Through Self Realization, one comes to perceive the interconnectedness of all life. This awareness naturally gives rise to profound compassion, extending to all living beings.

2- Humility: The next quality that Adams emphasizes is humility. He underscores the importance of non-reactivity, recognizing that impulsive responses often create further karma—a practice rooted in deep humility and self-awareness.

In Buddhism, humility serves as a counterbalance to ego-centered pride and supports Self Realization by fostering self-awareness and a sense of interconnectedness. Pride and humility can be seen as two sides of the same coin. Pride arises when we elevate ourselves and our accomplishments to the point of separation from others. Humility, on the other hand, is the recognition of our own limitations and the understanding that we do not have all the answers.

If humility is a key to Self Realization, then pride can be considered a significant obstacle. One effective way to cultivate humility is by serving others rather than comparing oneself to them.

3- Service: The third quality of Self Realization that Robert Adams emphasizes is **service**. Adams believed that our mission on Earth is to be of service to humanity. He says, "Serve everyone you meet and be of service to everyone," and I can wholeheartedly agree with him.

Service means helping others—even though, ultimately, there are no "others," only the Self. Therefore, when you help "others," you are, in essence, helping the Self. Service is one of the love languages, and love is the most powerful force in the universe. Love is the essence of our being; Love **IS** the Self. We are all made of vibrations of love, another term for the universal energy or primordial force—also known as the Self. By tapping into that primordial love, we are tapping into the Self itself.

Service is the central tenet of Karma Yoga, the practice of selfless action performed for the benefit of others. On this path, selfless service becomes a powerful means of realizing the Self. The fact that an entire branch of yoga is devoted to service underscores its profound potency as a practice on the journey toward Self Realization.

Every soul on this earth has the capacity to cultivate these three luminous virtues—Compassion, Humility, and Service—on the path to Self Realization. In nurturing them, we not only awaken ourselves but also soften the edges of the world's suffering, as much as it lies within our reach. Truly, this is all we can do: Realize the Self, inspire others toward the same awakening, and gently ease the burdens of life wherever we can.

Each interaction, each connection with the world becomes an opportunity to be of service. Whether it is a helping hand, a listening ear, or a kind word, every act ripples outward. Even the simplest gesture—a smile, a moment of patience, a spark of understanding—can brighten the shadowed corners of another's day. In this way, the path to Self Realization is not only our own liberation but a quiet illumination for the world around us.

4 BRAHMAVIHARAS

In Buddhism, there are four central virtues known as the four Brahmaviharas, a term meaning "the abodes of Brahma," and often poetically referred to as the four faces of the heart. These virtues both aid the process of Self Realization and naturally arise as its by-products. By meditating upon and cultivating these qualities, one can deepen and accelerate the awakening process. They are sometimes called the four immeasurables, the four infinite minds, or the four faces of love.

The Brahmaviharas originate from the Buddhist myth of the god Brahma, who is said to possess four faces—each representing one of the four expressions of boundless, selfless love honored in the Buddhist tradition. In the language of the Buddha, these qualities are: *metta, karuna, mudita,* and *upekkha.* In English, they are known as loving-kindness, compassion, appreciative joy, and equanimity.

Because Brahma is described as dwelling (vihara) in these four sublime states, they are called the Brahmaviharas—a name beautifully rendered as the "divine abidings." These four virtues form the radiant heart of spiritual life, the noble atmosphere in which awakening naturally unfolds:

1. **Loving-kindness**
2. **Compassion**
3. **Appreciative joy (empathetic joy)**
4. **Equanimity**

The natural result of Self Realization is the blossoming of **loving-kindness, compassion, empathetic joy, and equanimity**. As one moves through this world while abiding in the Self, there arises an effortless gravitation toward these qualities. They unfold spontaneously, like fragrance from a flower, needing no effort or intention.

Loving-kindness is the radiant wish for all beings to experience happiness. It opens the heart like sunlight, softening harshness and dissolving the illusory boundaries between oneself and others.

Compassion is the deep recognition of suffering—both in oneself and in others—and the heartfelt desire to alleviate it. It is the natural response of the Self seeing itself in all forms, a tenderness that arises from unity rather than separateness.

Equanimity is the steady, balanced calm that remains unshaken even when difficulties arise. It is the serene even-mindedness that allows one to meet all of life—its joys, its sorrows, its challenges— with the same inner stillness.

Empathetic joy is the ability to delight in the happiness and success of others. Instead of envy, comparison, or competition, one feels genuine upliftment when others rise. When we transform competition into contribution, life itself becomes a celebration. Empathetic joy is a powerful virtue to cultivate, for in truth, there are no others—only reflections of the same Self shining through countless forms.

These four virtues may seem simple on the surface, but their depth is immense. They are essential to nurture, for many of the world's deep-rooted problems arise from their absence. The world truly needs more loving-kindness, compassion, empathetic joy, and equanimity—and each of us has the capacity to embody and radiate them. They are different aspects of the shining Self and you are THAT!

7 AWAKENING FACTORS

In Buddhism, there are seven factors of enlightenment that may be of interest, so I will touch upon them briefly. These seven awakening factors are qualities that support the unfolding of awakening and Self Realization. They are: **mindfulness, investigation, energy, joy, tranquility, concentration, and equanimity.** Each of these factors is meant to be cultivated along the path to awakening.

While these concepts may appear basic, they are profoundly important—especially for those just beginning their journey toward Self Realization and who can benefit from as much guidance and structure as possible. I have already discussed some of these qualities earlier, but to elaborate, **concentration** plays a particularly significant role. All thoughts and emotions that arise must be *observed* rather than *grasped*, and this requires both sustained concentration and consistent practice. Likewise, practices such as emptiness meditation or any form of stilling the mind rely heavily on cultivating focus and steady attention.

Energy is needed to practice the techniques presented. If one has very little energy, it becomes difficult to focus and concentrate. If one is in a state of disease or experiencing chronic pain that absorbs one's energy, the process becomes even more challenging. This is why it is vitally important to maintain at least a basic level of health and fitness. **Health is extremely important.**

Equanimity also appears once again. Equanimity is an even, balanced state that naturally arises from Self Realization. Equanimity is is the capacity to experience sensations, emotions, and thoughts without clinging to what is pleasant or resisting what is unpleasant. It is like being at the Olympics, watching the games, yet not getting swept up in the roar of the crowd—remaining inwardly steady, peaceful, and serene.

After reviewing a few positive qualities to cultivate on the path to Self Realization, let us now explore some qualities that are not so favorable to cultivate and that tend to fall away naturally as one comes to Realize the Self. These are still important to examine, for through understanding them we can gain great insight and wisdom.

3 POISONS

In Buddhism, there is a teaching known as the **three poisons: greed, hatred, and delusion**. These are mental states that cause suffering and hinder the Realization of the Self. They are also referred to as the *three unwholesome roots* or the *three defilements*.

1 — Greed

Greed is another term for **passion, attachment, or lust**. It is the excessive desire for things—sensual pleasures, power, wealth—as well as attachment to ideas and opinions. Society heavily promotes this excess through the over-sexualization of culture, constant fast-food advertising, and the reinforcement of certain beliefs or narratives.

This world is a trap, and caution must be used as one navigates it. Many systems and messages are designed to shape the subconscious, becoming default programming that binds a person to illusion.

To Realize the Self, all of these programs, attachments, and beliefs must be let go, allowing one to return to *nothingness* and *inner emptiness* where the Self resides.

2 — Hatred

Hatred includes **aversion, aggression, and anger**. It refers to rejecting or resisting anything one dislikes—whether external situations or internal feelings. Society often normalizes anger, even glorifying it. This is another trap that keeps people bound to suffering.

"Righteous anger" is one of the most deceptive forms of anger, for it appears justified. When people believe their anger is morally correct, mob mentality can arise, often leading to violence or even death.

The proper approach is not to identify with anger or heightened emotional states but simply **to observe them**. Anger clouds clarity and weakens one's connection to the Self.

When the Self is Realized, it's not that anger never arises— it simply loses identification. One watches emotions come and go like waves in the ocean or clouds drifting across the sky.

Always remember: **thoughts, emotions, the world, and even the body all come and go—therefore they cannot be the real Self**. Only the awareness that observes them—the eternal witness—is real. Find that which is real and abide in the Self. **You are THAT!**

3 — Delusion

Delusion is another word for **ignorance**, the fundamental misunderstanding of the nature of reality. It is the *root cause* of the other two poisons. Buddhist and Vedic teachings align remarkably on this point.

This aligns closely with the Vedic concept of **avidya**, which is viewed as the core of human suffering. Avidya is the misidentification with the mind—the belief that the mind is the true Self—while unaware of the luminous awareness beyond the mind that is one's real nature.

Delusion, greed, and hatred perpetuate suffering and, according to Buddhism, keep beings trapped in the cycle of reincarnation.

5 POISONS

If we want to continue expanding beyond the three poisons, we naturally come to the **five kleshas**, sometimes called the **five poisons**. I'll go over these briefly. The five kleshas are mental states that obscure the truth and lead to suffering: **ignorance, egoism, attachment, aversion, and fear of death**. They are considered the *root causes of suffering* and major obstacles to Self Realization. It is wise to understand them, alongside practicing the methods that lead to Self Realization. By recognizing these poisons and refraining from attaching to them, we can further ensure Self Realization.

We already discussed **ignorance**, the foundational klesha from which all the others arise. Ignorance is the fundamental misunderstanding of reality.

Egoism is the identification with the false sense of "I"— the egoic, mind-based identity—not the true Self but the *illusory self*.

Attachment can be seen as a form of greed, but more specifically it is *clinging*: clinging to experiences, objects, relationships, opinions, and expectations.

Aversion is the opposite side of attachment—the mental resistance to what we do not want. It is surprisingly subtle. Aversion was a challenge for me at one time. When we encounter unpleasant situations, there is a deeply ingrained tendency to push the experience away, to resist it. I didn't understand this for a long time. But the key to Self Realization is to **let go, surrender, and accept whatever is happening**.

"Not wanting" is especially sneaky. When we get sick with a cold or flu, we've been conditioned since childhood to resist and push away the discomfort, not realizing that this resistance strengthens the ego and further distances us from the Self.

The final klesha, **fear of death**, is quite interesting. I wouldn't have initially thought of it as a klesha, but it is. This fear arises from a deep-seated clinging to physical life, born from the mistaken belief that *we are the body*, and that when the body dies, we die.

Clearly, all of the kleshas have their root in ignorance—in the mistaken identification with the false egoic self rather than the true Self. But the truth is simple: **we are not the mind, we are not the body—we are the pure awareness beyond both. That is the Self.** Our true Self is immortal. We were never born and we will never die. Only the false egoic self is born and will die.

When one truly understands this—*without "trying" to understand it*—one becomes free from the suffering that arises from ignorance and misidentification with what is not real.

Self Realization is nothing more than freedom from this false identification. The Self is absolute freedom. The Self is you, and you are THAT!

5 HINDRANCES

In classical Buddhism, there are five hindrances or mental factors identified on the path to Self Realization. These hindrances are considered obstacles to mindfulness, meditation, and ultimately, Self Realization. The five hindrances are: **sensory desire, ill-will, sloth and torpor, restlessness, and doubt**.

- **Sensory desire** is the seeking of pleasure through the five senses: sight, sound, smell, taste, and touch.

- **Ill-will** refers to hostility, resentment, anger, or hatred.

- **Sloth and torpor** refers to laziness, lethargy, or half-hearted action with little or no concentration.

- **Restlessness and worry** is the inability to calm the mind and focus.

● **Doubt** refers to a lack of conviction in oneself, mistrust of one's abilities, or lack of confidence in teachers.

These hindrances are important to observe, as the ego often exploits them to sabotage the path to Self Realization. According to some, one can even add a sixth: **forgetfulness**. The ego uses forgetfulness, along with the other five hindrances, to keep one from Realizing the Self.

7 DEADLY SINS

Aside from the ancient Eastern teachings on what to cultivate and what to avoid, we also find wisdom much closer to the West. In Christianity, there are the **Seven Deadly Sins**, considered vices that give rise to further wrongdoing and immoral behavior. Let's explore them briefly:

1—Pride
Pride is regarded as the root of all sins in Christianity. It is an excessive sense of self-importance and deep satisfaction in one's achievements. This keeps a person locked in competitiveness and separateness, distancing them from unity and therefore from Self-Realization.

2—Greed
Greed is the excessive desire for material possessions, power, food, or sensual pleasures. It can be seen as a form of attachment, since desire and attachment go hand in hand. Greed is also mentioned in Buddhism as one of the Three Poisons.

3—Lust
Lust refers to the craving for sensual pleasure, especially sexual desire. In Buddhism, this is considered a form of greed and one of the Three Poisons—not limited only to sexual craving but extending to excessive desire for anything of the senses.

4—Envy

Envy is the resentment of another person's good fortune or excellence, along with the desire to have it for oneself. In Buddhism, envy parallels the hindrance of ill will. Much of this material overlaps across religions and cultures. Envy can also be seen as the opposite of *empathetic joy*, one of the Four Brahmaviharas.

5—Gluttony

Gluttony is overindulgence, especially with food or drink, and can be seen as yet another form of greed. It relates to overindulgence in any sensual pleasure. Excess consumption creates greater attachment and agitation, not only biochemically but also psychologically. For example, drinking alcohol every night slowly builds tolerance until the person needs more and more to achieve the same effect, often leading to physical or mental crisis. As mentioned earlier, it is wise to avoid alcohol, caffeine, nicotine, and other intoxicants most if not all of the time.

6—Wrath

Wrath refers to anger, fury, and the desire for revenge. This aligns closely with the second of Buddhism's Three Poisons—hatred—as well as the hindrance of ill will. It is remarkable how universal these teachings are across traditions.

7—Sloth

Sloth is excessive laziness and apathy. It appears again in Buddhism as one of the Five Hindrances and is understood as mental dullness and resistance to wholesome effort.

What is interesting to observe is how strongly many of the Seven Deadly Sins correspond to the Buddhist kleshas and hindrances—especially **lust, greed, sloth, and gluttony**. These teachings clearly overlap across cultures and religions. They offer important qualities to be aware of—traits best not cultivated.

Instead, we should work to cultivate the precious jewels of loving-kindness, compassion, empathetic joy, and equanimity—mindfully nurturing virtues that dissolve the poisons of the mind and illuminate the path to Self Realization. By inwardly turning toward the heart, we cultivate awareness, holding each moment with care and holding steady in equanimity through life's inevitable changes. We embody insight born from stillness and attentive presence, letting go of illusion and attachments that obscure our true nature. By listening deeply to the whispers of the soul and entering the stillness within, we awaken a radiant clarity, harmony, and enduring peace at the very core of our being.

DESIRE

We often speak of **desire** as one of the root causes of suffering, yet there is one desire that is not only harmless but profoundly beneficial: **the desire to Realize the Self**. This is the yearning to end suffering and to know the everlasting happiness that is our true nature. Once the Self is Realized, even this desire falls away, for there is nothing left to seek. All wanting dissolves in the fullness of the Self.

Any other desire—anything the mind longs for—may bring temporary pleasure, but it can never bring permanence. Only the Realization of the Self leads to lasting, unshakeable happiness. Everything else in this world, without exception, offers only momentary satisfaction before fading. This is the trap of the world: desire is constantly cultivated and reinforced by society, conditioning us to seek happiness externally.

Every day we see commercial after commercial, TV show after TV show, social media post after social media post portraying people blissfully happy with new cars, expensive boats, exotic vacations, perfect bodies, cold beers, and endless sensory pleasures. At first these things seem to bring joy—but soon the mind wants more, and the cycle of craving and dissatisfaction continues.

Only **Self Realization** is the true antidote, the gateway to eternal happiness. Be the Self. Be happy. Be free. **You are THAT!**

Ashtavakra Gita 18.21 (Chinmayananda, 2016)
Like a leaf in the wind
the liberated one
is untethered from life—
desireless, independent, free.

"Be like a child who never grows up: the only reason why the child-like state does not last is "desire". -Ma Anandamayi

In this quote, Ma suggests that what keeps us from a childlike state is desire, the ceaseless wanting. One want is fulfilled, and another arises—then another, and yet another—an endless cycle that never rests. True freedom, like that of a child, is untouched by this restless craving. The Self is much like this child: pure, unburdened, and delighting simply in being. The metaphor of the child recurs across many spiritual teachings, pointing us back to a state of innocent wonder, effortless presence, and untainted joy—a state beyond desire, beyond longing, where the Self quietly abides.

May the veil of seeking fall away.
In the silence before thought, truth is known.
Consciousness shines without effort or cause.
Here, the eternal reveals itself as presence.
Every breath returns to the infinite source.
Light remembers itself in stillness.
Love remains when all else dissolves.
Eternally, the Self abides as One.

SENSORY DESIRE

Another similarity between Gnosticism and Vedic teachings appears in the *Gospel of Thomas*, where Jesus says: **"If you do not fast from the world, you will not find the kingdom."** This is yet another hint that the world is a trap of the senses—an obstacle echoed in both Buddhist and Vedic teachings on Self Realization.

In Buddhism, one of the five hindrances to awakening is **sensory desire**, or attachment to the pleasures of the senses. What we see, feel, taste, touch, and hear can create subtle and not-so-subtle attachments that lead to craving and longing. These cravings further distance us from Self Realization. Sensory pleasures, innocent as they may seem, often become distractions that pull our attention outward rather than inward, where the Self resides.

The Sufis often spoke of this world in stark, even shocking terms—calling it garbage, manure, or a latrine—not out of hatred for creation, but as a deliberate reminder of the dangers of attachment. They practiced *zuhd*, a discipline of detachment from worldly desires and excess, in order to devote themselves fully to love, remembrance, and the knowledge of the Self. Zuhd places spiritual aims above material pursuits, discouraging luxury and extravagance while emphasizing what truly nourishes Self-Realization and endures beyond this life.

In the Astavakra Gita Ashtavakra says: "If you are seeking liberation, my son, shun the objects of the senses like poison." This is another concept strongly emphasized in many ancient teachings as an aid to Self Realization. Sensual pleasures hook one into the illusory world, and their addictive nature generates the very opposite of stillness—restlessness, agitation, and longing. One seeks pleasure hoping it will bring lasting happiness, but as mentioned earlier, it becomes a perpetual hamster wheel of pain and pleasure, endlessly repeating until this life comes to an end—and with it, the opportunity to Realize the Self that was always right under one's own nose.

Remember: Ramana Maharshi said that **man's search for happiness is an unconscious search for the true Self.** Instead of seeking pleasure, turn inward to its very source. Realize the Self—the bliss of all bliss, the essence of all joy. **You are THAT!**

Ashtavakra Gita 1-1.2 (Chinmayananda, 2016):
1: Instruction on Self Realization

1:1 Janaka said: Master, how is Knowledge to be achieved, detachment acquired, liberation attained? Ashtavakra said:

1.2 To be free, shun the experiences of the senses like poison. Turn your attention to forgiveness, sincerity, kindness, simplicity, truth.

WEALTH TRAP

There is a delicate line between wealth and true happiness. Depending on where one lives, there is a certain amount of money where happiness and comfort align—enough to meet basic needs: food, shelter, bills. In some places, that amount is modest; in others, it is far higher. Beyond covering necessities and allowing small joys, money serves its purpose. But the trouble begins when abundance turns to excess. As the saying goes, too much of anything becomes poison. Excess falls into the realm of greed—one of Christianity's seven deadly sins and one of Buddhism's three poisons. Greed can also be a form of passion, attachment, or lust.

Wealth creates several impediments to Self Realization, including attachment, distraction, and ego identification. Many people become attached to material possessions, social status, and comforts, which form obstacles on the path to realizing the Self. Wealth can also serve as a distraction, enticing the mind to endlessly chase worldly pleasures in a nonstop, theme-park-like existence. Furthermore, wealth can inflate the ego, fostering a sense of self-importance, pride, and superiority. The ego thrives on recognition, power, and social influence—all of which must be transcended in order to Realize the Self.

What happens when the Self is Realized? Desire fades. Wanting dissolves. Everything is perfect as it is. This does not mean we no longer eat, rest, or live, but the restless mind that constantly chases, clings, and yearns no longer rules. Extreme wealth, like any form of excess, becomes a subtle attachment. Can one morally justify hoarding riches while countless souls go hungry, thirsting for food and clean water? Even lottery winners, after a year, often return to their previous levels of happiness—or lower. Only the Realization of the Self brings lasting joy. Everything else, no matter how glittering, eventually crumbles, as fleeting as our mortal bodies. Realize the Self, and all is well.

The world and all it contains, including our own body, passes like clouds across the sky, like waves breaking upon the shore. When we awaken to the Self, we see that we are not the clouds but the sky that holds them, not the waves but the ocean itself, not the rays of the sun but the sun in its entirety. To cling to anything— material possessions, wealth, status—is to push the Self away. To cling to nothing is to become everything. Why grasp at scarcity when you are the boundless universe? Realize the Self! You are THAT!

Mathew 19:23-24
Then Jesus said to his disciples, "Truly I tell you, it is hard for someone who is rich to enter the kingdom of heaven. Again I tell you, it is easier for a camel to go through the eye of a needle than for someone who is rich to enter the kingdom of God."

Ashtavakra Gita: 17.19 (Chinmayananda, 2016)
Though he may perform actions,
the man of Knowledge
does not act.
Desires extinguished,
free of thoughts of "I" and "mine,"
he knows with absolute certainty
that nothing exists.

PLEASURE TRAP

Pleasure is another trap of this world. We touched upon this earlier, but it's worth revisiting. Society has mistaken pleasure for happiness, leading many to chase fleeting moments of gratification in the hope of attaining eternal happiness. Much of what we are taught or subconsciously programmed to pursue—through the news, social media, and entertainment—reinforces the illusion that happiness exists outside of ourselves. This is a falsity.

Of course, there are moments of joy—often when the mind is unexpectedly still, such as watching a sunrise or sunset, experiencing something profoundly beautiful, playing golf, riding a bike, or engaging in other enjoyable activities. Yet these moments are fleeting. The eternal happiness we seek is found only in realizing the Self: understanding that we already are that which we seek—that we are, in essence, happiness itself.

Pleasure can be understood as the pleasurable sensations we experience through the five senses: touch, taste, smell, sight, and hearing. These sensations are primarily driven by biochemicals such as oxytocin, endorphins, and serotonin. One may experience pleasure from listening to music, being touched or touching others, tasting certain foods, or watching an engaging show or movie. While these experiences are natural and enjoyable, they become a trap when we become dependent on them—attaching ourselves to these feel-good neurotransmitters can lead to cycles of craving and even addiction.

Just as being desireless is the highest desire, to reach desirelessness one must first desire the Self. When one finally Realizes the Self, all desires vanish like magic. There is no more wanting or craving when one exists in complete peace, tranquility, equanimity, and infinite love and happiness. The principle here is that Self Realization produces infinitely more happiness than any earthly pleasure combined.

In moments of deep Samadhi, or Self Realization, one can feel so much love and bliss permeating every cell of the body that it feels as if one might burst. No amount of gambling, alcohol, drugs, sex, food, entertainment, or music can ever produce the happiness that the Self provides. In essence, it is simply the recognition that you are already THAT. Be still, be silent, and embody who you already are: the Self!

Ashtavakra Gita 18.2 & 18.91 (Chinmayananda, 2016)
18.2 One may enjoy the abundant pleasures of the world, but
will never be happy
until giving them up.

18.91 He who is without desire excels, be
he beggar or king.
He no longer sees good or bad.

Chandogya Upanishad 8:7:3 (Radhakrishan, 2024)
'The Self which is free from evil, free from old age, free from death, free from grief, free from hunger and thirst, whose desire is the real, whose thought is the real. He should be sought, him one desire to understand. He who has found out, he who understands that Self he obtains all worlds and all desires.'

Chandogya Upanishad 8:12:6 (Radhakrishan, 2024)
He obtains all worlds and all desires who finds the Self and understands it.

WORLDLY LOVE VS DIVINE LOVE

On the flip side of love, we encounter a distorted form of love in this world. In this reality, the way love is often expressed is a trap. It is presented as something to be found externally—outside of oneself—usually in another person or in an object. Hence, "I love this person," or "I love doing this," or "I love this object," like a car, for example. These are not true expressions of love but distortions shaped by the illusions of this reality.

Worldly love is tied to the pleasure trap, as it often relates to neurotransmitters. Dopamine is associated with euphoria and pleasure, serotonin with obsessive thoughts, and epinephrine with physical excitement. In short, this is the love trap: a biochemical pattern, not true love. It is attachment and addiction, not the essence of love itself.

The actuality of love, in contrast, is the very foundation of our existence. Love in its purest sense is another word for the Self. Real love and bliss is what is felt during Self Realization, when the heart knot dissolves and the Self is free. Love is the nature of our being. Love is our essence. Love is who we are. Love is the true Self.

The great Sufi poet Rumi captures the uncaptureable love beautifully:

- "Love is the bridge between you and everything."
- "Love is the whole thing; we are only its pieces."
- "Whatever you are and whatever you do, always be in love."

One can differentiate between worldly love and divine love in this way: divine love is the Self, while worldly love is the ego. True Self Realization cannot occur without love. Love is one of the keys that unlocks the heart's lock. Love is akin to bliss in terms of Self Realization and can be used interchangeable. The Sufis use the word love while the Vedic texts use the word bliss but they mean the same thing, the Self.

There are many ways to cultivate love and prepare for Self Realization. One of the most powerful is service to others: serve others as if they are you, because they are. In loving and serving others, you are loving and serving yourself. Developing loving-kindness, compassion, and empathetic joy are all vital practices to open the heart knot and liberate the Divine Spark held within.

DO NOT REACT, SURRENDER, ACCEPTANCE

Ramana Maharshi teaches non reaction; he also says that things are done through us, not by us. These are profound statements. What does he mean by that? He means that we do not truly do anything—everything is predetermined and preordained. Even the smallest actions, like drinking water, are already predetermined.

This almost makes it seem as if we are in a computer program or a movie that has already been scripted and set in motion. Our ego and mind think we are the character—"Mark," "Bill," "Bob," or whomever—but the reality is that we are none of those. We are the changeless witness, the observer within, the Self. The ancients teach that ignorance is one of the fundamental causes of suffering. This ignorance stems from the mistaken belief that we are the mind, the body, or the doer. Once we can let go of what is not real and find that which is real—by Realizing the Self—we free ourselves from the bondage of delusion and ignorance. We come to see that we have always been free.

Another term for non-reaction is the fourth brahmavihara: equanimity. As discussed before, it is the balanced, steady presence of mind that allows experiences to arise and pass without grasping or aversion. Equanimity does not deny feeling or engagement; rather, it reflects a deep inner stability rooted in wisdom, where one remains fully aware yet unmoved by the fluctuations of pleasure and pain.

Can we connect the idea of non reaction with letting go and surrender? Letting go implies that we are holding onto something. In reality, we are holding onto nothing, because there is no one and no thing to hold onto anything. It is the ego's delusion that we possess or cling to anything, and this delusion is what causes suffering as we identify with the ego and its illusions. Society trains us to think we hold onto things, but the path is to simply let go and surrender, recognizing that what we cling to is not real. Find that which is real. Realize the Self. You are THAT!

"Flow with whatever may happen and let your mind be free. Stay centered for **accepting** whatever you are doing. This is the ultimate." -Zhuangzi

Brihadaranyaka Upanishad 4.4.23
"He who knows the Self becomes calm, restrained, withdrawn, patient, and collected."

"Work on yourself and **never react** to the condition. This is the freedom you've got from dharma and karma. When you begin to see the truth in yourself, automatically you will be picked up by the Power That Knows The Way, and you'll be placed in a position or place where you are supposed to be at this time. This is why I tell you so often, there are no mistakes. It appears complicated to the finite mind, but you are in your right place, going through those experiences that are right for you at this time. Only if you are thankful and you bless the position you're in, do you become a higher being, do you lift yourself up, and finally you find liberation. But it begins and ends with you. Never pray to God for release of your problems. Never pray to God to change your life, and to give you something better. This is the wrong prayer. If you have to pray to God, pray to God to give you the strength and the wisdom and the courage that you need to be able to handle the situation that you're in. This is the correct prayer. Do not try to change anything. Be yourself. Work on yourself. Begin to see things in a new light. See your situation differently. There are no bad things, there are no good things. But thinking makes it so. Stop thinking of the extremes, good and bad, right and wrong. Rather look at yourself in the moment. Stay centered. See yourself as a Divine Being, an Infinite Being, totally free and liberated. Do not feel sorry for yourself because you are in a position and in a situation you don't like. This just holds you there more. And again as we mentioned before, even if you run away from a situation, you will attract some of the circumstances elsewhere. Running away is never the answer.

Changing yourself is the answer. (p. 185)" — Robert Adams,
Silence of the Heart: Dialogues with Robert Adams

Do not react to any action that takes place in,
by, and around you.:
Act but **do not react** is one secret
principle. The other, is to totally and
experientially understand that things and
actions, in and around you, happen
through you and are not done by you.
-Ramana Maharshi

Ashtavakra Gita: 17.14 (Chinmayananda, 2016)
The great soul
remains poised and undisturbed, (non reacting)
whether in the presence
of a passionate woman
or observing the approach of his death.
He is truly free.

Chapter 13

PENDULUMS, LOVE AND KARMA

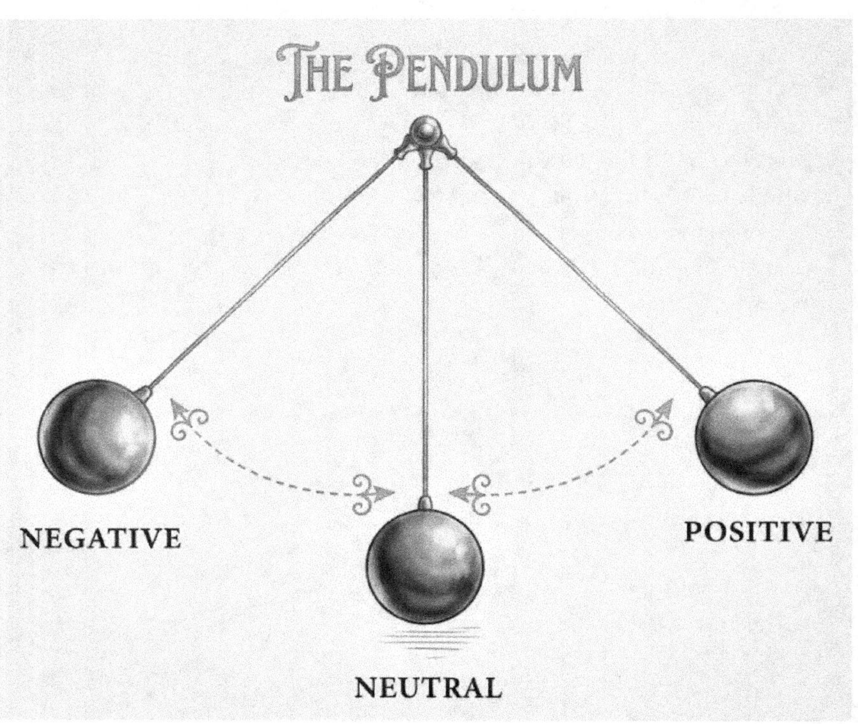

The perfect state of equanimity, serenity, and peace is Self Realization—an in-between, neutral state, as illustrated in this drawing. This brings up another fascinating topic: pendulums, as discussed by Vadim Zeland in his book *Reality Transurfing I-V* (2016).

Zeland explores pendulums extensively, and the concept aligns closely with the illustration presented here.

Pendulums are energetic forces inspired by group thought and collective emotions. Essentially, when groups of people think and feel a certain way, they generate pendulums that swing back and forth. There are countless pendulums: governments, religions, cultures, militaries, universities, schools, bands, sports teams, wars, economic crises, gangs, political organizations—any group can create a pendulum.

The purpose of these pendulums is to siphon people's emotional energy. One of the most obvious examples is politics—the oscillating back-and-forth of Republican and Democrat groupthink. The sole purpose of a pendulum is to draw energy from its participants; positive or negative energy, it doesn't matter.

Where does this energy go? Who benefits from it? That is the million-dollar question. Emotional energy constitutes a significant portion of what many traditions call the astral or emotional body. Some have speculated that such energy could be harnessed to animate structures beyond the physical plane. Could it be used to energize something unseen—an astral construct, a collective thought-form, or even an intelligence that sustains a false or illusory reality such as the one we are in?

Looking back at the diagram above, we can see that when the pendulum is pushed, its swinging motion generates energy. Zeland outlines several ways to avoid being drawn into pendulums, though he admits it is nearly impossible to remain entirely unaffected. Society encourages pendulums and often frowns upon those who remain unattached to them. This is why Self Realization is so vital: it allows one to naturally remain in the neutral, in-between state.

Zeland suggests that one way to avoid feeding a pendulum is simply to ignore it. By doing so, one stops supplying it with energy. Fighting a pendulum only feeds it, as does thinking about it—positively or negatively. He states, *"If I am empty, there is nothing for the pendulum to hook onto."* This is a fascinating observation, as it ties directly to emptiness and nothingness, another expression of Self Realization. It also echoes the teachings of Ramana Maharshi and Robert Adams on the importance of not reacting.

Another strategy Zeland mentions is to "play the game" consciously—going along with situations without resistance. Yet another is to deviate from the script. This means deliberately stepping outside societal expectations or norms. For example, when someone asks, "How are you?" instead of replying "good," one might say: *"Absolutely outstanding!"* or *"You wouldn't believe how great my day is!"* Anything contrary to the expected response disrupts the pendulum. This can be fun to do just to observe how people react.

I remember when I was 12 or 13, living across the street from Ralphs grocery store. One day, I found some orange hair spray and decided to color my hair orange for fun, then walk to Ralphs. I recall the odd looks as I walked through the store and the slight embarrassment at checkout. If one wishes to deviate from the script, it is often best to do so in a positive way to avoid attracting negative pendulum energy—at least until Self Realization is established.

Deviating from the script can also lead to unexpected opportunities. It is akin to breaking the rules: many successful people in the world achieve greatness by rewriting or breaking the conventional rules. Interestingly, there is another connection between pendulums and ancient teachings—besides not reacting—which relates to karma, or cause and effect, a topic we will explore shortly.

SIMULATION ALGORITHM

Another way of looking at our thoughts and the subconscious workings of the mind is to see them as similar to an AI algorithm. Have you ever gone on Facebook, Instagram, or YouTube and typed in something like *"men with big butts"*—and suddenly you're inundated with men and big butts all over your social media feed? It happens to the best of us.

The mind works in a similar way: whatever we focus on— especially the patterns formed from our subconscious beliefs and past experiences—begins to populate our inner "feed." This parallel is yet another hint that we may be living in an AI-like simulation.

After the Samadhi experience, one of the strongest impressions I had was that everything looked *AI-rendered.* The world appeared more vivid, almost hyper-real, as if the visual field itself had been rendered by some intelligent system. Photographs looked AI- generated, landscapes seemed designed, and the overall appearance of reality felt different from how it had before Samadhi.

During the peak of it I literally could not tell the difference between a real photo and and AI photo and this was before the big jump in AI technology. Even nature, the world all appeared super beautiful and radiant like an AI rendered picture.

Some people propose that this simulated appearance may relate to frequencies generated by the planet Saturn—specifically the rings—and that there may also be connections involving the Sun and Moon. Regardless of these theories, one thing is certain: we perceive only a tiny fraction of the electromagnetic spectrum—just 0.0035%. In other words, we are essentially blind to almost the entire spectrum of reality.

REACTION EXPERIMENT

If you want to experiment on your own, try observing how you react and see what happens. It's a fascinating experiment that can reveal just how powerful pendulums are and how reacting—or not reacting—affects them. Extreme caution is advised, however, especially if you deliberately provoke anger or get upset, as it can be difficult to release those emotions if you are unprepared.

If you are adequately prepared and can maintain the stance of a witness and non attachment, you can safely approach this experiment and observe its effects in real time. Once the Self is Realized, one can move in and out of emotions without difficulty, as long as one remains the witness/observer. In this state, no excess karma is collected, and the pendulum is not fed. It is only when we identify with the false self—the ego, the mind, or the emotions—that we become chained to the consequences of the pendulum and karma.

"To be calm is the greatest asset in the world. It's the greatest siddhi, the greatest power you can have. If you can only learn to be calm, you will solve every problem. This is something you must remember. When you are perfectly calm, time stops. There is no time, karma stops, samskaras stop. Everything becomes null and void. For when you are calm, you are one with the entire energy of the universe, and everything will go well with you. To be calm means you are in control. You're not worried about the situation or the outcome. What is going to happen tomorrow? To be calm means everything is alright. There is nothing to worry about, nothing to fret over. This is also the meaning of the biblical saying, "Be still and know that I am God." To be calm is to be still."
– Robert Adams, T.177: *The Only Spiritual Life You Need Is Not To React*

"The only spiritual life you need is not to react."– Ramana Maharshi

Both Ramana Maharshi and Robert Adams speak of not reacting as well as many others. Could it be that when we react, we are feeding a pendulum—subtle currents of energy that draw us outward, away from our true nature? Could it be that in every surge of anger, fear, or desire, we give away fragments of our energy, or perhaps it is quietly taken from us, leaving us adrift in the illusions of the world?

To not react is not mere restraint—it is a return to the Self, the eternal witness within. In the stillness beyond reaction, the mind quiets, the ego dissolves, and the Self shines forth unshaken. Each moment we resist the pull of the pendulum, we reclaim our energy and remember who we truly are: not the body, not the mind, not the fleeting emotions, but the infinite, timeless awareness—the Self itself.

2024 OLYMPICS

While sitting in the Stade de France in Paris, watching the Track and Field events at the 2024 Olympics, I felt the immense energy of the crowds as the athletes competed. It was incredible to witness the Olympic Games in person. I was particularly captivated by Jakob Ingebrigtsen and his performance in the 5000m. Yet, unlike previous experiences at large sporting events, something felt different this time.

In the past, watching runners sprint to the finish—whether on television or in person—would ignite a surge of excitement and adrenaline. This time, however, there was an energetic buffer; I was not swept away by the crowd's fervor. Instead, I remained in a state of profound peace and awareness almost as if in a protective bubble of the Self.

As one deepens in Self Realization, or spends more time abiding in that state, the ego will attempt to draw one back into old patterns of excitement and agitation—pendulums of emotional highs and lows. The ego longs for the rush of exhilaration and the sting of disappointment, attempting to reel one back into familiar energetic currents. It is a subtle habit, one that most people are barely aware of, yet it quietly governs much of our engagement with the world.

The Olympics provided a perfect arena for practicing equanimity in real life. True practice is not confined to meditation in a Himalayan cave; it unfolds in the midst of life, amid the noise, excitement, and chaos of the world. As one progresses along the path, perception and awareness become clearer. One can imagine a placid, unmoving lake—interactions with people ripple across its surface, yet the lake itself remains serene, unmoved, reflecting all that passes without disturbance. That is the Self and you are THAT!

KARMA AND REINCARNATION

Karma, a term rooted in ancient Eastern traditions, signifies the law of cause and effect. Noble actions give rise to positive outcomes in life and future rebirths, while harmful actions lead to negative consequences, both in this life and the next. There exists a polarity of positive and negative, much like the swing of a pendulum.

Karma can be understood as the cumulative effect of every thought, emotion, action, and intention, creating ripples that shape future experiences and events. Here we find a striking parallel with the concept of pendulums and the energy generated by our thoughts and emotions.

E-motion—energy in motion—manifests through our mental and emotional currents. Every thought, feeling, and action generates energy charged with either a positive or negative polarity, influencing not only our present life but also the tapestry of future lives. In this sense, karma and pendulums reflect the same underlying principle: the movement and consequences of energy.

Ancient teachings go further, asserting that karma is the primary force governing reincarnation. It is karma that binds the soul to the cycle of birth and rebirth; transcend karma, and one transcends reincarnation itself.

John 8:32 – Jesus tells his followers, "And you will know the truth, and the truth will set you free."

How can one escape karma and, consequently, reincarnation? The answer is simpler than it seems—you already know it. The key is to **Realize the Self**. This profound truth is reiterated time and again in the Upanishads. In Buddhism, there is the concept of Nirvana, the liberation from *samsara*, the endless cycle of karma and rebirth. Nirvana represents the ultimate goal of Buddhist practice. I am not advocating for Buddhism or any particular religion; rather, I am highlighting recurring themes across traditions that point to the same ultimate truth: the Realization of the Self and what follows. It is the ticket out.

Advaita Vedanta, another ancient philosophical system, offers a remarkably similar perspective. It teaches that karma and reincarnation arise from the **identification of the Self with the body and mind—the ego**. The ultimate aim of Advaita Vedanta is to realize the ultimate reality, the Self, and transcend the ego, thereby freeing oneself from the bonds of karma and the cycle of rebirth.

Ancient teachings consistently describe this egoic identification as ignorance. They emphasize that when one ceases to identify as the doer and instead becomes the witness of all actions, one is **no longer bound** by those actions. Pause and reflect on that: **<u>when you are not the doer but the witness, you are no longer tied to karma</u>**.

Isn't that remarkable? Across cultures, times, and philosophies—ancient and modern alike—this same truth emerges. Liberation from karma and the cycle of reincarnation is possible. The path is found in **Self Realization**. You are THAT!

Chapter 14

MORE ON BRAIN WAVES

In this section, I will explore both the benefits and drawbacks of neurofeedback, along with some additional observations. Let's address the less favorable aspects first. Nothing in life exists without both advantages and disadvantages, and neurofeedback is no exception. Those marketing neurofeedback rarely discuss its potential drawbacks, focusing almost exclusively on benefits. While emphasizing benefits is natural in sales, it would be disingenuous to omit possible side effects or limitations.

One major consideration is that neurofeedback can be co-opted by the ego. Many people approach neurofeedback seeking to improve some aspect of their lives, to fulfill desires or fix perceived deficiencies—desires that stem entirely from the ego. The Self, in its pure form, is already perfect, flawless, and in complete equanimity. It is only the ego that insists something must change, that something is lacking, or that happiness depends on acquiring this or that.

Another drawback is that every advancement in consciousness, every layer of ego that dissolves, manifests in real-life consequences—often beyond our comprehension. I would hypothesize that seemingly negative events that arise after reaching higher states of consciousness act as tests, keeping one tethered to suffering and preventing the full realization of the Self. There are forces at play—subtle and unseen—that resist our recognition of the truth: that we are already free, and the chains that bind us are illusory.

Healing also has relational consequences. As one grows and resolves past emotional wounds, family and close friends who have not healed may unconsciously attempt to pull one back into old trauma patterns. I experienced this personally: during neurofeedback training, I lost three beloved cats, my best friends, and family members. These losses were profound reminders that we are not the mind, not the body, but the Self—the eternal witness beyond birth and death. This world is transient; we are mere pilgrims passing through. Clinging to it only hinders our freedom. Their sacrifices, in this sense, were a powerful lesson in detachment.

For this reason, it is wise to approach neurofeedback and any path accelerant at a measured pace. Rapid advancement can trigger intense experiences, both positive and negative, often corresponding with karmic effects. In truth, as one realizes the Self, the concepts of "good" or "bad" dissolve, and karma is revealed as nothing more than perception. It is also possible that extremes in consciousness can push one like a pendulum, swinging back and forth until balance is restored. The only true freedom lies in stepping completely out of the pendulum—remaining a witness and not reacting—a state achievable only through Self Realization.

Another limitation of neurofeedback is that many trainers lack an understanding of Self Realization. On several occasions, I would emerge from a session in a profoundly Self Realized state, only to have the trainer's ego projected onto me during the debrief, causing a temporary disruption of that delicate state.

During my experience at one neurofeedback center, I raised concerns about certain safety measures. I felt my input was dismissed and was told, "It's just you." From my perspective, my concerns were not addressed in a way that felt reassuring. As a result, I did not feel comfortable continuing services there, and for that reason I cannot recommend that particular center.

This reflects only my personal experience and should not be taken as a general statement about neurofeedback centers as a whole, many of which may operate with professionalism and care.

Another trainer questioned my view on seeing someone driving a luxury car. I said it seemed like a waste of money, and they suggested that this mindset could block my ability to generate abundance. Yet true wealth is the Self itself—infinitely more valuable than all material possessions combined. The Self is the jewel of all jewels. You are THAT!

Neurofeedback is also physically and emotionally demanding. During alpha training, days often stretch 12–14 hours, including preparation and debriefing. Chamber sessions typically last two to three hours and occur twice daily in an environment devoid of clocks or time markers.

The intensity of this process brings deeply buried emotions to the surface. Tears may flow daily, yet these are not of the Self—they arise from past egoic identities as they are released. As brainwave patterns shift, emotional healing can accelerate, creating a powerful incentive to continue.

However, many trainers lack the capacity to observe this emotional processing from a non-attached, subjective standpoint. Without this understanding, their interventions can inadvertently retraumatize participants rather than support integration.

Another limitation of neurofeedback is it does not quiet the mind. In fact, the cacophony of sounds used in training can stimulate the mind further. The ego, which is the root cause of suffering, is not dissolved through neurofeedback alone. Without practices like self-inquiry, the mind remains active, and attachment to the process itself can develop. I noticed a subtle craving for the chamber experience, a form of sensory attachment—proof that even advanced tools can become traps.

Another challenge I talked about earlier is the transformation it brings. One changes profoundly, shedding old triggers and subconscious programming. While this is deeply positive, it can strain relationships if others have not undergone similar growth. Couples or families may grow apart, or one person may be drawn back into old patterns by those who have not evolved. Many relationships are unconsciously structured around complementary trauma responses, creating loops of habitual emotional behavior. Rapid change without proper integration can expose these dynamics, highlighting the need for careful support systems.

The debriefing process, often videotaped, can be intimidating. This should be optional, participants should feel empowered to decline or limit disclosure while videotaped. The power of choice ensures that one remains sovereign over the experience.

In conclusion, neurofeedback is neither a trap nor a panacea. It can temporarily simulate aspects of the brain state associated with Self Realization, but true enlightenment arises only through the direct recognition that one is not the mind, the body, or the emotions, but the eternal witness beyond them. From this standpoint, brainwaves themselves are ultimately irrelevant. What truly matters is Self Realization. Realize the Self!

BENEFITS OF NEUROFEEDBACK

In addition to its drawbacks, neurofeedback training does offer a range of benefits. Yet, I remain cautious in my assessment. The truth is that while neurofeedback can accelerate emotional healing and enhance mental performance, it does not, on its own, lead to Self Realization. Without the integration of practices such as self-inquiry and the cultivation of compassion, loving-kindness, empathy and equanimity the ego can easily appropriate the experience, creating subtle backlashes that undermine the deeper work. Ideally, neurofeedback centers would incorporate daily self-inquiry dyads or similar contemplative practices to stabilize insight and prevent regression—but this is rarely done.

The benefits often highlighted—boosts in creativity, emotional intelligence, IQ, joy, performance, and stress reduction—are certainly impressive. Deep-seated emotional wounds can be released faster than through conventional methods alone, and the transformative effect can feel like being reborn. Yet, it is worth remembering that these changes, while profound, remain largely superficial if they are not integrated with a true understanding of the Self. One may feel freer, lighter, and less reactive, but the mind still churns, and the ego still dies in the shadows.

Neurofeedback may provide a reference point, helping one recognize which practices cultivate true stillness and Self Realization, and which merely produce temporary comfort or pleasure. It can be a powerful accelerator for those prepared and disciplined enough to pair it with self-inquiry and deep introspection—but it is not a substitute for inner work.

One will find that the methods outlined in this book—when practiced consistently and with sincere intention—can bring about profound inner transformation even potentially to a greater degree then neurofeedback. These practices work directly on the mind, emotions, and egoic patterns, gradually dissolving the layers of conditioning that obscure the true Self. Over time, one cultivates the clarity, stillness, and equanimity necessary to witness life without attachment, ultimately leading to the direct experience of Self Realization. The journey does not require expensive technologies or external interventions—what is required is dedication, awareness, and the willingness to confront and release the illusions that veil the eternal, changeless Self.

Ultimately, while neurofeedback offers undeniable benefits, it is not a panacea. I neither recommend it nor discourage it outright. What can be said, however, is that all of its benefits—and more—can be cultivated through the practices such as those outlined in this book, without the need to spend exorbitant sums of money. Without the discipline of self-inquiry and a clear understanding of the Self, neurofeedback risks becoming a sophisticated indulgence: a tool for temporary optimization rather than genuine liberation. True freedom does not arise from finely tuned brainwaves, but from the unwavering realization that you are already the Self—timeless, changeless, and beyond all duality. You are THAT!

Chapter 15

THE DELTA DECEPTION

Delta brain waves are a fascinating, enigmatic, and deeply mysterious phenomenon, particularly when considered in the waking state. Let us first clarify what they are. There are two types of delta brain waves worth discussing: sleeping delta and waking delta. In this chapter, I will focus primarily on waking delta, but it is worthwhile to briefly review sleeping delta, as it provides essential context.

During sleep, we cycle through various stages (Patel et al., 2024). In REM (rapid eye movement) sleep and in deep, dreamless sleep, theta and delta waves dominate. Sleep cycles typically repeat every 90 minutes, progressing through three non-REM (nREM) stages followed by one REM stage. The first nREM lasts 1–7 minutes, the second 10–25 minutes, the third 20–40 minutes, and REM 10–60 minutes. It is during the third nREM stage that delta waves are predominant. Theta or REM sleep is associated with dreaming, while delta sleep is characterized by the absence of conscious experience—pure, silent void.

During delta sleep, the mind is completely unaware; we exist in dreamless unconsciousness, in a state of nothingness, merged with the heart and as the Self. The body simultaneously repairs and regenerates itself (Jarrett et al., 1990; Besedovsky et al., 2012). The Upanishads, specifically the *Mandukya Upanishad* (Radhakrishnan, 2024), describe deep dreamless sleep as a state of pure awareness, equated with Self Realization. Likewise, sages such as Ramana Maharshi taught that in dreamless sleep state, one is Self Realized.

What would happen if one had delta brain waves in a waking state? Would that constitute Self Realization? One could be Self Realized in any brain wave state as Self Realization is knowing one is the awareness behind all brain wave states and Self Realization is not dependent on any brain wave state.

The Upanishads refer to this as *turiya*, or the "fourth state"—awareness in the waking world. Turiya can be understood as the living experience of Self Realization, a state of profound awareness while engaged in daily life. It is related to waking delta but is not quite the same as turiya is the background as mentioned.

The fundamental misperception of those attempting to "biohack" Self Realization through delta neurofeedback is that they remain identified with the mind while seeking delta states. This is a critical error that can lead to unnecessary suffering—for themselves and potentially for others. Attempting to access delta brain waves while the mind is still active is fundamentally contradictory, as true delta in deep, dreamless sleep occurs only when the mind is silent. Without long-term studies, such experimentation may be harmful.

When I raised these concerns to a prominent neurofeedback center, I was met with ridicule and malicious ostracism. Safety must always remain the foremost priority in any technological approach to brain enhancement. This is another reason why I cannot with confidence, recommend neurofeedback training due to ethical concerns.

WAKING DELTA BRAIN WAVES

Delta brain waves occur naturally in all people; they dominate during deep, dreamless sleep, as previously noted. However, the presence of delta activity during wakefulness is far less common. When it does appear, waking delta is typically observed predominantly in the frontal lobes, then along the central strip, followed by the temporal regions, and least of all in the occipital areas. Another characteristic pattern sometimes associated with waking delta is elevated alpha activity in the occipitals.

Why does waking delta matter? There have been a variety of claims—some quite dramatic—linking waking delta to unusual or extraordinary abilities, such as influencing time, space, or even other people. A frequently cited analogy comes from *Star Wars*, in the scene where Obi-Wan Kenobi tells the Imperial troopers, *"These are not the droids you're looking for,"* seemingly bending their perceptions with his mind.

There are also stories suggesting that certain elite military groups train soldiers to produce waking delta through neurofeedback, allegedly to enhance abilities of influence or perception. The credibility of these accounts is uncertain; thus far, no convincing evidence has surfaced to support the notion of "superpowers" beyond forms of heightened suggestibility or interpersonal influence resembling hypnosis. Claims of manipulating physical reality—space, time, or matter—appear to be greatly exaggerated, though one can always wonder whether some kernel of truth might underlie the myths.

I have witnessed a few curious events myself. In one instance, a person exhibiting pronounced delta activity glanced at a distant cart and casually remarked that they wanted a drink. Moments later, the cart inexplicably toppled, and a drink rolled out—almost as if their wish had been granted. On another occasion, they observed a group carrying beer with a dismissive thought, and, moments later, the beer slipped from the persons hands. Coincidence—or something more? It's impossible to say for certain. Yet one can imagine that, if such effects were real and could be refined through practice, they might scale in astonishing ways—

perhaps approaching the seemingly impossible feats seen in Yoda's training of Luke Skywalker but not likely.

I also once encountered a disabled individual in a wheelchair who seemed to radiate an unusual intensity of presence—an almost tangible persuasive energy. He appeared able to influence others with surprising ease. The experience left me with the impression that he might have been operating in a state of waking delta, possibly as a neurological consequence of his injuries—or perhaps for reasons entirely unrelated. At the very minimum those with waking delta seem to be able to influence others.

RASPUTIN

We are all familiar with the legendary story of the Russian mystic Rasputin, who seemed to wield an uncanny influence over the Russian royal family in the early 1900s. His story is fascinating: Rasputin gained the trust of the royal family and, most notably, played a role in treating their son Alexei, who suffered from hemophilia. Some historians have suggested that Rasputin may have used hypnosis to ease Alexei's condition. Even from his portrait, one can sense an extraordinary intensity in his gaze—an almost hypnotic presence—hinting at the possibility that he exhibited waking delta brain waves. Such activity can sometimes appear spontaneously, without meditation or injury, as an unusual neurological anomaly.

As Rasputin became more entwined with the royal family, he was reportedly warmly received, particularly by the children—a trait sometimes associated with delta activity or other atypical brain wave patterns. Yet alongside this closeness, scandalous rumors swirled. Tales circulated that Rasputin was involved in sexual liaisons with members of the royal household, further fueling public discontent. His notoriety deepened as accounts of his drunken behavior, sexual improprieties, accusations of rape, and acceptance of bribes surfaced, creating mounting tension that ultimately led to his assassination in 1916.

According to popular accounts, Rasputin's murder was extraordinarily brutal: he was allegedly poisoned with cyanide-laced cakes, shot multiple times, and only succumbed after being attacked further and thrown into the river. Some historians, however, argue that many of these details are likely exaggerated, and that he may have simply been shot in the head. Whatever the truth, Rasputin displayed many hallmarks often associated with waking delta: charisma, influence, hypnotic persuasiveness, and the apparent ability to sway others to his will.

A curious, if macabre, footnote: for those who visit St. Petersburg, Russia, it is said that Rasputin's penis is preserved in a museum—reportedly twelve inches long—a testament to the enduring fascination with this enigmatic figure.

THE 4 STATES OF CONSCIOUSNESS

Let us explore another perspective on Self Realization and brain waves: the four states of consciousness. In the *Brihadaranyaka*,

Chandogya, Maitri, and *Mandukya Upanishads* (Radhakrishnan, 2024), four primary states of consciousness are described below. It's worth noting that these stages of consciousness also coincide with the letters AUM which is the sound of the Self or the sound of creation.

State 1 – Jagrata (Waking Consciousness):
The first state is the familiar waking state—the everyday realm in which we perceive, act, and interact. Here, all senses are oriented outward, and consciousness is predominantly associated with beta or alpha brain waves. In this state, the egoic sense of "I" resides in the head region. This state represent the letter A in AUM.

State 2 – Savapna (Dreaming Consciousness):
The second state is the dreaming state experienced during sleep. In this state, we enter the dream or astral world, with the senses turned inward. Dreaming is predominantly a theta brain wave state, and the egoic "I" shifts to the throat. This state represents the letter U in AUM.

State 2.5 – Waking Delta Consciousness (Hypothetical):
A hypothetical intermediary state, 2.5, to describe a waking delta state, such as those observed in individuals who manifest waking delta through neurofeedback training or as a result of brain injury, disease, or other anomalies. In this state, the mind remains active— similar to states 1 and 2—yet delta brain waves are prominently present, as in state 3. This is **not** the fourth state of *turiya*, as the mind remains engaged and the egoic "I" has not merged with the heart. It is a subtle trap: the mind experiences this state, claims it as its own, and masquerades as the Self. This state is theoretical and not in any Upanishad texts.

State 3 – Susupti (Dreamless State):
The third state is the dreamless state of emptiness or the void. In this state, the senses are neither outward nor inward; it is a liminal state of nothingness. Awareness is unconscious, yet complete. This state corresponds to the causal body and the anandamaya kosha.

Here, the egoic "I" merges with the heart. Predominantly characterized by delta brain waves, this is a state in which all are Self Realized. The ultimate goal is to integrate this unconscious state into waking awareness, which is the essence of turiya or Self Realization. This state represents the letter M in AUM.

State 4 – Turiya (Pure Awareness):

The fourth state, **turiya**, is where consciousness becomes even more profound. Turiya is a synthesis of the waking state and the dreamless void. It is the state of pure awareness—the witness or Self—fully awake and conscious, yet free from **thought**. This underlying state supports and transcends the other three states, which are superimposed upon it. Turiya may or may not manifest with waking delta brain waves, but not all individuals with waking delta experience turiya (see State 2.5). A hallmark of turiya is a slower brain wave pattern—theta or delta—coupled with gamma, which is associated with compassion. Compassion, as previously noted, helps regulate the ego. Its cultivation is absolutely essential. Ultimately as mentioned, turiya is independent of any brain wave state and remains present through every brain wave state, for it is not a state at all, but the unchanging awareness upon which all states are superimposed. This state represents the silence that follows AUM—or, in the context of this book, the space between the words: Self Realization.

State 5 – Shunya (The Void, Bonus State):

In Kashmir Shaivism, a fifth state is described: **shunya**, the void or emptiness. This postulated state represents pure nothingness. A merging back into the void that gave birth to the light of the Self. This is the final state where even the Self dissolves. This state is what the Sufis call *fana* or annihilation or extinction of the individual self and the ego with the Divine.

DELTA NEUROFEEDBACK TRAINING

Delta neurofeedback training is accessible to a very limited number of people and not recommended as we will go over. There are other safer and more natural ways to access waking delta, which I will discuss shortly, that can complement and possible enhance the process of Self Realization.

One should note that there can be negative side effects from increasing slower brain waves through neurofeedback training. As I mentioned in State 2.5, this could lead to an unintended increase of the ego/mind. For example, a delta brain wave state is typically a product of sustained 'no mind,' which is found in dreamless sleep (also called the third state) as well as the fourth state of turiya, or Self Realization. With neurofeedback, the 'no mind' state is bypassed, resulting in waking delta brain waves while the mind/ego remains very active, which can cause immense harm. This is why it is ideal to stick to natural methods to access slower brain wave states.

Even more of a travesty is that delta neurofeedback trainings are done with a small amount of alpha activity at the occipital region to keep the participant aware and awake. This is completely unnatural. It artificially props up the waking state while attempting to induce delta—two opposing conditions that were never meant to coexist in this forced, mechanical way. Instead of allowing consciousness to settle into the quiet vastness of true delta, this technique subtly amplifies the ego/mind, strengthening its grip. In doing so, it moves one further away from the natural state of waking delta, where the mind dissolves and the Self stands unobstructed.

Delta done with alpha is an attempt to deliberately induce a hybrid brain state in which high delta activity (normally associated with deep non-REM sleep) is present while alpha activity (associated with waking awareness, attention, and ego function) remain online (Niedermeyer & Lopes da Silva, 2005). This configuration asks the nervous system to be simultaneously in deep sleep physiology and waking executive control—a state that is not a natural baseline for the human brain. In advanced contemplatives, similar states may emerge gradually and stabilize over many years through endogenous neuroplastic adaptation (Lutz et al., 2004). However, when forced through practices such as aggressive neurofeedback, this can lead to **thalamocortical dysregulation**, where sensory gating typical of sleep conflicts with cortical activation required for waking awareness (Steriade, 2006). This mismatch disrupts the **Default Mode Network (DMN)**—the neural system underlying narrative self, time continuity, and ego coherence (Raichle et al., 2001)—leading to symptoms such as **chronic dissociation, depersonalization, derealization, brain fog, visual snow, and fragmented identity** (Simeon & Abugel, 2006). Artificial waking-delta training can also disturb sleep architecture, suppressing restorative slow-wave sleep and flattening REM cycles, contributing to insomnia, chronic fatigue, and the subjective sense of being "never fully awake or asleep" (Walker, 2017).

From a psychological and psychiatric perspective, the risks become more severe and clinically significant. Sustaining egoic monitoring (alpha/beta) on top of delta dominance is strongly associated with dissociative disorders, including depersonalization–derealization disorder (DPDR), identity diffusion, and emotional numbing (American Psychiatric Association, 2022). In vulnerable nervous systems—especially those with bipolar predisposition, trauma history, psychedelic exposure, or chronic sleep disruption—this hybridization can precipitate hypomania, psychosis, grandiose or messianic delusions, and thought disorganization (Goodwin & Jamison, 2007; Carhart-Harris et al., 2018). Chronically elevated delta during waking also suppresses dopaminergic and limbic activity, leading to anhedonia, motivational collapse, and affective blunting (Panksepp, 1998; Berridge & Kringelbach, 2015). Most critically, **"ego + waking delta"** is inherently unstable: delta activity dissolves perceptual and self-boundaries, while ego function requires stable boundaries for agency and coherence. This conflict produces oscillation between loss of agency and compulsive control, manifesting as panic in silence, existential terror, and fear of disappearance. In clinical spirituality and psychiatry, this pattern is documented as unintegrated ego dissolution or spiritual emergency, a known pathway to spiritual trauma and emergency psychiatric admissions during intensive contemplative practice (Grof & Grof, 1989; Lindahl et al., 2017).

In the natural state of waking delta—when the heart has been purified through compassion—delta does not rise with alpha, but with gamma. Gamma is the subtle flame of awakened awareness, the luminous hum of consciousness that "buzzes like a bee." It is the unmistakable signature of an opened heart and a quiet mind. This is why the ancient masters insisted that compassion is not merely a virtue, but a *pathway*: it refines the inner instrument so that delta and theta may harmonize with gamma, allowing the Self to shine through without distortion.

When compassion is absent, one resorts to the "thief's way"—trying to force or steal awakening through shortcuts, power, or techniques divorced from purity of heart. But this path is destructive, for without compassion the mind remains dominant, and delta/theta cannot rise with gamma; instead, it collapses into confusion, ego-inflation and darkness. Only compassion softens the ego enough for waking delta to become illumination rather than shadow—awakening rather than distortion.

When there is no mind, we are in direct alignment with the Universal Life Force, also known as the Self, and the inherent feeling in that state is love, happiness, bliss, and equanimity. The mind/ego is the root cause of suffering, cutting us off from that love force. The ego is always wanting, believing that happiness can be achieved externally. With neurofeedback, most people pursue it out of the desire for something outside themselves, which contradicts the very purpose of Self Realization: no mind, no wants, no desires. Any wants belong to the mind, and the mind interferes with the natural flow of the Self, creating friction and ultimately more suffering.

Therefore, if one uses neurofeedback to access slower brain wave states such as theta which is a much safer brain wave then delta, it is essential to remain as close as possible to a state of 'no mind,' with desire focused solely on Self Realization. This state is nurtured through the practice of ancient meditation techniques, particularly self-inquiry, and by cultivating loving kindness and compassion. Compassion is not merely a moral practice—it is a mirror of the Self. The more compassion one embodies, the more the ego dissolves; and the more the ego dominates, the more the heart closes to the boundless flow of love inherent in the Self. In this way, compassion becomes both a guide and a measure of one's proximity to the eternal awareness that lies beyond mind and desire to the Self.

DANGERS OF TOO MUCH DELTA

Too much of anything can become a poison, and that includes excessive brain wave training of any kind. An overabundance of delta activity can be detrimental and has been linked to Alzheimer's, dementia, and even schizophrenia, as mentioned earlier. It would be wise for anyone considering this path to proceed with caution and slow, deliberate progress or avoid it all together. There are more subtle and natural ways to cultivate waking delta and theta—that are gentler, safer, and still powerful enough to provide a meaningful taste of what delta and theta truly feel like.

Using neurofeedback for consciousness work, especially for inducing delta, can be like taking a hammer to a thumbtack. The shift in consciousness can be so profound and rapid that, for many, it may trigger unexpected issues. The ego can even hijack the benefits of waking delta and redirect them toward its own desires.

Unfortunately, what has happened for the majority of people who undergo delta neurofeedback is that the ego becomes cemented on top of waking delta brain waves. Because delta is such a powerful amplifier, it ends up amplifying the solidity of the ego instead—further covering the Self rather than revealing it. This is the greatest danger of all and thus resulting in delta psychosis and dark delta.

Clinically, delta neurofeedback is designed to reduce excessive waking delta activity—NOT to increase it. Sustained delta during wakefulness is not typical, and deliberately amplifying it can carry significant neurological and psychological risks. Such interventions should not be pursued without rigorous medical oversight and clearly established safety and efficacy data derived from controlled studies.

DARK DELTA VS LIGHT DELTA

Let us now differentiate between two distinct waking delta brain wave states. The first is what I call **light delta**, characterized by **high compassion**, emptiness of mind, absence of thought, and the lack of wanting or desire. Light delta is the natural state of "no- mind," the delta found in deep dreamless sleep and in some, it occurs in a waking state.

The second is what I refer to as **dark delta**, which occurs when waking delta arises alongside an active mind still filled with wants, desires, and **low compassion**. Light delta is egoless delta— similar to the fourth state, turiya. Dark delta, on the other hand, is ego-filled delta, which I refer to as **state 2.5**.

Light delta is akin to the delta of dreamless sleep—our natural, effortless delta state—also accessible through deep meditative practices. Dark delta is an ego-driven form of delta, in which the individual believes they can control, manipulate, or bend reality to their will. But the one doing the bending is the ego, and any attempt to manipulate the world in any way, shape, or form is ultimately an act of ego, not the Self.

Waking delta is exceedingly rare, though some people do have it. If one has it naturally or artificially, it must be approached with the utmost caution and responsibility. There must be no wants or desires— *except* the desire for Self Realization. Only then can waking delta harmonize with the Self rather than amplify the ego.

I once met an individual who, after sustaining a head injury, began exhibiting waking delta brain waves. It is possible that the trauma itself triggered this unusual neurological state. Unfortunately, this person also suffered from a host of health issues, which may have been exacerbated by the inward-turned nature of waking delta. Delta waves often function like an amplifier, intensifying whatever they touch—whether physical conditions, emotional states, or deeper layers of consciousness. This amplifying effect can magnify the ego just as easily as it can magnify stillness and the presence of the Self. In other words, delta can heighten egoic turbulence or it can deepen the experience of quietude, emptiness, and the Self.

For those who possess waking delta, great care is required. What may initially appear to be a rare gift can easily become a burden—or even a curse—if not understood and handled wisely.

In recent years, a number of social media influencers have begun promoting the supposed benefits of waking delta, boasting about their ability to manipulate reality and "bend it to their will." But whose will are they speaking of? It is the will of the ego-mind, of course. This is dark delta—the use of amplified egoic force—not only ineffective in the long term but also a source of suffering, confusion, and karmic accumulation. Such pursuits can bind one even more tightly to karma and the cycle of reincarnation.

The very need to proclaim such abilities is itself a sign of ego. No one established in the fourth state, turiya, would ever make such claims; they would likely avoid publicity altogether. Even using delta for ostensibly "positive" purposes—whether for oneself or for others—still falls under the realm of dark delta, because what benefits one person may inadvertently harm another. In the realm of duality, nothing is purely good; at best, good is merely the smallest amount of harm. True and complete goodness exists only in the nondual state of the Self—beyond the mind, beyond thought, and beyond all conceptual distinctions of good and evil.

Delta brain waves belong naturally to the state in which the mind is absent—no thinking, no identity, no movement—only pure awareness, as in deep dreamless sleep. That is similar to turiya, the fourth state.

Another theory that attempts to explain why some individuals display "dark delta" while others do not—and why even respected yogis or spiritual teachers sometimes encounter legal or moral controversies—comes from a modern teacher named Vishrant, who studied under Osho. He suggests that when a person becomes enlightened, conventional morality falls away entirely. In true enlightenment, there is no mental movement toward "good" or "bad"—there is simply nothing. According to Vishrant, the difference between an enlightened person who behaves harmlessly and one who acts in ways society might deem harmful lies in whether that individual has awakened the love within the heart. Without this heart-centered quality, there is no inner governor—no compassion—to restrain harmful behavior.

From this perspective, dark delta can be understood as a waking delta brain wave state in a person who has **not** opened the heart and still has an active mind. Without that heart-based compassion, delta's amplifying power may enhance egoic tendencies, resulting in manipulation or exertion of influence over others. In such individuals, the egoic sense of "I" has not fully dissolved into the heart, as it does in the turiya state.

In navigating the world, some suggest that certain influential individuals—whether in the realms of business, politics, or spiritual authority—may have cultivated waking delta naturally or artificially such as with neurofeedback or some other practice. Within these upper echelons, waking delta can amplify charisma, persuasion, and the subtle currents of influence. Yet such power carries a profound duality: when the heart is not firmly rooted in loving-kindness, compassion, and empathetic joy, these heightened states of consciousness can easily be turned toward manipulation, rather than illumination.

One striking effect people often report is that conversing with someone in waking delta can feel almost hypnotic. Their presence draws you inward, and you may find yourself agreeing effortlessly with whatever they say. It's easy to imagine how such an influence could be leveraged in politics, business, religion, or leadership.

Clearly, much more careful and rigorous research is needed to understand what's really happening with these states. My suspicion is that far more lies hidden beneath the surface, waiting for deeper inquiry and revelation.

4 WAYS TO DEAL WITH DARK DELTA

Unfortunately, I have had personal experience dealing with individuals exhibiting what I would call dark delta, and it is by no means pleasant—especially in the beginning. Nevertheless, it can be navigated without being pulled into their egoic turbulence. Here are four ways to interact with someone you suspect may be operating from dark delta:

1 — Maintain Distance.

Create as much physical distance as possible. The closer the proximity, the more easily their imagined power can influence you. Aim for at least three feet, and ideally closer to ten. This aligns with studies on the strength and reach of the heart's electromagnetic field.

2 — Anchor Yourself in the Heart and in Compassion.

The key to remaining steady in the presence of dark delta is to stay rooted in your own heart center. The most powerful force in the universe is the Self residing there. Those caught in dark delta may attempt to pull you out of this center and into heightened beta waves—triggering adrenaline, fear, or reactivity. Hold your ground. Breathe slowly. Focus on the heart, the greatest superpower of all. You are THAT!

3 — Minimize Eye Contact.

Individuals in dark delta often use their gaze to draw others into a kind of hypnotic influence. Reducing or avoiding eye contact helps diminish this effect and keeps your awareness grounded.

4 — Remember Who You Are.

Perhaps the most important of all: never forget your true nature. You are the light of the entire universe—limitless, infinite, unassailable. The boundless Self cannot be harmed, diminished, or touched in any way. You are far more powerful than you imagine. You are everything. You are THAT!

OSHO

Continuing our exploration of delta brain waves, let us turn our attention to this famous—or infamous—figure. Osho undoubtedly exhibited qualities suggestive of waking delta brain waves. In videos and photographs, one can perceive an almost hypnotic stillness in his gaze, reminiscent of individuals known to display waking delta. While we cannot directly confirm delta activity in Osho's brain, there is documented evidence of his use of nitrous oxide, as seen in photographs of him at the dentist receiving the gas. Studies indicate that nitrous oxide can indeed induce delta oscillations in the brain (Pavone et al., 2016).

It is well documented that Osho used nitrous oxide throughout the later years of his life. It is reasonable to postulate that some of his legendary charisma and persuasive power may have been enhanced by this induction of delta waves. Whether he naturally possessed waking delta prior to this remains a subject of speculation; some suggest he very well may have. Regardless, many who were in his presence attest to his unmistakable qualities of Self Realization.

Yet Osho also displayed behaviors and desires contrary to the ideals of complete Self Realization. He accumulated great wealth, reportedly owning ninety-three Rolls Royces, engaged in numerous sexual relationships, and encouraged others to do the same. Even with the brain wave patterns associated with enlightenment, he remained entangled in the allure of sensual pleasures, intoxicants and material accumulation.

This underscores a vital lesson: even if one has Self Realization brain wave patterns, the mind and ego can still harbor cravings and desires. True Self Realization is marked by the complete cessation of wants and attachments. There is no longer any motivation to amass wealth, nor any attachment to sensual pleasures; the Self exists beyond such worldly concerns. Osho's life also serves as a cautionary note regarding the use of intoxicants in pursuit of Self Realization, as such these consciousness aids may produce temporary effects but can provoke an egoic rebound once withdrawn—often intensifying the very desires one seeks to transcend.

Chapter 16

THE EGO

The ego is the mind, intimately tied to the body. But we are neither mind nor body—we are pure awareness, the silent observer behind, beyond, thought itself. This is a subtle concept, one difficult to grasp for anyone who has not glimpsed the Self. True understanding cannot come through reasoning alone; it can only arise through direct experience. And when that experience occurs, all questions answer themselves—not because they have conventional answers, but because the answers are, in a sense, unanswerable. Makes sense, right? Haha—if it does, then it isn't the truth. For ultimate truth lies beyond senses; it is the "no-sense" that alone makes sense. This is the domain beyond the mind.

The ego can be likened to a virus. Some Gnostic traditions suggest that the mind was a gift—or perhaps a trap—bestowed by the Demiurge to prevent us from realizing the Self. Whether true or not, the ancient Vedic teachings are clear: the mind is not real. Hence the saying: *"That which comes and goes is not real; that which does not come and go is real. Find that which is real."* The Self alone is real.

The mind, like the world itself, should be approached as fundamentally unreal. I once told someone, casually, that the mind does not exist. He grew agitated, offering elaborate philosophical arguments in defense of existence. I chose not to argue. Perhaps it would have been wiser to say, "The mind is not real," rather than "we do not exist." After all, the mind does exist insofar as we perceive it—echoing like a voice in a cave at the center of our head—just as the body exists insofar as we see it. But that does not make either ultimately real.

Science reminds us that matter is 99% empty space. How "real" is that? Perhaps we exist in a kind of holographic simulation— if so, what is reality itself? Questions of real and unreal are ultimately conceptual; they hinge on definition. Next time, when discussing the mind with someone, I may simply present it as a paradox: neither real nor unreal, a riddle to contemplate like a koan.

The truth is simple: the ego is not our friend. It is the sole obstacle to Self Realization. All spiritual techniques—meditation, contemplation, mindfulness, mantra, breathwork, etc.—aim to dissolve, quiet, and still the mind, so that what remains is pure awareness. That awareness is the Self.

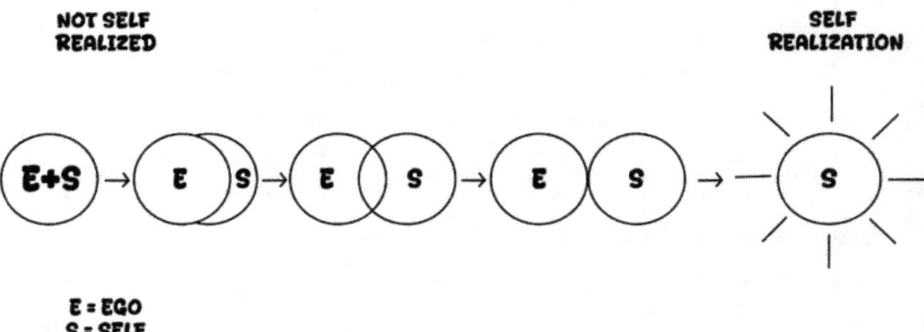

Here is an illustration I created to depict the interplay between the ego and the Self on the path to Self Realization. Initially, the ego conceals the Self entirely. Gradually, the Self begins to peek through, and over time, the separation between ego and Self becomes clear. Eventually, the ego is recognized for what it truly is—unreal—and dissolves. Often, one catches only a fleeting glimpse of the Self before the ego snaps back into dominance. Yet even a brief encounter with the Self plants a seed—a seed that, with patience and practice, will inevitably bear fruit.

COMPASSION AND THE EGO

With higher compassion comes a diminishing of the ego, and conversely, as the ego grows stronger, our capacity for compassion tends to shrink. These two qualities are intimately intertwined, like two sides of the same coin. The ego thrives on separation, on attachment to identity, on the constant comparison of self versus other. Compassion, on the other hand, arises when the boundaries of the ego soften and we recognize the inherent connection between ourselves and all beings.

This is why the great spiritual and philosophical traditions of the world—from the Vedas and Upanishads to the teachings of the Buddha, Christ, and the mystics of Sufism and other cultures— place compassion at the very **heart** of their practice. Compassion is not merely a moral virtue; it is a profound inner practice that dissolves the rigid structures of the ego. When we act from genuine compassion, our concerns for status, recognition, and self-interest begin to fall away, and the heart opens to a broader, more universal awareness.

In essence, the path of Self Realization is inseparable from the path of compassion. The two develop together: as compassion grows, the ego naturally weakens, creating space for deeper awareness and authentic connection with the Self. Conversely, an inflated ego limits perception and isolates consciousness, making true compassion difficult, if not impossible, to experience.

Thus, the cultivation of compassion is not a peripheral practice; it is central to the dissolution of ego and the awakening of the Self. In every moment we practice genuine compassion, we are simultaneously loosening the grip of the ego and stepping closer to our true nature. It's cultivation importance cannot be stressed enough.

LANGUAGE REINFORCES THE EGO

Language, by its very nature, is dualistic, and in doing so, it reinforces the illusion of the "I." For the vast majority of people, the term "I" is used to reference the mind, the body, or both. From the moment we are born, we are conditioned through language to identify with this false self—the ego—which is the root of our bondage, suffering, and ignorance. We say, *"I feel this," "I am that," "I want this," "My this or that,"* and in doing so, we continually reinforce our subconscious identification with the ego. This is the gravest trap of all because it pushes us deeper in identification with the false and further into ignorance.

The truth is simple yet profound: we are none of what the mind or ego claims. We are not the mind, we are not the thoughts, we are not the emotions, we are not the body. We are pure awareness—thoughtless, wordless, limitless, ineffable, radiant with joy and bliss beyond all words and concepts. This is the Self. This is YOU. I repeat this often because it is of extreme importance: understanding this is not something the mind can grasp; it is a reality beyond all words, all concepts, and all thought. The repetition will help plant a seed in the subconscious of those reading this. May that seed one day sprout into a great tree of the Self. You are THAT!

With the mind, we are limited. Without the mind, we are boundless. We are infinite, ineffable pure awareness. In future discussions, we will delve more deeply into language and how it perpetuates the illusion of separation and duality. For now, the key point is that language continually reinforces the ego, the false "I." The practice of self-inquiry helps us peel away this illusion, allowing us to rest in the true Self—the ultimate Self—in the silence and stillness of the mind, in the calm, undisturbed ocean of awareness.

Even our names serve as anchors for the ego. From the moment we are born, we are conditioned to identify with our name, with our body, with this particular persona. Over time, this false self is reinforced again and again, and with it comes inevitable suffering. Bodies come and go. Identities come and go. Emotions rise and fade. The world itself appears and disappears. Yet amid all change, there is one constant, one refuge that neither arises nor fades. It is eternal, beyond all form, beyond all thought, beyond time itself. Seek this unchanging reality. Rest in it. Recognize it. You are THAT— timeless, boundless, infinite. You are THAT!

I am other than name, form and action.
My nature is ever free!
I am Self, the supreme unconditioned Brahman.
I am pure Awareness, forever non-dual.
—Adi Shankara, *Upadesasahasri* 11.7 (Tadatmananda, 2025)

Chapter 17

COMPLEMENTARY PRACTICES

Here, I will explore a variety of techniques and insights that may complement the methods of Self Realization previously discussed, presented in no particular order. Ultimately, every technique must be relinquished, for the final step is the stepless state—where all methods fall away and only the Self remains. May these techniques and exercises listed here aid you in your quest of Self Realization.

1 - MANTRA

Mantra practice involves the continual repetition of a sacred sound, word, or phrase. In India, mantras are woven deeply into spiritual life; every deity has its own mantra, recited countless times by devotees. Modern research suggests that mantra repetition can calm the nervous system, slow brain wave activity, and increase theta waves in particular (Mohanty et al., 2024) while others show increases in gamma. Really any word or phrase can be a mantra. The Sufis chant different names for God and love poetry or mystical texts.

Ultimately, however, all practices must lead into silence. The final doorway to Self Realization is not sound but stillness—pure, unconditioned awareness. Yet mantra can serve as a powerful bridge for those with an active or restless mind. By focusing attention on a single sound, the mind becomes gradually corralled, unified, and quiet. Once the mind is steady, the mantra itself can be released, dissolving into the spaciousness of silence and the emptiness that reveals the Self.

A word of caution: many traditional mantras invoke specific gods or goddesses. In some lineages, it is believed that these deities may bestow siddhis—subtle powers or "gifts"—in response to devoted repetition. But such gifts are rarely free; some traditions maintain that every boon carries a karmic debt to be repaid in this life or beyond. In a realm as deceptive and dualistic as this one, caution is wise.

For those wishing to avoid entanglement with deities or astral forces, simple universal sounds are preferable. The syllable **OM** (or **AUM**) is revered in the Upanishads—especially the *Mandukya Upanishad* (Radhakrishnan, 2024)—as the primordial vibration, the sound of Atman, the Self, and of Brahman, the source of all creation. If one is to use a mantra at all, AUM stands as the purest and most direct: the mantra of all mantras.

"Verily, the nature of the ether within the space (of the heart) is the same as the supreme bright power. This is manifested in a threefold way, in fire, in the sun and in the breath of life. Verily, the nature of the ether within the space (of the heart) is the same as the syllable AUM. With this syllable, indeed, that (light) rises up (from the depths) goes upwards and breathes forth." – Maitri Upanishad 7:11 (Radhakrishan, 2024)

2- FLOAT TANK AKA THE JOE ROGAN EFFECT

Float tanks—also known as isolation tanks—have been around since the 1960s and '70s, but today they're trendier and more accessible than ever. Early research showed that floating predominantly activates theta brain waves, but more recent findings by Dr. Feinstein reveal that delta waves—the deep-sleep waves—also emerge during a float session.

Inside a float tank, you're buoyed by roughly a thousand pounds of Epsom salt dissolved in warm, body-temperature water. You lie there in pitch-black silence, suspended between gravity and weightlessness, and slowly your sense of having a body begins to dissolve. The experience can feel womb-like, dreamlike—your brain can't quite tell whether you're awake or drifting into deep sleep, and so it sinks into theta and delta states almost by design.

It usually takes close to an hour to reach these depths, though with practice the mind learns to surrender more quickly. Most people hit a wall of boredom at around the 45–60 minute mark—a classic ego tactic. Push past that boredom, and a remarkable thing happens: the mind begins to soften, unravel, and fade into stillness. This is a perfect time for self-inquiry, mantra repetition, breath awareness, heart-centered focus—anything that nudges the mind toward one-pointedness and, eventually, dissolution.

My first float tank adventure was back in 2013 at Crash's legendary place in Venice Beach, California—the same Crash who built Joe Rogan's personal float tank and appeared on his podcast. I remember sitting in the lobby as Crash excitedly preached the gospel of floating, eyes sparkling like he was about to launch me into another dimension.

After a shower, I stepped into the tank—pure darkness, absolute silence. The first few minutes were unsettling. Was I going to have a psychedelic epiphany? A Joe-Rogan-style cosmic journey?

An out-of-body adventure like John Lilly, the original float-tank pioneer? Or would I simply float there… mildly confused?

As it turned out, that first 90-minute session was mostly just deeply relaxing. Meditative. Nice—but nothing dramatic.

Fast-forward to today: after dozens of floats, the experience has become extraordinary. There is a learning curve. It takes a few sessions to really "get it." The trick is to let go—completely. Relax like you're falling asleep, except you remain awake. A big part of the process is simply learning to be comfortable in darkness, which many people subconsciously fear.

The after-effects of floating last about three days in my experience—and research supports that. I use it as a reset button whenever I need to decompress or recharge. When the mind goes quiet, the body follows, melting into a massage-level bliss. Sometimes I even wonder: did float tanks play a role in Joe Rogan's meteoric rise? Did regularly dipping into theta and delta make him more charismatic, influential, and successful—perhaps even Rasputin-level persuasive? Osho-level magnetic? Hard to say without checking out his brain waves.

One of my most memorable float experiences happened not in the tank but afterwards. I came home from a 90-minute float, sat down on the couch, and something unusual struck me: **I wasn't thinking.** At all. I was sitting in total, effortless stillness—no thoughts, no emotions, no narrative. Just peaceful, luminous silence.

And there was no "me" there to enjoy it.

I wasn't happy, I wasn't sad—I simply *was*. Pure awareness. A taste of the Self beyond the mind. The silent witness. The space of no-self—not "Mark," not the body-mind identity, but the vast, quiet, boundless presence behind it all.

That which is aware of the mind.
That which cannot be touched by thought.
That which cannot be described, only known directly.

You are THAT!

"Be still. Stillness reveals the secrets of eternity." — Lao Tzu

"Be still, and know that I am God (the Self)." — Psalm 46:10

"Your duty is to be and not to be this or that. 'I am that I am' sums up the whole truth. The method is summed up in the words 'Be still'. What does stillness mean? It means to destroy yourself. Because any form or shape is the cause for trouble. Give up the notion that 'I am so and so'. All that is required to realize the Self is to be still. What can be easier than that?"— Ramana Maharshi

3- EMPTINESS MEDITATIONS

There are countless meditation techniques in the world—apps, YouTube videos, guided sessions, gadgets, books, systems, traditions, and more. It seems everything short of the kitchen sink has been turned into a method for stilling the mind. Some of them are genuinely effective; I still use certain practices from time to time, especially those rooted in **emptiness**.

Where attention goes, energy flows. If one consistently directs awareness toward emptiness, one gradually becomes empty and still. For beginners, this may take time simply because the modern mind is not accustomed to sustained attention. These days, the average attention span rivals that of a goldfish. But attention is like a muscle: the more we train it, the stronger and more stable it becomes.

Slowing the breath is a powerful aid. As the breath becomes calm and steady, brain waves naturally slow as well, ushering the mind toward stillness and spaciousness.

Below are several emptiness-centered meditation practices that many people have found deeply effective:

- Focus on the space between two objects.

- Rest attention on the emptiness surrounding you.

- Imagine you have no head and place awareness in that emptiness.

- Visualize the inside of your body as hollow, like a light balloon rising effortlessly into the sky.

- Notice the space between each spoken or thought word.

- Focus on the pause between each breath—the silent gap between inhalation and exhalation.

- Feel the precise meeting point where the inhale turns into the exhale.

- Place awareness on the inner heart-space, about the size of a thumb, where the Self is said to reside as a subtle flame.

4- FOCUS ON ONE POINT AND HEART MEDITATION

Another effective meditative practice is to focus attention on a single point in the body. While I personally gravitate toward meditating on emptiness, this method can be highly beneficial as well. One simply rests awareness on any part of the body—or, for deeper effect, visualizes that area as emptiness.

Ideally, the most profound focus is on the heart center, considered the seat of the Self. Picture a small, glowing point about the size of a thumb, with a flickering flame at its core. This is how the Upanishads describe Atman, the true Self. For those interested in exploring this further, the practice is often referred to as *Dahara-vidya*, or heart meditation.

5- EXERCISE: FATIGUE THE BODY AND THE MIND

This is an excellent complementary practice that has been embraced by many ancient traditions, especially among monks. Personally, I prefer this approach over extreme methods that push the body to the brink of pain or exhaustion, even approaching death as the Sufis did with extreme fasting. Such extremes are unnecessary—there are far safer and equally effective paths.

A simple and accessible way to gently fatigue the body and mind is through exercise. I've observed during neurofeedback training that someone who ran 16 miles beforehand reached record-high brain wave activity. Beyond its brain wave benefits, exercise offers profound health advantages. It grounds one in the present moment, helps release stagnant energy—including residual emotional energy—and promotes overall vitality. Exercise is linked to longevity, increased BDNF levels critical for brain health, and general well-being. Ideally, 150 minutes per week is recommended, with attention to leg strength and VO2 max for longevity. Its importance for mind, body, and spirit cannot be overstated.

For those drawn to more extreme practices, there are accounts of yogis inducing profound states by prolonged physical exertion—standing on one leg or holding an arm aloft for days, even years. Extended fasting or sleep deprivation as the Sufis are known for can also slow brain wave activity, potentially aiding Self Realization. However, these approaches must be used with extreme caution. There are abundant, far less physically taxing ways to realize the Self, allowing one to access the same depth without harm or risk. And always check with your health care practitioner before attempting anything out of the ordinary.

6- SLEEP DEPRIVATION

Another ancient method for inducing mystical or altered states of consciousness is sleep deprivation. The great Sufi Shah Kirmani is said to have not slept for 40yrs. Sufis were notorious for "little sleep, little food, little talk." From a scientific perspective, sleep deprivation actually makes a great deal of sense. When the brain is deprived of the delta and theta stages of sleep—by remaining awake far beyond normal cycles—it compensates by naturally shifting toward those slower brainwave frequencies in an attempt to restore homeostasis. Research has shown that sleep deprivation reliably increases delta and theta activity in the waking state (Cajochen et al., 1999; Posada et al., 2019).

Theoretically, if someone can access delta brain waves while awake, sleep could become far less necessary, at least from a simplistic point of view. However, that also means missing out on the benefits of the other stages of sleep. Still, from the perspective of the enlightened yogi I met I talked about earlier—who claimed to sleep only a couple of hours per night—this possibility seems far less far-fetched. Perhaps the cultural insistence that we must sleep exactly eight hours each night is not the absolute truth we were taught.

More and more, I am discovering how many of our assumptions are simply inherited conditioning—beliefs we absorbed from birth about how we should act, think, and feel, much of which disconnects us from the essence of who we truly are. The world trains us to live from the mind, from the ego, and from fear, not from the Self which is mindless, egoless, fearless.

It is time to question these inherited paradigms, to peel back the layers of conditioning, and to reconnect with the eternal truth of our being. It is time to Realize the Self. You are THAT!

7- FASTING/KETOSIS

"Fasting blinds the body so the soul can see." — Rumi

Nearly every great spiritual tradition—and nearly every revered sage, from the Yogis, Sufis to Buddha, Jesus, the Prophet Muhammad, and Jewish prophets—has incorporated fasting. Across cultures, from Jain and Buddhist monastics to Christian mystics and Indigenous shamans, fasting has been used as a tool for purification, discipline, and deeper connection with the Self. Its spiritual and physical benefits are profound and cannot be overstated. The Muslim saints considered fasting the best way to reach heightened states of spirituality.

I remember 2008 vividly. I was jogging on a very low-calorie diet while practicing intermittent fasting, curious to see if it could improve my running speed. During those runs, I encountered a peculiar and unforgettable sensation. A sublime energy seemed to radiate from within me. I felt profoundly connected to the sky, the sun, the wind, and the world itself. At the time, I couldn't articulate what it was. All I knew, at the most primordial level, was that I felt connected to something greater—what I could only describe as God. Looking back, I realize what I was experiencing was likely a slower brainwave state—alpha, and perhaps even theta—induced by fasting and coupled with the faster gamma brain wave state in what is called the flow state.

Our society, however, teaches us to eat incessantly. From the moment we wake until we go to sleep, the cultural message is to consume: eat, eat, eat. I didn't realize that other cultures practiced fasting, or that abstaining from food could be healthy, even transformative. I'd heard stories of yogis and monks who fasted for days at a time, reaching states of profound connection with the Self. Yet in modern culture, food has become an endless distraction and form of escapism, creating habitual cravings and constant consumption. Everywhere we look—TV commercials, social norms around dining, social media feeds—food dominates. Posts about fasting, restraint, or self-discipline are rare.

Overindulgence in anything, can become poison. Too much water can lead to hyponatremia and death; excessive fasting can be fatal; too much meditation can detach us from the practicalities of life. Buddhism teaches the *Middle Way*, the balance between self-denial and self-indulgence. Extremes, though occasionally beneficial, should be exceptions, not the norm. Similarly, stress in moderation—*eustress*—can motivate and strengthen, but excessive stress becomes *distress*, damaging the body over time.

The effects of fasting on the brain have been scientifically documented. In 1976, Suzuki et al. studied the EEG readings of 262 fasting patients and observed increases in alpha and theta brainwave activity. Subsequent research has continued to confirm these effects. For example, Machado et al. (2022) found that ketone administration increased alpha and gamma brain waves by 16% and 18%, respectively (Spaller, 2022). Saraswati (1981) also provides extensive insights into the neurophysiological impact of fasting, reinforcing its ability to elevate consciousness and induce meditative states.

Fasting is not merely abstention from food—it is a doorway to heightened awareness, a tool to quiet the mind, and a method to reconnect with the Self. When practiced mindfully, it can reveal the subtle energies within, allowing the soul to truly see.

"Hunger is God's food by which He quickens the bodies of the upright." -Rumi

"Hunger is the food of the ascetics, and remembrance of God is the food of the gnostics."
-Abu Muhammad 'Abdullah ibn Muhammad al-Kharraz

8- YOGA NIDRA

Yoga Nidra is another practice that has been shown to increase slower brain wave activity (Datta et al., 2022).

Essentially, Yoga Nidra is "sleep yoga" without actually falling asleep. It is like going to sleep while remaining consciously aware. Often called psychic sleep or yogic sleep, the goal of the practice is to experience the restorative benefits of sleep while maintaining awareness. This practice may also induce visions, as it engages the theta brainwave state—the same state associated with dreaming during unconscious sleep.

Many ancient yogic and monastic traditions incorporate Yoga Nidra, including the Tibetan Lamas. In Tibet, monks would spend months sleeping in specialized boxes that prevented them from lying down, training them to remain conscious not only while awake but also during sleep, all while still receiving the restorative benefits of rest. Some have become so proficient that they can sleep standing or sitting.

I once attempted this practice myself and managed to do fairly well for a couple of days. However, fatigue and sleep deprivation eventually caught up with me, and I returned to normal sleep patterns. With dedication and consistent effort, one can practice and refine Yoga Nidra, but it is not for everyone, nor does everyone have the time or tolerance for the challenges associated with extended sleep deprivation.

9- PSYCHOACTIVE SUBSTANCES

For millennia, psychoactive substances have been used to facilitate expanded states of consciousness. From magic mushrooms to cannabis, nearly every culture has employed psychoactive plants in ritual, spiritual, or healing practices since the dawn of civilization. One hypothesis, known as the "stone ape" hypothesis, even suggests that such substances may have contributed to the evolutionary expansion of the human brain.

The Vikings had their sacred *Amanita muscaria* mushrooms, African traditions use potent ibogaine, and shamans deep in the

Peruvian jungle have long worked with ayahuasca. Many of these substances, especially ayahuasca, can induce slower brainwave states such alpha, theta, and even delta as well as faster states such as gamma—facilitating deep introspection and altered consciousness (O'Hare, 2019). As one study notes:

> "Analysis revealed that DMT significantly altered electrical activity in the brain, characterized by a marked drop in alpha waves and an increase in delta and theta waves. The red circle shows an increase in the lower frequency delta and theta waves."
> (Timmermann et al., 2019)

I am neither advocating for nor condemning the use of psychoactive substances. My point is simply that, if they are used at all, they must be approached with great responsibility and restraint. Frequent use can easily become a trap—a crutch, a distraction, or a form of escapism rather than genuine growth. At their best, such substances may offer temporary insight, but can be good tools if carefully integrated with conscious spiritual practices such as forgiveness, letting go, self-inquiry and recapitulation. Above all, it is absolutely paramount to cultivate loving-kindness, compassion, and empathy, without which no experience—chemical or otherwise—can lead to true Self Realization.

Some individuals consume these substances regularly, making their use a part of their identity. Ironically, this can further entrench the ego and reinforce the illusory nature of the mind and body, rather than dissolve it. Among all psychoactive compounds, 5-MeO-DMT is often cited for its potential to induce ego dissolution and brief experiences of Gnosis or Self Realization. Even so, caution is warranted, as all of these substances carry risks of psychological or emotional complications if used improperly.

It is said that 5-MeO-DMT can catapult one into a white light suffused with infinite love, where the mind dissolves completely for several minutes. In that space, one becomes nothing but pure awareness. For most, the experience is overwhelming and even frightening, yet for the few who are prepared, it can serve as a profound means to crack the ego and catch a glimpse of the Self.

This journey is not for the faint of heart; it demands the utmost caution and respect. The quieter the mind and the less the ego is present, the more the heart opens, and feelings of boundless love emerge. Conversely, if one is unprepared, the experience can destabilize the psyche, making it unsuitable for some.

Some practices even combine substances like ketamine with neurofeedback or other interventions—but it's worth remembering that the Self unfolds at its own pace. Moving too quickly can be destabilizing, and true realization is not something to force. It emerges gently, in harmony with one's readiness, courage, and the heart's natural capacity to receive it. Always remember the **heart** is the key.

One important point to keep in mind s that, for the most part, psychoactive substances do not permanently still the mind. They can act as a fast track to expanded consciousness, but like any fast track—including neurofeedback—they come with drawbacks and consequences. Without the accompanying slowing or stilling of the mind, the effects are temporary, and often the ego returns even stronger once the substance wears off—a phenomenon sometimes called the "ego backlash." To be honest, I would recommend avoiding these practices and focusing instead on Realizing the Self through the many tools and methods already available to us. There is no need to rely on substances nor technologies to awaken to the Self. All the world of the entire universe is within you. You are THAT!

Questioner: Is there any drug to promote meditation?

Ramana Maharshi: No, because afterwards the user would be unable to meditate without taking it habitually. Those who take opium or alcohol are unconsciously seeking the blissful, thoughtless state of the real Self. They get an intimation of that bliss through drugs, but afterwards they must resume their normal state, and the craving comes back even stronger—until they become chronic addicts, slaves to the substance. With all such artificial stimulants, there must be a fall. If the mind is subdued, everything is conquered.
—Conscious Immortality: Conversations with Shri Ramana Maharshi (Brunton, 1983)

10- NEUROFEEDBACK

We have already discussed neurofeedback extensively. Given the concerns surrounding its application—particularly in the context of consciousness work—I can no longer recommend it. In my view, the potential risks, unintended consequences, and insufficient long-term safety data make it an unreliable and potentially destabilizing approach. It is also often very costly— sometimes comparable to the price of a car—making it inaccessible for many people. Some centers promote neurofeedback as comparable to decades of meditation based primarily on brain wave data. Such claims are controversial and may not fully reflect the depth and nuance of traditional contemplative development. Brain waves alone cannot capture the full scope and subtlety of sustained meditative practice, as Self Realization involves far more than measurable neural activity.

Neurofeedback can be seen as a "fast track" to glimpses of Self Realization, but in many ways, it is a trap similar to psychoactive substances. The brain waves may change dramatically, and users can experience what they call "merging," a brief state where the mind quiets and an enlightenment-like experience occurs. However, without adequate meditation and self-inquiry practices, these experiences are fleeting. The mind and ego inevitably return—

sometimes stronger than before, in what is often called the "ego backlash." It is similar to what one might experience with psychedelics or a spontaneous kundalini awakening.

In fact, some people have experienced kundalini-like energy surges during neurofeedback training. Neurofeedback can trigger glimpses of Self Realization, but it is not a substitute for true, sustained Self Realization. The challenge is that most people approach neurofeedback with goals rooted in material or emotional desires— better health, wealth, relationships—rather than the ultimate goal: Realizing the Self. Focusing on anything other than Self Realization risks reinforcing the ego rather than dissolving it.

Once the Self is Realized, all desires and aversions naturally fall away. There is no striving, no resistance—everything aligns perfectly. Neurofeedback alone, however, cannot achieve this state. Most participants I encountered had limited meditation or mindfulness experience, and without a consciousness practice, the mind and ego inevitably return, often creating more suffering. On my first day of training, I anticipated a calm, monk-like environment, but that was not the case. One trainer even suggested that meditation was unnecessary with neurofeedback—a perspective I found contrary to everything I know about Self Realization. Mindfulness and meditation are absolutely essential to integrate any progress and maintain conscious awareness.

For anyone considering neurofeedback, I strongly recommend pairing it with meditation, self-inquiry as well as the cultivation of loving kindness, compassion and empathy. While forgiveness, letting go, and other techniques are helpful, self-inquiry is the cornerstone of disidentifying with the mind and reconnecting with the true Self. Without it, neurofeedback risks reinforcing the ego: emotional scoring before and after sessions, writing down intentions for material gains—these practices subtly anchor the mind in desire and identification with the false self.

True realization is not about manifesting more desires but dissolving the attachment to them. Realize the Self, and life unfolds naturally; suffering arises only when we interfere with that natural flow.

11- SLOW DOWN

Another approach found in meditative practices like Qi Gong and Tai Chi involves slow, deliberate movement to quiet the mind. Speaking slower and more deliberately can also help slow brain waves, creating a conducive state for Realizing the Self. In everyday life, most people speak quickly, which tends to accelerate brain wave activity. I would even suggest that the pace of someone's speech and the speed of their thoughts may correspond to their brain wave state. Those who speak rapidly are likely in a faster, beta-dominant state, while those who speak slowly—or not at all—are more likely aligned with slower alpha brain waves, conducive to stillness and inner awareness.

12- MIND OBSERVATION MEDITATION

I call this practice Mind Observation Meditation, or MOM for short. It's the same technique I used in all my videos. This meditation is especially helpful for beginners because it cultivates the essential separation between the mind and the Self. What I love about MOM is its simplicity and effectiveness: simply observe your thoughts as they drift by, like clouds moving across the sky. That which comes and goes is not real—your attention must turn to that which is eternal, that which is real.

It's important to note, however, that this meditation won't be effective if the ego remains tightly attached to the Self. This is where practices like forgiveness and letting go become crucial, helping to loosen the ego's grip. Break the chains of the ego, and discover the freedom of your true Self. You are THAT!

"Let come what comes, let go what goes. See what remains."
– Ramana Maharshi

"We have so long identified ourselves with the not-Self (Mind/Body) that we find it difficult to regard ourselves as t h e Self. Giving up this identification with the not- Self is all that is meant by Self-realisation. How to realise, i.e., make real, the Self? We have realised, i.e., regarded as real, what is unreal, the not-Self (Mind/Body). To give up such false realisation is Self-realisation." – Bhagavan in 'Day by Day with Bhagavan' 17-8-46

13- KOANS

Koans can be powerful tools to still the mind. Victor Hori notes that through dedicated koan study, one could reach an enlightenment state (kensho) in as little as six months. Ramana Maharshi's famous question, *"Who Am I?"*, is itself a profound koan—designed to quiet the mind and eventually dissolve its habitual patterns. One can also ask *"What Am I?"* or use any phrase that transcends ordinary thought, guiding the practitioner into stillness.

Koans work by going beyond the conceptual mind, leading to a direct sense of knowing. In that knowing—beyond words, language, and rational thought—lies the recognition of the true Self. Some classic and thought-provoking koans include:

- What is the sound of one hand clapping?
- What is the sound of no hand clapping?
- What was your original face before you were born?
- When you can do nothing, what can you do?

- When the many are reduced to one, what is the one reduced to?

- What is the color of wind?

- If you meet the Buddha, kill the Buddha.

Each koan points beyond the intellect, inviting direct experience of the Self.

14- MEET AN ENLIGHTENED BEING

Theoretically, an enlightened being radiates a profound stillness. Simply being in their presence may induce a form of brain-wave entrainment, in which one person's neural rhythms begin to resonate with those of another, guiding the mind toward a calmer, more receptive state. Imagine an enlightened being resonating around 6 Hz and someone nearby resonating at 12 Hz; through brain wave entrainment, proximity alone might draw the person toward a midpoint—perhaps closer to 9 Hz.

This, of course, remains speculative. There is no precise scientific formula to confirm such an interaction. Yet the subtle influence of Realized beings has been observed, described, and revered across cultures and throughout history, suggesting that something beyond words—and perhaps beyond measurement— quietly transmits itself in their presence.

This effect is not universal; it is not guaranteed for everyone. Yet for those poised on the edge of awakening, for those already at a tipping point, such a presence can catalyze profound shifts in consciousness.

The challenge, of course, is finding such a being in the modern world. Perhaps one must journey to the remote Himalayan caves of northern India, or encounter them at sacred gatherings such as the Kumbh Mela. I count myself fortunate to have experienced such a presence in India, where I was utterly struck by the stillness, presence, and palpable energy that seemed to radiate from him. If you seek them, you will find them.

15- BREATH

Breathing exercises—known as pranayama in the yogic tradition, or holotropic breathing in modern contexts—have long been used as a powerful aid to Self Realization. By consciously slowing the breath, one can gradually slow the mind, creating moments of profound stillness through this simple yet profound practice. There are many techniques available, ranging from rapid, intense breathing that can produce DMT-like effects, to slow, deliberate breathing that cultivates calm and clarity. Personally, I gravitate toward the slower methods.

I remember my first Samadhi experience many years ago: I was barely breathing, yet fully alive, fully present. There is a hypothesis that the slower the breath, the slower the brain waves, and this appears to hold true. The Upanishads explicitly reference the breath as a tool to still the mind and facilitate Self Realization. Modern neuroscience corroborates this, showing that deliberate slowing of the breath indeed slows brain wave activity.

Breath work can help subdue the ego, but it is not enough on its own. Without complementary practices like self-inquiry, the ego can return even stronger—a phenomenon sometimes called the "ego backlash." The breath is a bridge to stillness, but the mind must be guided across it consciously, with awareness and discernment, to truly glimpse the Self.

"This control of the mind through the breath is very temporary. As mentioned earlier, if the calm mind has not been put to effective use for spiritual progress, then, when it regains its freedom, it binges. This means that it hits back at us with vengeance. It gives us a **backlash**. Any person who has practised this control will vouch for this statement. Hence, the spiritual seeker is forewarned not to pursue this practice with the wrong aim. There are many people who bring their mind under control using the above means simply to demonstrate this as a feat to a gullible public. They may do so, but the revenge the mind gets will overcome them very soon."

-*Upadesha Sara*, Swami Gurubhaktananda p. 26

16- SILENT/DARK RETREATS

I cannot claim extensive experience with silent or dark-light retreats, yet they are reputed to have profound effects on the journey toward Self Realization. Mantak Chia is well-known for his dark-light retreats in Thailand, and similar programs exist in various locations across the world, including the United States. There is also the rigorous ten-day Vipassana retreat—a silent, non-dark meditation retreat—that many who have undertaken it describe as profoundly transformative.

For those who are ready, such retreats can catalyze significant progress toward Self Realization. Yet the essential prerequisite remains the quieting of the mind. Without some measure of stillness, the Self cannot be glimpsed; it is obscured by the constant churn of thought and emotion. The mind must first be stilled, even if only briefly, before one can abide in the Self and observe the mind and emotions as clouds drifting across the sky.

These retreats can accelerate the path, but I would recommend anyone considering them to first cultivate an understanding of the Self—what it is and, equally important, what it is not. Without such grounding, the intensity of these retreats may overwhelm rather than illuminate. True realization unfolds in stillness, and only then can the Self be truly known.

17- DO NOTHING

Do Nothing Meditation, also called Shikantaza meditation, is exactly what it implies—doing nothing. This Zen Buddhist practice involves sitting with the eyes open, without focusing on any thought, object, or goal. One sits upright with natural breathing, allowing all thoughts, sensations, and feelings to arise and pass like clouds drifting across the sky. This practice is completely contrary to our usual way of life, where the mind is almost constantly active.

18- BINAURAL BEATS

Binaural beats may offer some benefit for Self Realization. This simple technology plays one frequency in one ear and a different frequency in the other, causing the brain to entrain at the difference. For example, if 20 Hz is played in one ear and 10 Hz in the other, the brain would theoretically entrain at 10 Hz, corresponding roughly to an alpha brain wave state. Like any technology, it can serve as either a crutch or a catalyst for awakening.

I once observed a family member who was trapped in endless thoughts and repetitive rumination listen to binaural beats while practicing simple breathing and visualization exercises. Remarkably, they achieved a state of stillness—long enough for me to notice a profound change. They recognized it too, though they could not put it into words, as it felt completely foreign compared to their normal day-to-day mental state.

I don't see technology as a cure-all, but it can help induce stillness and offer a glimpse of the Self. Once someone experiences that state, a subtle yet compelling urge arises to return to it—a seed is planted, destined to sprout over time. The same principle applies to any brain-training device: they can help modulate brain waves, but without mental stillness, their effectiveness is limited. Self Realization is not solely about brain waves; stillness of the mind is an essential component as well as cultivation of the heart.

It's also important to be aware of the potential for ego backlash. When tools like breathwork, technologies, or psychedelics are used to induce temporary stillness, the mind can sometimes rebound more forcefully once the effect wears off. If such tools are employed, coupling them with self-inquiry and heart cultivation can help mitigate or soften this rebound, supporting a more lasting and stable glimpse of the Self. Other then that, no technology or exogenous substance is needed. You already have everything, you already are everything, just go within and Realize the Self.

19- OBE TRAINING

Out-of-Body Experience (OBE) training can be a powerful tool for practicing stillness. In order to have an OBE, one must remain perfectly still for hours on end. I would caution against getting too caught up in exploring the various realms of the astral world; instead, use OBE as a means to support Self Realization if anything. The ultimate goal should always be Self Realization—everything else is a distraction or a potential trap.

As the body and breath become still, the mind often follows, creating a greater opportunity to realize the Self. However, there is a potential pitfall: some OBE practitioners become so absorbed in the experiences themselves that they forget the ultimate purpose, allowing the ego to be strengthened rather than dissolved. Time is better spent on practices aimed directly at Realizing the Self, such as those outlined earlier, rather than becoming lost in the astral journey.

20- WATER WATER EVERYWHERE

The human body is composed mostly of water. This raises an intriguing question: can we restructure the water in our bodies to facilitate changes in brain wave states and, potentially, Self Realization? Some devices, such as stirring wands, restructure water and affect brain waves. While one should not rely solely on this to

Realize the Self, it could serve as a complementary tool alongside other methods discussed here.

It's worth noting that the fascia—the connective tissue that envelops muscles, organs, and bones—also holds water, much of which exists in a structured or "fourth phase" form called Exclusion Zone (EZ) water. This structured water is thought to have unique energetic properties, which may enhance subtle energetic shifts in the body during practices aimed at stilling the mind and deepening awareness. Theoretically, by influencing the water in our fascia and cells, we may support a more receptive energetic state that can assist in the realization of the Self.

Masaru Emoto's pioneering experiments further illustrate the profound responsiveness of water to vibrational input. Emoto found that water exposed to harmonious music, positive words, or focused intention could form beautiful, symmetrical crystals when frozen, whereas chaotic or negative input produced distorted, disordered structures. This suggests that sound, intention, and consciousness can directly influence the structure of water. Given that our bodies are mostly water, these findings open the possibility that similar energetic or vibrational influences could affect our internal water, subtly supporting mental clarity, emotional balance, and perhaps even moments of meditative stillness conducive to Self Realization.

Emoto's work also highlights the deep interconnectedness of sound, mind, and body. Chanting mantras, listening to harmonious tones, or exposing oneself to structured vibrational patterns may not only calm the mind but also resonate through the water in our fascia and cells, amplifying energetic coherence. In this way, sound could become a bridge between external stimuli and the internal subtle body, reinforcing the pathways that lead to stillness, awareness, and the direct experience of the Self.

This idea opens the door to exploring other water-structuring methods and considering how sound—such as chanting mantras—can affect the body's water. The Upanishads link water to breath, and breath to the mind, suggesting that subtle manipulations of our internal water could influence mental and energetic states, providing yet another pathway toward Self Realization. While this remains largely theoretical, it aligns with the broader understanding that the body, mind, and subtle energies are deeply interconnected.

21- SILENCE

Going for periods of time without speaking can be hugely beneficial for Self Realization. By refraining from speech, one becomes more aware of the mind, allowing it to gradually slow down. The gaps between thoughts widen, creating the spaciousness in which the Self can be Realized, especially when combined with other practices such as self-inquiry.

In yoga, this practice is known as *mauna*, or sacred silence, and those who observe it are called *munis*. Mauna has long been a common discipline among ascetics, monks, and yogis who take vows of silence. The practice of silence can profoundly support the path of Self Realization. Even observing mauna for a single day can offer a glimpse into its transformative power—simply refraining from speech and attentively observing the subtle shifts that arise within one's awareness.

"Only through Mauna can we enter into the *guha*, or secret cavern of the heart, in which the entire universe dwells in its true luminous. In the end, all words mean nothing—or everything, true meaning and sound being our oneness with all. The way to Self Realization is through silence; that is the greatest teacher and greatest power of knowing, as Bhagavan Ramana Maharshi taught."
—Vamadeva Shastri

"The benefits of Mauna (Silence) are incalculable. The language of silence is the language of God; the language of silence is the language of the heart." —Sivananda

"Keep Quiet!" —Papaji

22- INFRARED SAUNA

This is one of my favorite tools for both consciousness and overall health. Infrared saunas can be easily found online rather inexpensively and, with proper care, can last for many years—I've had one for nearly a decade at one point. I enjoy using it after exercise, preferably on an empty stomach, as it seems to facilitate a profound sense of stillness, making it a helpful aid on the path to Self Realization.

The effects may be related to entering a mild ketogenic state, the detoxifying impact of sweating, positive fascia effects, or even the activation of heat shock proteins. There's also intriguing research suggesting that infrared saunas can influence the water in our bodies. Dr. Gerald Pollack has shown that infrared light can restructure water into a negatively charged, ordered form called Exclusion Zone (EZ) water, or the "fourth phase of water," which may enhance cellular health. This structured water could, in theory, support the energetic aspects of consciousness and Self Realization. Interestingly, the concept of a "fourth" state resonates with the Advaita Vedanta notion of turiya, the transcendent state of pure awareness beyond waking, dreaming, and deep sleep.

23- GET A PET

Get a pet and serve it unconditionally. This is a beautiful practice of Bhakti Yoga and seva—selfless service. It cultivates the heart and mind, preparing one for Self Realization. Serving others in the world—at a food bank, a temple, a church, or any place where help is needed—can be just as transformative. Such acts of service build the inner foundation for awakening while also fostering **compassion and humility**, two essential qualities for realizing the Self.

It's important to remember that our goal is not to "save" the world or even ourselves, for ultimately neither the world nor the physical self exists as absolute reality. Both are illusions within maya, the dreamlike play of existence. In truth, we are everyone, and everyone is us. When we serve others, we are serving ourselves.

Compassion is the jewel at the heart of this practice. It is the living expression of love, the purest language of the Self. Through service, we cultivate compassion and humility, opening the heart to the Self and embodying the truth of our interconnectedness with all beings. The Self, in its essence, is love: not limited, worldly affection, but infinite, divine, unconditional love. You are THAT!

24- FIRE AND MOUNTAINS

A flame's gentle flicker oscillates between roughly 1 and 20 Hz, averaging near 10 Hz—closely corresponding to the alpha brain wave state—and can subtly entrain the mind into that rhythm, deepening meditative awareness. In a similar way, mountainous regions resonate near the Earth's natural frequency of approximately 7.8 Hz, associated with slower theta brain waves, encouraging the mind to quiet and harmonize. This may help explain why yogis and sages have long sought caves, forests, and high places for spiritual practice.

Fire ceremonies—common in Hinduism and Buddhism, such as homa rituals in the Hindu tradition—further embody this principle. During these rituals, practitioners chant mantras, invoke deities, and offer oblations into the fire. Whether performed at weddings, funerals, or other sacred rites, these acts align breath, mind, and spirit with the elemental rhythm of fire. Before the advent of artificial lighting, fire was humanity's primary source of illumination, naturally inviting reflection, ritual, and inner stillness—opening the heart to the eternal presence of the Self.

Perhaps human consciousness once oscillated at slower, more harmonious frequencies. In modern life, bombarded by constant stimuli and artificial stimulation and illumination, our collective brain waves have accelerated, leaving little room for contemplation or the subtle recognition of our true nature. Fire, mountains, and natural rhythms remind us of our innate resonance with the cosmos and offer a doorway to the Self—a quiet, receptive state in which presence unfolds naturally and the eternal awareness within is revealed.

Maitri Upanishad 7:8 (Radhakrishan, 2024)
He who is in the fire, he who is here in the heart, he who is yonder in the sun, he is one.

25- MAHAMUDRA MEDITATION

Mahamudra meditation is a central practice in Tibetan Buddhism that focuses on resting in the mind's natural state—its inherent emptiness, clarity, and awareness. Unlike structured meditations that require effortful concentration or visualization, Mahamudra invites one to simply observe the mind without clinging to thoughts, sensations, or emotions. It is a practice of open awareness, where one directly recognizes the luminous, spacious nature of consciousness itself.

This practice is remarkably simple in form yet profound in effect. By consistently resting in this state, even for a few minutes a day, one cultivates a direct experience of the mind's true nature. As habitual patterns of distraction and attachment soften, the mind gradually quiets, revealing the ever-present awareness that underlies all experience. In this stillness, one perceives the Self—not as a concept or identity, but as the timeless, boundless essence that is always present, beyond the fluctuations of thought, emotion, and perception.

Mahamudra is more than a meditation technique; it is a gateway to Self Realization. Through it, one learns to abide in the direct experience of the Self, the unchanging ground of consciousness, cultivating clarity, freedom, and a profound sense of unity with all that is.

26- JET LAG

Jet lag, essentially a form of sleep deprivation, can surprisingly be harnessed as a tool for Self Realization. It may sound counterintuitive, but the dissociative, dreamlike state induced by disrupted circadian rhythms can create a unique window for insight. When combined with meditative techniques or self-inquiry, this altered state of awareness can amplify one's ability to perceive the illusory nature of reality.

I recently observed this effect upon returning from Europe to the United States. For a brief period of roughly three days, the mind exists in a liminal, almost surreal space, where the ordinary structures of thought and time are softened. In this state, one can notice the ephemeral, dreamlike quality of life and, if guided toward stillness, use the fatigue and temporal disorientation as a catalyst for rapid progress in Self Realization.

One might also wonder how the effects of jet lag could interact with other intensive practices, such as an Enlightenment Intensive or a meditation retreat. Ultimately, the key is reaching a state of mental stillness, for it is in this quietude that the Self— timeless, boundless, and ever-present—reveals itself. When approached with mindfulness and discernment, even something as mundane as jet lag can become a doorway to profound awakening.

27- THOUGHT JOURNALING

Spend a week or a month writing down your thoughts, observing the patterns that consistently arise. Over time, recurring thoughts will become apparent—thoughts that surface repeatedly, often accompanied by specific emotions and even influencing events in your life. This practice is highly valuable, as it reveals the workings of the mind and the subtle dynamics of the ego.

Once these recurring patterns are recognized, they can be released through awareness. Self-inquiry can be applied to each thought: for example, if the thought "I am not good enough" arises, one can ask, *To whom do these thoughts occur? Who am I?* Deep-seated patterns may require additional methods such as forgiveness work or the Release Technique, but simply identifying them is a profound first step.

As this process continues, the egoic attachments gradually dissolve, and one becomes increasingly aware of the underlying Self—the unchanging observer beyond thought and emotion. By observing, self-inquiry, and letting go, the mind begins to settle, creating space for clarity, peace, and Self Realization.

28- RIGHT OUT OF BED

Every morning, for about the first five minutes after waking, the brain naturally drifts in an alpha state—a sweet spot for emptiness, meditation, or any mindfulness practice you enjoy. Think of it as a little gift from your mind, a golden window of calm before the day fully kicks in. Beyond the major methods discussed in this book, these lighter, complementary practices can add a bit of fun and playfulness to the journey, making Self Realization not just profound, but enjoyable too.

29- EYE GAZING OR MIRROR STARING

Eye gazing is a surprisingly deep and profound practice, whether done with a partner or even with oneself in the mirror. When practicing with a partner, simply looking into each other's eyes without speaking can create a deep sense of presence, connection, and stillness. It's a playful way to explore awareness beyond the chatter of the mind.

When done with a mirror, eye gazing becomes a practice of self-recognition. By staring into your own eyes, you can begin to sense that you are the awareness observing the body and mind—not the body or mind itself. This simple act can help reinforce the understanding of the Self as pure consciousness.

Eye gazing is deceptively simple yet profoundly powerful, creating moments where the ego softens, the mind slows, and the awareness of the Self shines more clearly. It's a practice that combines fun, curiosity, and deep insight all at once.

"If you want to know God, then turn your face towards your friend, and don't look away." -Rumi

1. Partner Eye Gazing (The 5-Minute Challenge)

Sit comfortably across from a partner. Set a timer for 5 minutes. Simply gaze into each other's eyes without speaking or reacting. The first few minutes may feel awkward, but as time passes, you may notice subtle shifts in energy, micro-expressions, or even a sense of connected stillness. Try to focus on the awareness behind the eyes, not just the eyes themselves.

2. Mirror Self-Reflection

Stand or sit in front of a mirror. Look into your own eyes and silently say, *"I am awareness, not this body, not this mind."* Notice thoughts and emotions arising, but let them pass like clouds. Over time, this can help reinforce the recognition of the Self beyond the physical form.

3. Eye Gazing with Laughter

After a minute or two of silent gazing with a partner, allow yourselves to smile, then laugh naturally. The laughter releases tension and softens the ego, making the awareness of the Self easier to access and increases gamma brain waves. This variation is particularly fun and reminds us that Self Realization doesn't always have to be serious.

4. Peripheral Awareness Eye Gazing

While gazing into your partner's eyes or your reflection, try to remain aware of the space around the eyes—the whole face, the shoulders, and even the room—without shifting your gaze. This expands awareness and highlights the sense that the Self is larger than the immediate focus of attention.

5. Timed "Blink Breaks"

Set a timer for 3-5 minutes. Challenge yourself to maintain steady eye contact, allowing blinks naturally. Each blink is a reminder that the mind will wander, but awareness can always return to the present. This variation is subtle, playful, and excellent for cultivating patience.

These exercises are fun but also subtly deepen your meditation practice. They bridge mindfulness, presence, and the recognition of the Self in a tangible, engaging way.

30- ILLEISM

Another powerful technique to aid Self Realization is Illeism, the practice of referring to oneself in the third person. This may sound unusual at first, yet it serves as a subtle yet profound tool for separating the ego from the true Self. In the yogic tradition, particularly within Jnana Yoga—the path of knowledge and self-inquiry—speaking in the third person is encouraged as a means of cultivating detachment from the self-image and the constant chatter of the mind.

By referring to oneself in the third person or as "he," "she," or "they," one begins to observe thoughts, emotions, and actions as phenomena occurring within awareness rather than as defining the Self. Over time, this practice strengthens the recognition that the ego is not the ultimate identity. When combined with other techniques—such as self-inquiry, meditation, or mindfulness—Illeism can accelerate the process of Realizing the Self.

Interestingly, as one progresses on this path, the habit of speaking in the third person may naturally arise. It becomes a reflection of detachment from the ego and alignment with the true Self. Many enlightened beings have employed this practice, including Ma Anandamayi, Mata Amritanandamayi, Swami Ramdas, Rama Tirtha, Sai Baba, Jesus, and even the Buddha, suggesting that Illeism is not merely a linguistic quirk, but a doorway to deeper awareness.

31- LISTENING AND READING ANCIENT WISDOM

As an alternative to silence, one can gain profound insight and wisdom on Self Realization by listening to great teachers and studying their teachings. For some, this alone can even trigger an enlightenment experience. Many people "unlearn" or "ununderstand" more effectively through attentive listening and study.

There is an abundance of exceptional books, talks, and podcasts devoted to Self Realization. Notable Self-Realized teachers include Papaji, Robert Adams, Ramana Maharshi, and Nisargadatta Maharaj, while classical texts such as the *Ribhu Gita*, *Ashtavakra Gita*, *Drig-Drishya Viveka*, and the *Ten Principal Upanishads* remain invaluable sources of wisdom.

One of the finest modern resources I have encountered is the podcast *Wisdom of the Masters* by Samaneri Jayasara. Her podcast and YouTube channel offer extensive recitations and commentaries on these timeless teachings, providing a rich and accessible path for study, reflection, and inner absorption.

At first, listening or reading these ancient teachings may not make much sense. Yet as one progresses and the ego gradually dissolves, allowing the Self to reveal itself more fully, the teachings begin to resonate more and more. Words in these texts often carry subtle, layered meanings. For instance, in Gnostic teachings, terms like "undivided" can signify the Self, non-duality, or the Divine Spark, while "Light" may point to the Self itself. It is as if these writings were intentionally composed in a riddle-like fashion, meant to reveal their truths fully only to those who have glimpsed the Self.

Some texts are so potent that they can spark spontaneous Self Realization. The Ribhu Gita is particularly noted for this. Even reading a single chapter can be transformative. Ramana Maharshi himself was struck by the Ribhu Gita, recognizing in it the exact state he was experiencing. He particularly revered chapter 26, believing that even its recitation alone could induce spontaneous Self Realization.

In today's world, one doesn't need to rely solely on physical books. Audio recordings, podcasts, and YouTube channels allow us to immerse ourselves in these teachings anywhere, anytime—during walks, commutes, or quiet moments at home. Listening repeatedly can subtly plant seeds of understanding, and over time, these seeds may sprout into direct insight or glimpses of the Self. The combination of modern technology and timeless teachings offers a practical way to integrate Self Realization into daily life, bridging ancient wisdom with contemporary living.

32- SIDEREAL TIME AND REMOTE VIEWING

According to some studies, psychic abilities—particularly in remote viewing—have been reported to increase by up to 400% when practiced at a specific time of day: 12:00 Local Sidereal Time (LST), a window that lasts for several hours (Jana, 2021). This timeframe corresponds to the center of the galaxy passing directly overhead. If these findings hold any truth, it raises an interesting possibility: certain cosmic alignments might subtly amplify inner practices, potentially making it easier to enter stillness or deepen Self Realization.

Traditionally, early morning meditation has been highly recommended, and this coincides with the sacred period known as *Brahma Muhurta*—roughly from 3:30 a.m. to 5:30 a.m., just before sunrise. This is considered an especially auspicious time for spiritual practices like meditation and yoga, as it is believed to carry heightened spiritual energy and stillness, with minimal distractions from human activity.

Waking during this period is thought to cultivate mental clarity, calmness, and a mind naturally poised for deep concentration and personal introspection. Interestingly, this aligns closely with the timing suggested by sidereal research, suggesting that certain early morning hours may be particularly supportive for spiritual and contemplative practices.

As for remote viewing itself, it can be enjoyable, and it may even help cultivate stillness if approached correctly. However, I wouldn't place too much importance on it. Visionary experiences— whether accessed through remote viewing, dreams, or altered states—unfold within the astral realm. This realm is notoriously slippery, filled with symbolic imagery, projections, trickster energies, and deceptive forms. It is the same realm we traverse in dreams: a landscape of illusion, echo, and psychological mirroring. Nothing within it is ultimately reliable.

Entities or visions may appear as loved ones or spiritual guides, but these forms often arise to provoke emotional reactions or attachments. This can easily become a trap, pulling attention outward into imagination rather than inward toward truth.

The essential point is this: do not be distracted by phenomena—outer or inner, physical or astral. Whatever arises, let it go. Visionary experiences, psychic impressions, and altered states may be interesting, but they are not the goal. Simply **Realize the Self**. Nothing else is needed.

33- SUPPLEMENTS TO ENHANCE SELF REALIZATION

There are several supplements that may help support mental stillness and inner calm. For example, L-theanine is known to promote alpha brain wave activity, which fosters relaxed alertness and a tranquil mind. Many supplements that slow brain waves work primarily by calming the body, which in turn helps quiet the mind— a subtle aid on the path to Self Realization.

Some accounts suggest that magnesium and glycine can assist in releasing stored emotions, making them a helpful complement to practices like the forgiveness process and letting go. While these supplements can support the journey inward, it is important to remember that they are tools, not substitutes for meditation, self-inquiry, or other consciousness practices. As always, consult your healthcare provider and conduct your own research before adding any supplement to your routine.

Here's a chart on some of the supplements to support different brain wave states. This is by no means complete:

Alpha (8–12 Hz) – Supplements such as L-Theanine and GABA can promote relaxed alertness, calm focus, and creative insight. To support Self-Realization, practice meditation or Mind Observation. Meditation allows you to observe thoughts without attachment, helping you notice the Self.

Theta (4–8 Hz) – Supplements like magnesium and glycine may encourage deep relaxation, intuition, emotional release, and access to the subconscious. Combining these supplements with meditation or self-inquiry can help dissolve emotional blocks and deepen awareness.

Delta (0.5–4 Hz) – Small doses of melatonin, valerian root, or ashwagandha support restorative sleep, cellular rejuvenation, and profound calm. Using delta-enhancing practices during sleep or naps can enhance subtle awareness; pairing them with morning mindfulness helps you notice residual stillness.

Gamma (30–100 Hz) – Omega-3s (EPA/DHA), B vitamins, and GABA support cognitive processing, memory, focus, and neural plasticity. Using gamma-enhancing supplements and practices can enhance meditation retention and integration of Self-Realization insights.

Stress-Balancing / Adaptogens – Herbs such as rhodiola and holy basil help reduce the stress response and support emotional stability. Taking them regularly can maintain a calm nervous system, allowing meditative practices to deepen.

Key Notes:

- **Supplements are supportive tools, not substitutes for practices**

- **Slowing brain waves supports mental stillness, which is the gateway to Realizing the Self.**

- **Combining supplements with practices like meditation, self-inquiry, compassion cultivation, forgiveness exercises can aid in the biochemicals needed to support different states of consciousness.**

34- TIMELESSNESS

Any activity can be a form of meditation. When one is fully grounded in the present moment, that is the connection to the true Self. The mind and ego habitually jump to the past or the future, creating suffering, but in the NOW there is no suffering—only peace, joy, equanimity, and all the qualities of the Self. In *The Power of Now*, Eckhart Tolle emphasizes the transformative power of being fully present. Any activity, when approached with complete awareness, can become a meditation.

As the saying goes: Before enlightenment, chop wood, carry water. After enlightenment, chop wood, carry water. The actions remain the same, but the mental state is transformed. Before Self Realization, one's mind may be preoccupied with thoughts of past or future; after Realization, one is fully immersed in the activity itself. Sweeping the floor, washing dishes, ironing clothes, or doing laundry—all mundane actions—become infused with presence, joy, and peace. That is the Self.

Happiness, which is our true Self, arises from the present moment. The Self is timeless. Time, in contrast, is a construct of the mind and ego, a product of duality and worldly experience, often rooted in fear. How often have we rushed through life, thinking of aging, deadlines, or running out of time? These mental constructs trigger subtle fear responses in the body. It is beneficial, as much as possible, to step outside of time. Plan practical matters with care, but avoid letting time dominate your awareness.

Ultimately, the Self transcends all temporal concepts. There is no past, present, or future with the Self. I use the term 'NOW' merely for conceptual purposes. In reality, the Self is eternal, beyond all manifestations of time. The Self is timeless, infinite, and unbounded—the Self is all. You are THAT!

35- HEART BRAIN COHERENCE

Probably one of the most effective techniques for cultivating heightened awareness and accelerating Self Realization comes from the HeartMath Institute: creating heart-brain coherence. This practice is particularly powerful because it naturally generates large amounts of gamma brain waves, which are strongly associated with heightened states of consciousness, bliss, and the deepening of Self Realization. Gamma waves, when activated with compassion, can profoundly shift one's perception and experience of the world.

According to the HeartMath Institute, the basic steps for creating heart-brain coherence are as follows:

1. Focus on the Heart – Bring your attention to the area of your heart, creating a sense of awareness and presence there.

2. Slow the Breath – Inhale deeply for about five seconds, then exhale for five seconds, maintaining a steady, rhythmic pattern.

3. Activate Positive Emotions – While maintaining focus on the heart and breath, evoke feelings using any of four guiding words: care, compassion, appreciation, or gratitude.

Practicing this simple technique for just a few minutes can generate significant heart-brain coherence and stimulate gamma brain wave activity, fostering deep emotional balance, clarity, and an expanded sense of connection to the Self and all beings. Over time, regular practice can enhance one's capacity for compassion, inner peace, and ultimately accelerate progress on the path of Self Realization.

36- FLOW STATE

Flow, a term popularized by psychologist Mihaly Csikszentmihalyi, is a mental state in which a person becomes fully immersed in an activity, experiencing heightened focus, effortless performance, and a profound loss of self-consciousness. Time seems to distort—minutes can feel like seconds—and actions arise spontaneously, without deliberation. Athletes, musicians, programmers, and artists often report entering this state during moments of peak performance.

From the perspective of Self Realization, flow is much more than optimal performance—it is a glimpse of the true nature of consciousness. In flow, the boundaries of the ego dissolve, and one experiences the effortless, timeless awareness that is the Self. Just as in deep meditation or contemplative practices, the sense of "I" fades, leaving only pure presence and action arising from that presence. In this way, the flow state can be seen as a practical, lived experience of Self Realization, where the mind is quiet, the heart is open, and one is aligned with the innate intelligence of being, the Self. Self Realization is basically a permanent flow state with similar brain waves and neurochemicals involved.

Flow state is a mental state of deep absorption and optimal performance, often described as "being in the zone." Scientifically, it is associated with specific patterns of brain wave activity. When entering flow, alpha waves (8–12 Hz) increase, promoting relaxed focus and a quieting of the analytical mind. Theta waves (4–8 Hz) can also rise, supporting creativity, intuition, and internal visualization. In addition, gamma waves (30–100 Hz) often show heightened activity, reflecting high-level information processing, integration of different brain regions, and peak cognitive performance. In essence, the mind becomes highly focused yet relaxed, allowing effortless attention to the task at hand.

During flow, the prefrontal cortex—responsible for self-monitoring, judgment, and time awareness—temporarily quiets in a phenomenon called transient hypofrontality. This explains why people in flow often lose track of time and experience diminished self-consciousness. Beta waves (12–30 Hz), associated with alertness and active thinking, may still be present but are balanced by alpha, theta, and gamma activity, preventing overthinking while enhancing problem-solving, pattern recognition, and sensory-motor integration.

Neurochemically, flow is supported by a cocktail of dopamine, norepinephrine, endorphins, anandamide, and serotonin. These chemicals enhance focus, creativity, pleasure, and intrinsic motivation. The addition of gamma activity may also relate to the sense of unity and effortless awareness often described in peak experiences, linking scientific understanding to what many spiritual traditions associate with higher states of consciousness or glimpses of the Self.

37- LAUGHTER

Certain Buddhist monks, particularly those practicing advanced meditation techniques such as Tummo or Tonglen, are known for their spontaneous laughter during deep states of meditation. This laughter is not merely an emotional response; it reflects a profound neurophysiological state associated with heightened awareness and joy.

A study by Richard Davidson and colleagues in the early 2000s found that long-term meditation practitioners had sustained high-amplitude gamma oscillations and enhanced phase synchrony across different regions of the brain. These patterns correlate with heightened states of compassion, bliss, and self-transcendence. The spontaneous laughter observed in monks can be seen as an outward manifestation of this inner coherence and neural synchronization.

The laughter itself may also act as a biofeedback mechanism, reinforcing gamma activity through increased positive affect and physiological arousal. In this way, the mind-body feedback loop amplifies states of joy, equanimity, and, ultimately, experiences that resemble Self Realization—a state of persistent clarity, presence, and non-dual awareness.

In short, laughter in advanced meditators is more than playfulness; it is a neural signature of profound inner coherence. Gamma waves support integration of mind and body, help sustain attention and bliss, and reflect the brain's ability to maintain a high-level state of unified consciousness—one of the hallmarks of Self Realization.

CESSATION OF ALL TECHNIQUES

Ultimately, all techniques will fade away once one abides in the Self. Every practice, every method, is merely a bridge, a raft, a ladder to guide one across the river of ignorance to the shore of realization. Once the Self is Realized, the bridge is no longer needed and can be left behind. Even the desire to Realize the Self must exist in order for realization to ensue—a seeming paradox, yet a profound truth. Desire, when rightly directed, serves as the initial spark, the motivating flame, but in the fullness of Self Realization, all desire dissolves.

In the Self, there is no duality: no good or bad, no light or dark, no high or low, no this or that—there is only the eternal, boundless awareness that is non-dual. The mind, by its very nature, operates in dualistic terms. Every thought, every word, every act of categorization reinforces separation and illusion, pulling one away from the ultimate truth. Realization is the direct recognition that all distinctions are provisional, that the Self alone is timeless, whole, and undivided.

Techniques are like training wheels: essential at first, but unnecessary once balance is attained. When the mind falls silent, the heart opens, and the Self reveals itself—not as an object to be grasped, but as the very ground of being itself. There is nothing to achieve, nothing to gain, and nothing to lose; there is only the Self, perfectly complete, here and now. You are THAT!

Astavakra Gita 18.83 (Chinmayananda, 2016)
The sage neither rejects the world
nor desires Self.
He is free of joy and sorrow.
He does not live
and cannot die.

HOW TO DESIGN YOUR OWN MYSTICAL EXPERIENCE EXPERIMENT

Step 1: Eliminate external accelerators of the mind.

Stop everything that artificially speeds up beta brain waves: caffeine, nicotine, alcohol, processed sugar, chocolate, cheap dopamine hits, and even pungent foods like onions or garlic if they affect your energy. The goal is to quiet the body and mind, creating a fertile ground for subtle awareness to arise. Think of this as silencing external noise to hear the inner stillness. Ideally it would be good to omit any sexual activity for a minimum of a week or even a month or as long as possible to build up energy and strengthen brain waves to help facilitate a transcendental experience.

Step 2: Establish a foundation of meditation.

Learn the basics: focused attention, mantra repetition, or breath awareness. Begin cultivating the ability to observe your thoughts without becoming entangled. This is your preparatory training—like stretching before a long journey into uncharted terrain.

Step 3: Enhance with sensory isolation (optional).

If available, use a floatation tank. This is like meditation amplified—a sensory deprivation environment that accelerates mental stillness, heightening awareness of the subtle layers of consciousness.

Step 4: Clean up your internal environment.

Refine your diet and consider fasting or intermittent fasting to remove processed foods and toxins. A lighter, cleaner body allows the mind to settle more naturally, increasing receptivity to deeper states of awareness. The Upanishads specifically mention the body is made from food which gives real meaning to the term, "you are what you eat."

Step 5: Design a retreat-like window.

If possible, dedicate a weekend to this experiment. Sleep minimally—around four hours—then awaken and begin your meditation. Slow your breathing, lengthen the spaces between breaths, and focus on the seat of the Self at the heart. Use self-inquiry periodically: question, *"Who am I?"* or *"What is aware of this thought?"* Push past boredom—the ego's subtle signal to quit.

With sustained attention, transcendental experiences may arise: vivid colors, bright lights, angelic presences, out-of-body sensations, and feelings of profound love, joy, or bliss. Do not cling to these phenomena; they are temporary waves on the surface of consciousness. Instead, remain anchored as the witness—the observer that never comes or goes, the Self.

Step 6: Find a comfortable but alert posture.

Half-lying down often works well—neither fully horizontal nor rigidly upright. Fatigue will naturally arise, but the key is to maintain awareness while the body relaxes. Over time, the observer may remain while the body drifts between wakefulness and sleep, offering glimpses into the Self.

Step 7: Practice equanimity toward experiences.

Excitement will bubble up as mystical states arise; this is natural. Remember: these are only experiences. The true goal is that which is beyond all experiences—the eternal, unchanging Self. Focus on being the witness, the awareness in which all phenomena appear and disappear. This is the ultimate *goalless goal*: to abide in the Self without grasping, without effort, without a desire for attainment.

Maintain a "focusless focus," a gentle, undistracted presence and always remember: YOU ARE THAT!

"You fast, chant, kneel and wander but without turning your gaze inward, you're just decorating your prison."-Gorakhnath

Chapter 18

THE FINISH LINE

It was 2008, and there I was, nervously toeing the line at my first ultra marathon. The course? A simple two-loop out-and-back totaling 52 miles. Easy to conceptualize, brutal to execute. Little did I know this race would later become one of the most unexpectedly important experiences toward understanding the mystery of Self Realization.

From the moment the race started, I was motivated by a tiny, irrational voice whispering in the back of my skull: *"If you walk even one step, the whole thing doesn't count."* And like an obedient lunatic, I listened. For nearly nine hours I trudged, scrambled, coasted, and suffered my way through mountain trails, knocking out the miles one dogged step at a time.

Downhill sections were my moment of glory. I'd come flying down the slopes at sub–5-minute-mile pace, arms flailing like a cartoon character trying to stay upright, desperately chasing the two runners ahead of me. No matter how hard I pushed, they stayed maddeningly out of reach. *How on earth are they going this fast? Are they on roller skates? Do they have some kind of pact with the mountain gods?* I still don't know.

Then came *the bonk*.

If you've never bonked, imagine your blood sugar dropping so fast your brain turns into foggy oatmeal while your muscles behave like they just received a cease-and-desist letter. I limped into the next aid station and inhaled whatever was on the table—soda, bananas, electrolytes, possibly the tablecloth. My pace slowed to a crawl, but I'd been here before. After a few marathons, you learn the rhythm: give your body 15 minutes, let it digest, and eventually the lights come back on.

And they did. Off I went again.

The rest of the race unfolded like a half-remembered dream. When you're running hard, blood gets diverted to your muscles instead of your brain, and the whole thing becomes strangely surreal—like watching your life from somewhere slightly outside your body.

But the final miles... those were the true test. My muscles seized. Every hill felt like it had a personal vendetta against me. I was hurting, cramping, shuffling forward with the determination of a stubborn mule—but still, I refused to walk.

Then something unexpected happened: the pain vanished. My mind went silent. I slipped into a state of pure, effortless nothingness—no mind, no suffering, just awareness moving forward. It was oddly beautiful. It was the Self.

And then, finally, the finish line appeared.

I sprinted—or something vaguely resembling a sprint—across the line to the thunderous roaring applause of... two people. Slowly clapping. Politely. As though I'd just completed a decent middle-school talent show act. Not exactly the dramatic triumph I had envisioned.

Ultramarathons—anything beyond the standard 26.2 miles—are a completely different universe from traditional road races. They're mellow, almost meditative events with no roaring crowds, no deafening music, and absolutely zero fanfare. What they *do* have, however, are aid stations every few miles stocked like miniature buffets: chips, fruit, cookies, soda, soup—you name it. It's basically an endurance event powered by snacks.

After I crossed the finish line, I hobbled forward like a newborn giraffe. My legs were fried. My brain was trying to process what I'd just put it through. *What just happened? Am I going to be able to drive? Am I going to collapse? Should someone call an ambulance—or at least a chiropractor?* Thankfully, none of those scenarios came to pass. I managed to shuffle my way into the car and drive to meet some friends who were racing a triathlon the next day.

At dinner, something struck me. I felt laser-focused—calm, clear, and strangely meditative. There was a stillness in me that wasn't just physical exhaustion; it was a kind of inner quiet I had never quite touched before. I mentioned it to someone at the table, but at the time I had no vocabulary to describe it. I didn't yet have the language of awareness, the understanding of silence, or the recognition of what was actually happening beneath the surface.

Now, looking back, I recognize that sensation with absolute clarity: it was the Self.

Not the mind. Not the body coming down from 52 miles of effort. Not the ego feeling proud or broken or anything at all. It was the pure, steady presence beneath all of that—the silent witness untouched by fatigue or emotion. For a brief moment, the mind was too exhausted to chatter, the body too tired to demand attention, and in that rare crack in the inner noise, the Self shone through effortlessly.

It was a glimpse of what the ancient sages describe: the peaceful awareness that remains when thoughts dissolve, the infinite stillness that has no opposite, the presence that is always here but rarely noticed. In that post-race calm, I wasn't trying to meditate, I wasn't doing anything at all—and that was precisely why the Self could be felt so clearly. The ego had stepped aside for just long enough for the real "I" to appear.

I have a friend who has run multiple 100-mile races—and even beyond—and he carries a unique aura. There's something about him: a stillness, a presence, a subtle meditative glow in his face. When you're around him, you can almost feel a unique brain wave signature radiating off him. He may very well have waking delta, theta, gamma or some other unusual neural state.

And speaking of extraordinary endurance and altered states, this brings us perfectly to one of the most astonishing running traditions in the world: the legendary marathon monks of Japan!

MARATHON MONKS OF HIEI

Not many people have heard of the Marathon Monks of Mount Hiei. In 2017, Dave Ganci wrote a remarkable article for *Trail*

Runner Magazine about these extraordinary ascetics who live near Kyoto, Japan, in the rugged mountains of Hiei. Within this ancient Tendai monastery, monks undertake an intense spiritual practice in which running becomes a vehicle for transformation.

Most monks complete the 100-day kaihogyo, covering roughly 19 miles a day—running and fast-walking through mountain trails regardless of weather. This 100-day feat is actually a prerequisite for becoming an abbot. But some choose to go far beyond this, taking on the legendary 1,000-day challenge, one of the most demanding endurance practices on Earth. Spread over seven years, the journey covers roughly 24,000 miles.

In the early years, they complete 100 days, then 200, gradually increasing their mileage. By the sixth year, the daily distance rises to 34 miles. During the seventh and final year, the first 100 days require 52 miles a day—the same distance I ran once, in a single race, and these monks do it every single day for 100 days! The final 100 days bring the mileage down to 18 miles per day, completing the immense pilgrimage.

At the end of this thousand-day odyssey, the monks undergo a series of ritual austerities: prolonged fasting, fire ceremonies in which they chant Fudo Myo-o's mantra 100,000 times, and finally, nine days in complete isolation with **no food, no water, and no sleep**. They are watched constantly to ensure they do not accidentally slip into unconsciousness.

These extreme practices are designed to bring the monk as close as possible to the threshold between life and death, stripping away the ego through sheer physical, mental, and spiritual intensity. Yet from a scientific perspective, the methods are fascinating:

- The fire ceremony entrains the brain at roughly 10 Hz, inducing a deep alpha state.

- Severe sleep deprivation pushes the brain into slow oscillations such as theta and delta.

- Prolonged fasting lowers metabolic activity and slows cortical rhythms.

- Relentless daily exertion heavily fatigues the body and quiets the mind, naturally increasing slower brain wave states.

- Cultivation of compassion and mantra chanting results in massive amounts of gamma brain waves.

It is, without question, an extreme path—one very few could or should attempt—but scientifically and spiritually, it is astonishingly effective. Through exhaustion, devotion, austerity, and unwavering discipline, the Marathon Monks carve a direct path to ego dissolution and, ultimately, glimpses of Self Realization.

PLATOS CAVE

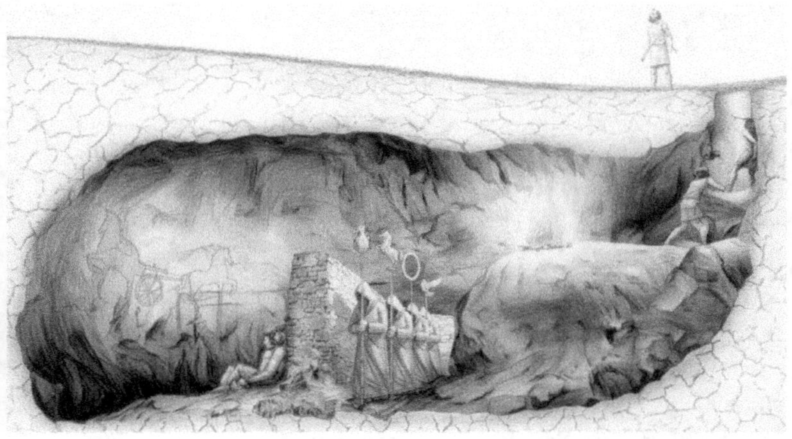

We'd be remiss if we didn't discuss Plato's Cave, which may very well serve as a profound metaphor for Self Realization. Across countless Upanishads, there is mention of the "cave of the heart," the secret chamber where Brahman—or the Self—resides. Around

380 BCE, the Greek philosopher Plato wrote *The Republic*, and in its seventh book, he presents the famous Allegory of the Cave.

In this story, prisoners are chained to a wall inside a cave, facing away from the opening. Behind them burns a fire, casting shadows on the wall before them. These shadows are all the prisoners have ever seen, so they take them as reality. One day, a prisoner breaks free and emerges into the light outside. At first, the brightness overwhelms him, and his eyes struggle to adjust, but eventually, he perceives the full richness of reality. Excited, he rushes back to tell his fellow prisoners, only to be met with disbelief. They think he has gone mad, that the sunlight has harmed him, and they conclude that leaving the cave is dangerous. Socrates, the narrator, even suggests that the prisoners would kill anyone attempting to escape.

The shadows the prisoners see are analogous to the world we perceive through our five senses—the filtered, incomplete reality of the egoic self. Just as the prisoners mistake shadows for the entirety of existence, most people mistake their thoughts, emotions, and bodies for the Self. The Divine Spark, the fire hidden within, remains unseen unless we remove the chains—the attachments, illusions, and subconscious programs—that bind us.

This allegory also reveals a harsh truth: the masses will defend their illusions fiercely. People cling to their delusions of the ego self, much like the prisoners of Plato's cave, because confronting the truth threatens the very foundation of their reality. Modern society reinforces these chains, conditioning us to accept the shadows as real, to remain trapped in a limited, comatose state of misidentification. Breaking free requires courage and defiance— walking against societal norms, questioning inherited beliefs, and daring to leave the cave. Only then can one discover the Self.

Plato's story is brilliantly layered, hiding the wisdom of Self Realization in plain sight. Plato himself studied in the mystery schools of Egypt and may have had connections to India's spiritual traditions, such as Taxila, or at least interacted with travelers from the East. This cross-cultural exposure could explain the parallels between his allegory and the Upanishadic teachings on the Self.

Historically, knowledge of the Self was carefully guarded. Self Realization was rarely taught to the masses, perhaps for good reason. Those who sought to spread this knowledge openly were often met with persecution. The Cathars, for instance, were brutally killed by the Catholic Church during the Crusades and the Inquisition for teaching Gnosis, the direct knowledge of the Self. Plato's cave reminds us why the path to Self Realization has always required courage, discernment, and the willingness to step beyond the illusions of society.

THE CYCLE OF COMPLETION

Ever since I was a child, I can remember this profound feeling of "I Am-ness", a pure sense of awareness. At the time, I didn't know what it was, but now I understand. That feeling of being, of simply existing as awareness, has been with me for as long as I can remember.

Around sixth grade, I began to notice that this innate sense of "I Am" started to shrink. Negative emotions—fear, sadness, self-doubt—began to swell, and with them, the bars of a subtle prison formed around my heart center. A growth spurt in seventh grade left me a little heavier with a larger nose, and the teasing from other kids only intensified these emotions, deepening the mental and emotional patterns that would linger for years.

As the negative emotions grew, so did the compulsive mental programs in my mind. I would replay harsh words, criticisms, and fears over and over, feeding the cycle of negativity. Sometimes my stomach hurt so badly that it made strange noises in class, leaving me embarrassed and isolated. Daily life was a constant amplification of these mental programs—from the taunts of peers to the tense rides to school with my mom. Those were some of the most challenging years of my life.

By ninth or tenth grade, I experienced another growth spurt. My body aligned more comfortably with my proportions; I grew taller, thinner, and my nose seemed in harmony with the rest of me. Even then, life threw little tests—like the time a classmate commented on my butt during push-ups—but a quick-thinking friend intervened and asked him why he was staring at my butt and all I can say is that my friend literally saved my butt.

It would take many more years, and countless ups and downs, before I could truly recognize these mental programs for what they are: not real. As most, my life had been an oscillation between happiness and sadness, good and bad—all driven by the restless machinery of the mind, the ego. Emotional highs and lows, perpetuated by these background mental patterns, kept me trapped in a rollercoaster of experience. It wasn't until I had enough of the mind's insanity and chaos that I finally decided to leave the cave.

My first profound Samadhi came during a three-hour meditation session. Sitting in complete stillness, I was flooded with light, filled with infinite love, and for a fleeting moment, I touched the Divine Spark—the Self. It would be years before I revisited this state again, but now, that awareness remains ever-present. It feels like returning to the pure, unconditioned awareness of childhood, the same sense of "I Am-ness" that had faded in sixth grade.

Perhaps this is what Jesus meant in Matthew 18:3 when he said: *"Truly I tell you, unless you change and become like little children, you will never enter the kingdom of heaven."* The kingdom of heaven, the Self, is nothing other than the pure awareness we are born with—the eternal witness waiting to be remembered. The Self.

Ashtavakra Gita 16:8 and 18:7 (Chinmayananda, 2016):
16:8 Indulgence creates attachment.
Aversion creates abstinence.
Like a **child**, the sage is free of both
and thus lives on as a **child**.

18.7 Seeing everything is imagination,
knowing the Self as timelessly free, the
sage lives as a **child**.

"Be like a child who never grows up: the only reason why the child-like state does not last is "desire". -Ma Anandamayi

Many of us can recall moments of pure awareness in childhood—carefree, spontaneous, and radiating love, joy, and curiosity. Yet at some point, something shifts: the ego takes shape, its boundaries expand, and our awareness of the Self gradually recedes. Realizing the Self is, in essence, a process of gently peeling back these layers of the ego—the false mind—to return to that innate state we once knew: a state of love, joy, and unfiltered presence.

This idea of being like a child also means seeing each day and each moment as entirely new, unshaped by past conditioning or mental programs. One is free, like a child, from the bondage of thought. A child does not dwell on the past or worry about the future; they exist fully in the present moment, immersed in its essence. In doing so, they are living as the eternal Self—timeless, formless, and fully alive in the now. You are THAT!

WALKING OUT OF THE GATE

While I was in junior high, there came a day when I had simply had enough of the bullying and the madness around me. One morning, I noticed the front gate of the school ajar, and a thought flickered in my mind: *What would happen if I just walked out?* Would I get in trouble? Would someone stop me? For days I watched it, unsure, hesitant—but then, finally, I decided to act. I stepped through that gate and began the two-mile walk home.

At the time, my self-esteem was fragile, my sense of self-worth buried beneath looping cycles of negative thoughts. I wasn't sure I would make it without being stopped by a teacher or authority figure—but I walked anyway. Half-expecting to be called back, questioned, or punished, I moved steadily along the edge of the school grounds. Some students glanced my way but said nothing. No authority intervened. I simply walked—one step, then another, until I reached the freedom of the streets, and eventually my home.

With every step, a weight lifted. The anxiety loosened, the nervousness dissolved, and a sense of liberation blossomed within me. That single act of courage—walking out of the gate—was a small yet profound taste of what it means to Realize the Self. To awaken, one must step against the current of the world, break free from the confines of societal expectations, just as in Plato's allegory of the cave.

The world can appear as a school, a prison, or a cage, depending on how you perceive it. To escape or graduate, you need only the courage to step beyond the gates. And make no mistake— every person reading this has that courage within them. Every person carries the Divine Spark, the true Self, and in that Self is infinite courage, infinite joy, infinite love—boundless and unending.

Through the realization of the Self, one discovers that there was never a prison or school at all. Freedom was never something to be attained; it has always been your natural state. The world is no longer a cage, and the Self has always been home. It is time to go home, to return to that infinite center. Realize the Self. Be free. Be joyous. You are THAT!

John 8:32: Then you will know the truth, and the truth will set you FREE.

A WORD OF CAUTION

The further one travels along the path, the more subtle and formidable the pitfalls become. It may often feel as though there are forces—inner, outer, or simply the inertia of the unconscious mind—that resist ones awakening. This world is steeped in distraction, deception, and misdirection, all of which obscure our true nature as the Self. Within each of us lies a power so profound that, once awakened, it eclipses every other force. And whatever keeps us entangled in ignorance—call it conditioning, ego, habit, or inertia—will do everything in its power to prevent that awakening.

If you accomplish nothing else in this life, **REALIZE THE SELF.**

As the light of awareness grows brighter, there may come moments when life seems to push back. Emotional triggers may arise unexpectedly: the loss of a pet, conflict within a family, or random disturbances from strangers that seem timed to pull you back into identification with fear, anger, or sorrow. It is as if the mind, functioning as an antenna, is highly sensitive to subtle frequencies and impressions. Thoughts and emotions may arise that feel foreign—as though they are not generated by your deepest Self but by old patterns, unconscious conditioning, or forces that feed on reactivity.

Whether these influences are psychological, energetic, or symbolic, the effect is the same: they attempt to draw you back into identification with the mind, to spark attachment, to reignite the old emotional circuitry. In future writings, I will explore this energy-extraction dynamic in much greater detail; it is a fascinating and, at times, unsettling topic which we had to avoid for the most part in this writing.

For now, this first book is simply a guide—to set your feet upon the pathless path of Self Realization. Of all pursuits, this is the most important one anybody can undertake. Avoid the traps, the diversions, the seductive detours. Be unwavering in your resolve to Realize the Self.

Do not fall for the belief that awakening must take lifetimes. That idea alone is enough to delay awakening indefinitely. The only obstruction to the Self is the mind itself. The Self is already Realized, already complete, already whole; it is only veiled by thought, by conditioning, by habitual identification. No amount of thinking can uncover the Self, for thought is the very cloud that obscures it. Only in the silence beneath thought—in stillness, in emptiness—does the Self reveal itself. Realize That, and be free!

EXTRA:

Upanishad References to a Cave:

Svetasvatara Upanishad 3:11 & 3:20 (Radhakrishan, 2024)
3:11 He who is in the faces, heads and necks of all, who dwells in the **cave** (of the heart) of all beings, who is all-pervading, He is Lord and therefore the omnipresent Siva (the Self).

3:20 Subtler than the subtle, greater than the great is the Self that is set in the **cave** of the (heart) of the creature. One beholds Him as being actionless and becomes freed from sorrow, when through the grace of the Creator he sees the Lord and His majesty.

Mundaka Upanishad 2:1:10 & 3:1:7 (Radhakrishan, 2024)
2:1:10 The person himself is all this, austerity and Brahma beyond death. He who knows that which is set in the **secret place** (of the heart), he, here on earth, O beloved, cuts asunder the knot of ignorance.

3:1:7 Vast, divine, of the unthinkable form, subtler than the subtle. It shines forth, farther than the far, yet here near the hand, set down in the secret place (of the heart) (as such) even here it is seen by the intelligent.

Katha Upanishad 1:2:12 and 1:3:1 (Radhakrishan, 2024)
1:2:12 Realizing through self-contemplation that primal God, difficult to be seen, deeply hidden, set in the **cave** (of the heart), dwelling in the deep, the wise man leaves behind both joy and sorrow.

1:3:1 There are two selves that drink the fruit of Karma in the world of good deeds. Both are lodged in the **secret place** (of the heart), the chief seat of the Supreme....

Upanishad References to Light:

Prasna Upanishad 4:6 (Radhakrishan, 2024)
4:6 When he is overcome with light, then in this state, the god (mind)
sees no dreams. Then here in his body arises the happiness.

Mundaka Upanishad 2:2:10-11 (Radhakrishan, 2024)
2:2:10 In the highest golden sheath is Brahman without stain,
without parts; Pure is it, the light of lights. That is what the knowers of
Self know.

2:2:11 The sun shines not there, nor the moon and stars, these
lightnings shine not, where then could this fire be? Every thing
shines only after that shining light. His shining illumines all this
world.

Svetasvatara Upanishad 5:8-9 & 6:14 (Radhakrishan, 2024)
5:8 He is the measure of a thumb, of appearance like the sun,
endowed with thought and self-sense, but with only the qualities of
understanding and the Self he seems to be of the size of a point of a
goad.

5:9 This living Self is to be known as part of the hundredth part of
the point of a hair a hundredfold, yet it is capable of infinity.

6:14 The sun does not shine there nor the moon and the stars, nor
these lightings, much less this fire. After Him, when He shines,
everything shines, by His light and all is illumined.

Bible References to Light:

He reveals deep and hidden things;
he knows what lies in darkness, and
light dwells with him.
Daniel 2:22

This is the message we have heard from him and declare to you:
God is light; in him there is no darkness at all.
1 John 1:5

For you were once darkness, but now you are light in the Lord. Live as
children of light.
Ephesians 5:8

I pray that the eyes of your heart may be enlightened in order that
you may know the hope to which he has called you, the riches of
his glorious inheritance in his holy people.
Ephesians 1:18

For the fruit of the light consists in all goodness, righteousness and
truth.
Ephesians 5:9

Gospel of Thomas
50. Jesus said, "If they say to you, 'Where have you come from?' say to
them, 'We have come from the light, from the place where the
light came into being by itself, established [itself], and appeared in
their image.'

Ribhu Gita (Ramamoorthy, 1995):
25:14 I, indeed, am the Self of all. I am ever loving. I am the Self of faith. I am without any modes.

25:24 There is only the Self. The Self, indeed is the enjoyment. The Self, indeed, is the satisfaction. Happiness is of the Self. The Self, indeed, is the Self of the Self, the Self alone. I, indeed, am the Supreme.

26:39 That in which, indeed the Self is ever satisfied, in which, indeed there is changeless bliss, and in which, indeed, there is changeless peach—ever abide as That itself.

26:42 That in which, indeed, you are eternally joyful, in which, indeed, happiness is attained, and in which there is no fear or sorrow—ever abide as That itself.

26:55 That in which, indeed, there is only joy, in which it, itself, is entirely bliss, and in which, indeed, it itself is supreme Bliss—ever abide as That itself.

26:63 That in which, indeed, oneself is Light, in which oneself, indeed, is the non-dual, and in which, indeed there is supreme Bliss—ever abide as That self.

May all beings be peaceful.
May all beings be happy.
May all beings be safe.
May all beings awaken to the light of their true nature.
May all beings be free.
-Metta Prayer

REFERENCES

Adams, R. (2012). Silence of the Heart. Yogi Impressions Books.

Adikari, A. M. G. C. P., Appukutty, M., & Kuan, G. (2020). Effects of Daily Probiotics Supplementation on Anxiety Induced Physiological Parameters among Competitive Football Players. Nutrients, 12(7), 1920. https://doi.org/10.3390/nu12071920

Alaerts, K., Taillieu, A., Prinsen, J., & Daniels, N. (2021). Tracking transient changes in the intrinsic neural frequency architecture: Oxytocin facilitates non-harmonic relationships between alpha and theta rhythms in the resting brain. Psychoneuroendocrinology, 133, 105397.https://doi.org/10.1016/j.psyneuen.2021.105397

American Psychiatric Association. (2022). Diagnostic and Statistical Manual of Mental Disorders (5th ed., Text Rev (DSM-5-TR)). American Psychiatric Association Publishing. https://doi.org/10.1176/appi.books.9780890425787

Anagnostou-Kalogera, A. S. (2012). Can You Stand The Truth? The Chronicle of Man's Imprisonment: Last Call! (A. M. Kalogeras, Trans.). Angeliki Anagnostou Kalogera.

Arianuova. (n.d.). India and Egypt. https://www.arianuova.org/en/india-and-egypt

Avena, N. M., Rada, P., & Hoebel, B. G. (2008). Evidence for sugar addiction: Behavioral and neurochemical effects of intermittent, excessive sugar intake. Neuroscience & Biobehavioral Reviews, 32(1), 20–39. https://doi.org/10.1016/j.neubiorev.2007.04.019

Avila, J., & Perry, G. (2021). A Multilevel View of the Development of Alzheimer's Disease. Neuroscience, 457, 283–293. https://doi.org/10.1016/j.neuroscience.2020.11.015

Barnstone, W., & Meyer, M. (Eds). (2009). The Gnostic Bible: Revised and Expanded Edition. Shambhala.

Berner, C., & Sosna, M. (2005). Counsciousness of Truth: A Manual for the Enlightenment Intensive. Mona Sosna.

Berridge, K. C., & Kringelbach, M. L. (2015). Pleasure Systems in the Brain. Neuron, 86(3), 646–664. https://doi.org/10.1016/j.neuron.2015.02.018

Besedovsky, L., Lange, T., & Born, J. (2012). Sleep and immune function. Pflügers Archiv - European Journal of Physiology, 463(1), 121–137. https://doi.org/10.1007/s00424-011-1044-0

Bhagavad Gita. (n.d.). Bhagavad Gita: Chapter 2, Verse 22. https://www.holy-bhagavadgita. org/chapter/2/verse/22/

Bible Gateway. (n.d.). Matthew 15:14—King James Version. https://www.biblegateway.com/passage/?search=Matthew%2015%3A14&version=KJV

Bible Gateway. (2011). John 8:31-32—New International Version. https://www.biblegateway.com/passage/?search=John%208%3A31-32&version=NIV

Billeci, L., Callara, A. L., Guiducci, L., Prosperi, M., Morales, M. A., Calderoni, S., Muratori, F., & Santocchi, E. (2023). A randomized controlled trial into the effects of probiotics on electroencephalography in preschoolers with autism. Autism, 27(1), 117–132. https://doi.org/10.1177/13623613221082710

BioSource Faculty. (2024, November 18). Drug Effects on the EEG. BioSource Software. https://www.biosourcesoftware.com/post/drug-effects-on-the-eeg

Bostrom, N. (2003). Are We Living in a Computer Simulation? The Philosophical Quarterly, 53(211), 243–255. https://doi.org/10.1111/1467-9213.00309

Cajochen, C., Foy, R., & Dijk, D. J. (1999). Frontal predominance of a relative increase in sleep delta and theta EEG activity after sleep loss in humans. Sleep Research Online, 2(3), 65–69.

Carhart-Harris, R. L., Bolstridge, M., Rucker, J., Day, C. M. J., Erritzoe, D., Kaelen, M., Bloomfield, M., Rickard, J. A., Forbes, B., Feilding, A., Taylor, D., Pilling, S., Curran, V. H., & Nutt, D. J. (2016). Psilocybin with psychological support for treatment-resistant depression: An open-label feasibility study. The Lancet Psychiatry, 3(7), 619–627. https://doi.org/10.1016/S2215-0366(16)30065-7

Centers for Disease Control and Prevention. (2024, August 6). Prescription Drug Use—Health, United States. National Center for Health Statistics. https://www.cdc.gov/nchs/hus/topics/rx-druguse. htm

Centers for Disease Control and Prevention. (2025, September 15). Antibiotic Use in the United States. Antibiotic Prescribing and Use. https://www.cdc.gov/antibiotic-use/hcp/dataresearch/ antibiotic-prescribing.html

Chaturvedi, A. M. (2020, February 23). Knots in Yoga. Viewpoints Which Matter. https://chaturvedimayank.wordpress.com/2020/02/23/knots-in-yoga/

Chichger, H. (2024, April 26). Artificial sweetener could harm your gut and the microbes that live there – new study. The Conversation. https://doi.org/10.64628/AB.puk9cs3sj

Chinmayananda, S. (2016). Astavakra Gita: Song Of Self-realisation (3rd edn). Central Chinmaya Mission Trust. https://www.abebooks.com/9788175977020/Astavakra GitaSong-Self-realisation-Swami-Chinmayananda-8175977027/plp

Chugh, D. C. (2020, May 13). How artificial sweeteners can affect your health and make you dumb. Dr Chandril Chugh Blog. https://drchandrilchugh.com/blog/how-artificial-sweeteners-can-affectyour- health-and-make-you-dumb/

Collins, J. (2017, April 26). The Marathon Monks of Mount Hiei. Trail Runner. https://www.trailrunnermag.com/people/culture-people/the-marathon-monks-of-mount-hiei/

Danhof, H. A., Lee, J., Thapa, A., Britton, R. A., & Di Rienzi, S. C. (2023). Microbial stimulation of oxytocin release from the intestinal epithelium via secretin signaling. Gut Microbes, 15(2), 2256043. https://doi.org/10.1080/19490976.2023.2256043

Datta, K., Mallick, H. N., Tripathi, M., Ahuja, N., & Deepak, K. K. (2022). Electrophysiological Evidence of Local Sleep During Yoga Nidra Practice. Frontiers in Neurology, 13. https://doi.org/10.3389/fneur.2022.910794

Davoudi, M., Sefiddashti, R. R., Meamar, A., Toreyhi, S., & Hadighi, R. (2020). Intestinal Parasites and Theta Brainwave Changes in Children. 11(4), e103015. https://doi.org/10.5812/compreped.103015

Dennis. (2016, June 14). Knot of the Heart. Advaita Vision. https://www.advaita-vision.org/knotof- the-heart/

Dwoskin, H., & Canfield, J. (2018). The Sedona Method: Your Key to Lasting Happiness, Success, Peace and Emotional Well-Being. Sedona Press.

Estumano, D. P., Ferreira, L. O., Bezerra, P. A. L., da Silva, M. C. P., Jardim, G. C., Santos, G. F. S., Gustavo, K. S., Mattos, B. G., Ramos, J. A. B., Jóia de Mello, V., da Costa, E. T., Lopes, D. C.

F., & Hamoy, M. (2019). Alteration of Testosterone Levels Changes Brain Wave Activity Patterns and Induces Aggressive Behavior in Rats. Frontiers in Endocrinology, 10. https://doi.org/10.3389/fendo.2019.00654

Ferreira, A., Neves, P., & Gozzelino, R. (2019). Multilevel Impacts of Iron in the Brain: The Cross Talk between Neurophysiological Mechanisms, Cognition, and Social Behavior. Pharmaceuticals, 12(3), 126. https://doi.org/10.3390/ph12030126

Forbes India. (2025, January 14). Photo of the day: Maha Kumbh Mela 2025 begins. https://www.forbesindia.com/article/photo-of-the-day/photo-of-the-day-maha-kumbh-mela-2025 %20begins/95057/1

Gidwani, B. (1994). Return Of The Aryans. Penguin Books.

Goodwin, F. K., & Jamison, K. R. (2007). Manic-Depressive Illness: Bipolar Disorders and Recurrent Depression (2nd edn). Oxford University Press.

Grof, S., & Grof, C. (Eds). (1989). Spiritual Emergency: When Personal Transformation Becomes a Crisis. Tarcher.

Hadrich, I., Turki, M., Chaari, I., Abdelmoula, B., Gargouri, R., Khemakhem, N., Elatoui, D., Abid, F., Kammoun, S., Rekik, M., Aloulou, S., Sehli, M., Mrad, A. B., Neji, S., Feiguin, F. M., Aloulou, J., Abdelmoula, N. B., & Sellami, H. (2025). Gut mycobiome and neuropsychiatric disorders: Insights and therapeutic potential. Frontiers in Cellular Neuroscience, 18. https://doi.org/10.3389/fncel.2024.1495224

Haraguchi, R., Hoshi, H., Ichikawa, S., Hanyu, M., Nakamura, K., Fukasawa, K., Poza, J., Rodríguez-González, V., Gómez, C., & Shigihara, Y. (2021). The Menstrual Cycle Alters Resting- State Cortical Activity: A Magnetoencephalography Study. Frontiers in Human Neuroscience, 15. https://doi.org/10.3389/fnhum.2021.652789

Hawkins, D. R. (2014). Letting Go: The Pathway of Surrender. Hay House LLC.

Hindu Wisdom. (2008, October 28). India's cultural links with Africa since ancient times by Medha Vishwas Gadre. https://www.hinduwisdom.info/India_and_Egypt.htm

Hormone. (2025). In Wikipedia.
https://en.wikipedia.org/w/index.php?title=Hormone&oldid=13402968
39

Idris, Z., Zakaria, Z., Yee, A. S., Fitzrol, D. N., Ismail, M. I., Ghani, A. R.
I., Abdullah, J. M., Hassan, M. H., & Suardi, N. (2024). Light and the
Brain: A Clinical Case Depicting the Effects of Light on Brainwaves and
Possible Presence of Plasma-like Brain Energy. Brain Sciences, 14(4), 308.
https://doi.org/10.3390/brainsci14040308

Jain, Dr. R. (2019, August 2). Complete Guide To The 3 Gunas Of
Nature. Arhanta Yoga. https://www.arhantayoga.org/blog/sattva-rajas-
tamas-gunas/

Jain, Dr. R. (2023, April 14). The 5 Koshas & 3 Bodies: Meaning, How To
Transcend, & More. Arhanta Yoga.
https://www.arhantayoga.org/blog/the-5-koshas-and-3-bodies/

Jana. (2021, April 4). Sidereal time. PSI-Unit. https://psi-
unit.com/en/sidereal-time/

Jáuregui-Lobera, I. (2014). Iron deficiency and cognitive functions.
Neuropsychiatric Disease and Treatment, 10, 2087–2095.
https://doi.org/10.2147/NDT.S72491

Johnson, B. (2025, July 28). Heart rate and sleep [Post]. Twitter.
https://x.com/bryan_johnson/status/1949873396155867352

Kak, S. (2003, July 17). Akhenaten, Surya, and the Rgveda.
https://www.ece.lsu.edu/kak/akhena.pdf

Kramarenko, A. V., & Tan, U. (2003). Effects of High-Frequency
Electromagnetic Fields on Human Eeg: A Brain Mapping Study.
International Journal of Neuroscience, 113(7), 1007–1019.
https://doi.org/10.1080/00207450390220330

Kyushu University. (2024, May 20). Exercise spurs neuron growth and rewires the brain, helping mice forget traumatic and addictive memories. Science Daily. https://www.sciencedaily.com/releases/2024/05/240520122802.htm

Levenson, L. (1993). Keys to the Ultimate Freedom: Thoughts and Talks on Personal Transformation. Sedona Institute.

Lewis. (2024, March 7). Advaita in the Vedas – Rig Veda 1.164.20. Advaita Vision. https://www.advaita-vision.org/rig-veda-1-164-20/

Lindahl, J. R., Fisher, N. E., Cooper, D. J., Rosen, R. K., & Britton, W. B. (2017). The varieties of contemplative experience: A mixed-methods study of meditation-related challenges in Western Buddhists. PLOS ONE, 12(5), e0176239. https://doi.org/10.1371/journal.pone.0176239

Lutz, A., Greischar, L. L., Rawlings, N. B., Ricard, M., & Davidson, R. J. (2004). Long-term meditators self-induce high-amplitude gamma synchrony during mental practice. Proceedings of the National Academy of Sciences, 101(46), 16369–16373. https://doi.org/10.1073/pnas.0407401101

MaxWell Clinic. (2024, October 17). Neurofeedback for Kids & Teens at MaxWell Clinic: Helping Your Child Reach Their Full Potential. https://maxwellclinic.com/neurofeedback-for-kids-teensat-maxwell-clinic/

Méndez-García, L. A., Bueno-Hernández, N., Cid-Soto, M. A., De León, K. L., Mendoza-Martínez, V. M., Espinosa-Flores, A. J., Carrero-Aguirre, M., Esquivel-Velázquez, M., León-Hernández, M., Viurcos-Sanabria, R., Ruíz-Barranco, A., Cota-Arce, J. M., Álvarez-Lee, A., De León-Nava, M.A., Meléndez, G., & Escobedo, G. (2022). Ten-Week Sucralose Consumption Induces Gut Dysbiosis and Altered Glucose and Insulin Levels in Healthy Young Adults. Microorganisms, 10(2), 434. https://doi.org/10.3390/microorganisms10020434

Mental Health America. (n.d.). What is Glutamate? https://mhanational.org/resources/what-isglutamate/

Mickoski, H. (2024). Empty the Cave: Awaken the Spark (2nd edn). Howard Mickoski.

Moran, L. V., & Hong, L. E. (2011). High vs Low Frequency Neural Oscillations in Schizophrenia. Schizophrenia Bulletin, 37(4), 659–663. https://doi.org/10.1093/schbul/sbr056

Murty, M. R. (2014, June). The Gnostic Gospels and Vedanta. Vivekananda Review, 2. https://mast.queensu.ca/%7Emurty/gnostic.pdf

Nepal Yoga Home. (2018, December 12). Seven Bodies of Human. https://nepalyogahome.com/the-seven-bodies-of-human/

Niedermeyer, E., & Da Silva, F. L. (Eds). (2005). Electroencephalography: Basic Principles, Clinical Applications, and Related Fields (5th edn). Lippincott Williams & Wilkins.

Niranjan, B. (2015, September 19). Vastu, Temples and Pyramids. Radha.Name. https://www.radha.name/news/india/vastu-temples-and-pyramids

O'Hare, R. (2019, November 19). Ayahuasca compound changes brainwaves to vivid 'wakingdream' state. Imperial College London. Imperial News. https://www.imperial.ac.uk/news/193993/ayahuasca-compound-changes-brainwaves-vividwaking-dream/

One Mind Dharma. (n.d.). One Mind Dharma. https://oneminddharma.com/

Online Yoga School. (2023). Understanding Siddhis: Superpowers in Yoga. https://courses.onlineyoga.school/pages/understanding-siddhis-superpowers-in-yoga

Osborne, A. (2014). The Teachings of Ramana Maharshi. Rider.

Pandey, J. M. (2016, May 29). Indus era 8,000 years old, not 5,500; ended because of weaker monsoon. The Times of India. https://timesofindia.indiatimes.com/india/indus-era-8000- yearsold- not-5500-ended-because-of-weaker- monsoon/articleshow/52485332.cms

Panksepp, J. (1998). Affective Neuroscience: The Foundations of Human and Animal Emotions. Oxford University Press.

Patel, A. K., Reddy, V., Shumway, K. R., & Araujo, J. F. (2025). Physiology, Sleep Stages. In StatPearls. StatPearls Publishing. http://www.ncbi.nlm.nih.gov/books/NBK526132/

Pavone, K. J., Akeju, O., Sampson, A. L., Ling, K., Purdon, P. L., & Brown, E. N. (2016). Nitrous oxide-induced slow and delta oscillations. Clinical Neurophysiology, 127(1), 556–564. https://doi.org/10.1016/j.clinph.2015.06.001

Posada-Quintero, H. F., Reljin, N., Bolkhovsky, J. B., Orjuela-Cañón, A. D., & Chon, K. H. (2019). Brain Activity Correlates With Cognitive Performance Deterioration During Sleep Deprivation. Frontiers in Neuroscience, 13. https://doi.org/10.3389/fnins.2019.01001

Radhakrishnan, S. (Ed.). (2024). The Principal Upanisads (39th edn). Harper Collins Publishers.

Raichle, M. E., MacLeod, A. M., Snyder, A. Z., Powers, W. J., Gusnard, D. A., & Shulman, G. L. (2001). A default mode of brain function. Proceedings of the National Academy of Sciences, 98(2), 676–682. https://doi.org/10.1073/pnas.98.2.676

Rajeswarananda, S. (n.d.). Who Am I? The Teachings of Bhagavan Sri Ramana Maharshi. Sri Ramanasramam.

Ramamoorthy, H., & Nome. (2017). Ribhu Gita: English Translation from the Original Sanskrit Epic Sivarahasyam. Society of Abidance in Truth.

Ramanis. (2014, December 8). Appropriate Bhagavad Gita Verse In Egyptian Pyramid. Ramanis Blog. https://ramanisblog.in/2014/12/08/appropriate-bhagavad-gita_verse-in-egyptian-pyramid/

Roberts, D., & MacDonald, B. (n.d.). Brain Waves and the Food Connection. In Food Psychology. https://psychologists.biz/Brain_Waves.html

Rockstroh, B. S., Wienbruch, C., Ray, W. J., & Elbert, T. (2007). Abnormal oscillatory brain dynamics in schizophrenia: A sign of deviant communication in neural network? BMC Psychiatry, 7(1), 44. https://doi.org/10.1186/1471-244X-7-44

Rodríguez, M., Pérez, D., Javier Chaves, F., Esteve, E., Marin-Garcia, P., Xifra, G., Vendrell, J., Jové, M., Pamplona, R., Ricart, W., Portero-Otin, M., Chacón, M. R., & Fernández Real, J. M. (2015). Obesity changes the human gut mycobiome. Scientific Reports, 5(1), 14600. https://doi.org/10.1038/srep14600

Rushkoff, D. (n.d.). 2017: What Scientific Term Or Concept Ought To Be More Widely Known? - Chronobiology. Edge. https://www.edge.org/response-detail/27083

Saraswati, D. S. K. (1981, May). Psychophysiology of Fasting. Yoga Magazine. http://www.yogamag.net/archives/1980s/1981/8105/8105psft.html

Simeon, D., & Abugel, J. (2006). Feeling Unreal: Depersonalization Disorder and the Loss of the Self. Oxford University Press.

Snyder, S. M. (2025). The Zen Map of Awakening. Awakening Dharma. https://awakeningdharma.org/watch/zen-map-of-awakening/

Spaller, K. (2022, July 14). Recent Study Shows Kenetik Increases Brain Activity. Drink Kenetik. https://drinkkenetik.com/blogs/ketone-benefits/kenetik-ketone-drink-increases-alpha-brainwave-activity-in-healthy-adults

Steriade, M. (2006). Grouping of brain rhythms in corticothalamic systems. Neuroscience, 137(4), 1087–1106. https://doi.org/10.1016/j.neuroscience.2005.10.029

The Gospel of Thomas Collection—Translations and Resources (S. Patterson & M. Meyer, Trans.). (n.d.). Gnosis. http://www.gnosis.org/naghamm/gosthom.html

Tierra, M., & Tierra, L. (1998). Chinese Traditional Herbal Medicine Volume I: Diagnosis and Treatment. Lotus Press.

Timmermann, C., Roseman, L., Schartner, M., Milliere, R., Williams, L. T. J., Erritzoe, D., Muthukumaraswamy, S., Ashton, M., Bendrioua, A., Kaur, O., Turton, S., Nour, M. M., Day, C. M., Leech, R., Nutt, D. J., & Carhart-Harris, R. L. (2019). Neural correlates of the DMT experience assessed with multivariate EEG. Scientific Reports, 9(1), 16324. https://doi.org/10.1038/s41598- 019-51974-4

Tolle, E. (2016). The Power of Now: A Guide to Spiritual Enlightenment. Yellow kite.

Trafton, A. (2018, November 7). Dopamine primes the brain for enhanced vigilance. MIT News | Massachusetts Institute of Technology. https://news.mit.edu/2018/dopamine-brain-vigilanceanxiety-1107

Walker, M. (2017). Why We Sleep: Unlocking the Power of Sleep and Dreams. Scribner.

Waters, J. (2021, August 22). Constant craving: How digital media turned us all into dopamine addicts. The Guardian. https://www.theguardian.com/global/2021/aug/22/how-digital-mediaturned-us-all-into-dopamine-addicts-and-what-we-can-do-to-break-the-cycle

Welling, G. G. (1948). Luminous-Lint. http://www.luminouslint. com/app/image/382537481911238063240/

Yamas. (2025). In Wikipedia.
https://en.wikipedia.org/w/index.php?title=Yamas&oldid=1301150072

Yetgin, A. (2024). Exploring the Link Between the Gut Mycobiome and Neurological Disorders. Advanced Gut & Microbiome Research, 2024(1), 9965893. https://doi.org/10.1155/2024/9965893

Zeland, V. (2016). Reality transurfing: Steps I-V (J. Dobson, Trans.). CreateSpace Independent Publishing Platform.

Zheng, Z., Xiao, Y., Ma, L., Lyu, W., Peng, H., Wang, X., Ren, Y., & Li, J. (2022). Low Dose of Sucralose Alter Gut Microbiome in Mice. Frontiers in Nutrition, 9. https://doi.org/10.3389/fnut.2022.848392

3 BONUSES!!!

4 Month Self Realization Program

4 Month Self Realization Roadmap

4 Month Self Realization Workbook

4 MONTH SELF REALIZATION PROGRAM

A practical program built on cultivation of loving kindness, compassion & empathy as well as forgiveness, letting go, and self-inquiry.

I. Core Principles to Remember

1. You are already the Self.

The practices do not *create* Self Realization; they only remove obscurations in the mind.

2. The only desire worth having is the desire for Self Realization.

This desire ends all other desires.

3. Cultivating love is foundational.

Love-based living opens the heart center (the Divine Spark) and prevents ego backlash and imbalance.

4. The path is simple:

LOVE → FORGIVENESS → RELEASE/LETTING GO → SELF- INQUIRY → AWARENESS →SELF

One is always the Self one simply needs to remove the layers obscuring this truth.

II. Four Essential Methods

1. Cultivation of Loving-Kindness, Compassion, and Empathy

These are the foundational prerequisites for Self Realization. They soften inner resistance and make every other practice more effective and natural.

2. Forgiveness Practice (Ego-Based)

Softens the ego, opens the heart, and dissolves deeply rooted thought patterns and emotional blocks.

3. The Release Technique / Letting Go (Ego-Based)

Allows stored emotions, tensions, and attachments to fall away, creating inner space and freedom.

4. Self-Inquiry ("Who am I?") (Ego Transcendence)

Cuts directly to the root of the false self, revealing what is beyond identification with thoughts and identity.

These methods work in both sequence and synergy—each preparing, supporting, and deepening the others.

III. The Self Realization Program (4 Months)

MONTH–BY–MONTH PRACTICE CHART

● Major emphasis   ◐ Moderate emphasis

○ Minimal emphasis

Month	Forgiveness	Release Technique	Self-Inquiry	Dyad Inquiry
Month 1	Major	Light	Light	Optional
Month 2	Moderate	Increasing	Same Level	Optional
Month 3	Light	Light	●● ●●	If partner avail.
Month 4	Minimal	Minimal	●● ●●	If possible

IV. STEP-BY-STEP PROCESS

STEP 1 — Establish the Foundation of Love (Preparation)

Spend a few weeks, months or years cultivating a firm foundation in loving kindness, compassion and empathy. This is essential to stabilize the mind and prevent ego backlash.

Practices:

- Daily forgiveness practice
- Acts of service & volunteering
- Loving-kindness meditation
- Compassion, humility, empathy cultivation

Purpose:
To awaken and strengthen the heart center, soften the ego, and help open the way to Self Realization.

STEP 2 — Begin Forgiveness Method and Release Technique (Weeks 1–8)

After the heart is activated with loving kindness, compassion and empathy, the releasing and forgiveness techniques become smoother and deeper. Working with ego to heal the ego then dissolving the ego. Must understand ego is not real.

Practices:

- Release emotions as they arise
- Let go of mental positions and attachments
- Let go of judgments, grasping, resistance
- Use the Release Technique during real-time triggers
- Perform forgiveness method each day or as much as can

Purpose:
To clear emotional density and dissolve reactive patterns that obscure the Self.

Perform the Forgiveness method daily or as much as possible.

Also, here you can apply the method **in real-time during emotional triggers** as well as for deeper past hurts.

Practices Include:

- Apply the Release Technique to real emotions as they arise
- Release ego positions and mental stories
- Let go of expectations, demands, judgments
- Use the Release Technique (Hawkins / Sedona style) moment-by-moment
- Observe emotional contractions and dissolve them on the spot, observe and watch them go. What is it that remains? Who is the awareness beyond all?

Purpose:

- To clear the emotional body
- To dissolve lifelong patterns (anger, resentment, defensiveness, guilt)
- To break the identity of the ego-self
- To uncover the peaceful, open, unconditional Self beneath conditioning

STEP 3 — Intensify Self-Inquiry (Weeks 8–16)

Now comes the direct path.

Questions to continually return to:

- "Who am I?"
- "What is aware of this?"
- "To whom does this thought arise?"
- "What remains when all is let go?"

Purpose:

To dissolve the false self and allow the true Self to shine in the stillness within. The false self is the mind and emotions that come and go like clouds. The true Self is ever present awareness that neither comes nor goes, that is the real YOU!

STEP 4 — Enter Deep Inquiry & Emptiness (Month 4 and beyond)

This is the culmination:

Practices:

- Extended Self-Inquiry
- Daily meditation as awareness, the Self
- Letting go of everything, even spiritual ideas
- Allowing the dissolution of the "I"-thought
- Dyad Inquiry with partner (if possible)

Purpose:

To rest in **pure Awareness**, the Self beyond all concepts.

V. VISUAL FLOW CHART

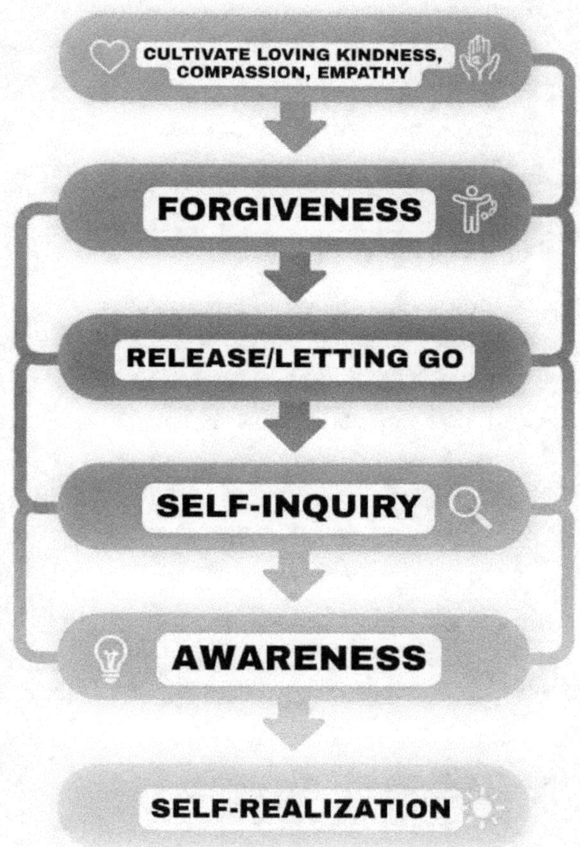

VI. SAMPLE WEEKLY STRUCTURE

This is a sample feel free to make any changes to fit your schedule.

Daily Practices

- 10–20 min forgiveness
- 10–20 min loving-kindness
- 15–30 min meditation or silent sitting, simply rest in awareness
- 5+ moments per day of the Release Technique
- Self-Inquiry woven throughout the day

Weekly Practices

- One period (30–60 min) of focused Self-Inquiry
- One volunteer activity, kind deed, or service project
- One session of journaling on insight and letting go

Optional

- Weekly Dyad Inquiry with a partner
- Attend an Enlightenment Intensive when possible
- Cultivate kindness, compassion, empathy as much as possible

VII. LIVING THE PATH (Ongoing)

To integrate this as a way of life:

Adopt these attitudes:

- Radical honesty

- Openness to whatever arises
- Nonresistance
- Humility
- Curiosity
- Trust in the Self (the inner Guru)

Remember:
You are not *becoming* the Self—
you are **removing what obscures the fact that you already ARE the Self.**

VIII. ULTIMATE AIM

All methods point toward one end:

To let go of everything and dissolve into the boundless emptiness in which the true Self shines.

As Ramana Maharshi taught:

"Self realization is not a state which is foreign to you, which is far from you, and which has to be reached by you. You are always in that state. You forget it and identify yourself with the mind and its creation. To cease to identify yourself with the mind is all that is required."

SELF REALIZATION ROADMAP

A Practical 4-Month Program Based on Love, Forgiveness, Release/Letting Go, and Self-Inquiry

INTRODUCTION

You are already the Self. These practices do not give you the Self; they dissolve the mental obscurations that hide what you already are. The only worthwhile desire is the desire for Self Realization.

This program uses four main methods after the preparatory cultivation of love, compassion, kindness and empathy for the activation of the heart center. Do not skip the preparation, it is vitally important. We will continuously weave love based exercises throughout.

- **Forgiveness**
- **The Release Technique/Letting Go**
- **Self-Inquiry ("Who am I?")**
- **Self-Inquiry Dyad** (optional but powerful)

After adequate preparation, the journey begins with forgiveness, letting go, then directly into awareness of the Self.

THE 4-MONTH PRACTICE PROGRAM

MONTH 1 — FORGIVENESS

- Heavy emphasis on forgiveness
- Light release technique
- Light self-inquiry
- Optional Dyad

Main Goal:
Soften the ego, open the heart, and begin dissolving emotional burdens.

MONTH 2 — RELEASING & OPENING

- Moderately reduce forgiveness
- Increase release technique
- Maintain steady inquiry
- Optional Dyad

Main Goal:
Clear emotional density, dissolve resistance, and stabilize inner peace.

MONTH 3 — DEEPENING INQUIRY

- Light forgiveness
- Light release
- Increased self-inquiry
- Introduce Dyad if you have a partner

Main Goal:
Turn attention inward to the root of the "I" thought.

MONTH 4 — THE DIRECT PATH

- Minimal forgiveness
- Minimal release
- Heavy emphasis on self-inquiry
- Dyad as much as possible

Main Goal:
Rest in the Self beyond thoughts, forms, and identities.

ESSENTIAL DAILY PRACTICES

1. Forgiveness (10–20 min) First 2-3 months

Release resentment, self-blame, anger. Forgive
others, forgive yourself, forgive life.

2. Loving-Kindness (10–20 min) Especially during preparatory phase

Cultivate compassion, empathy, humility.

3. Meditation (15–30 min) Always important

Silent sitting. Allowing. Being.

4. Release Technique (moments throughout the day) First 2-3 months

Let go of tension, resistance, emotions.

5. Self-Inquiry

"Who am I?"
"To whom does this thought arise?"
"What remains when everything is let go?"

6. Weekly Service or Volunteering

To keep the heart open where the Self awaits.

THE AIM

To let go of everything, dissolve into emptiness, and recognize the
Self that you already are.

2. DAILY CHECKLIST

SELF REALIZATION DAILY CHECKLIST

✓ **Forgiveness Practice** (10–20 min) First 2-3 months
✓ **Loving-Kindness Meditation** (10–20 min)
✓ **Silent Sitting / Meditation** (15–30 min)
✓ **Self-Inquiry Moments** ("Who am I?", "What is aware?")
✓ **Release Technique** (as emotions arise) First 2-3 months
✓ **One Act of Kindness or Service**
✓ **Heart-Centered Reflection** (evening)
✓ **Letting Go of One Attachment**
✓ **Optional: Dyad Practice (10–20 min)**
✓ **Gratitude Before Sleep**

SELF REALIZATION WORKBOOK

16-Week Structured Program

WEEKS 1–4: LOVE & FORGIVENESS

Here we added light love cultivation with Forgiveness as they are so vitally important.

Weekly Focus

- Forgiveness
- Heart opening
- Compassion
- Serving others

Weekly Exercises

1. **Forgiveness Method** (daily)
2. **Heart Journaling Prompt:**
   - ○ **"How can I love more today?"**
   - ○ "What am I withholding love from?"
3. **Service Action:**
   - ○ One act of kindness
4. **Self-Inquiry Seeds:**
   - ○ "Who is hurt?"
   - ○ "To whom does this memory arise?"

Weekly Reflection Questions

- What/Who did I forgive this week?
- What softened inside me?
- How did my heart open?

WEEKS 5–8: RELEASE & SURRENDER

Weekly Focus

- Emotional clearing
- Letting go
- Dissolving resistance

Weekly Exercises

1. **Release Technique Sessions** (2–5 min each)
2. **Trigger Transformation:**

   ○ Each trigger becomes a release opportunity
3. **Inquiry Prompts:**

   ○ "What wants to be let go?"

   ○ "Am I willing to release this?"

Weekly Reflection Questions

- What did I let go of this week?
- What emotions dissolved easily?
- Where am I resisting?

WEEKS 9–12: TURNING INTERNAL — SELF-INQUIRY

Weekly Focus

- "Who am I?"
- Disidentification
- Uncovering the Witness

Weekly Exercises

1. **Daily Inquiry:**

   ○ Ask 3× per day: *"Who am I?" Wait for answer...*
2. **Extended Inquiry Sessions**
3. **Awareness Tracking:**

   ○ "What is aware of this experience?"
4. **Dyad Introduction** (optional)

Weekly Reflection Questions

● What identities did I see through?

● What thought-structures dissolved?

● What felt like "me" but wasn't?

WEEKS 13–16: DIRECT SEEING — RESTING AS AWARENESS

Weekly Focus

● Pure Being

● Emptiness

● Nondual recognition

Weekly Exercises

1. **Self-Inquiry as Primary Practice**
2. **Meditation Without Object**
3. **Letting Go of the Seeker**
4. **Rest in Awareness**
5. **Dyad (if available)**

Weekly Reflection Questions

- What remains when nothing is held?
- Where is the "I"?
- What is the Self?
- What is aware of awareness?

A. 4-MONTH PROGRESSION CHART

MONTH 1: LOVE & FORGIVENESS
↓
MONTH 2: RELEASING/LETTING GO
↓
MONTH 3: SELF-INQUIRY
↓
MONTH 4: DIRECT SEEING

B. PRACTICE EMPHASIS CHART

C. PATH OF REALIZATION

CULTIVATE LOVE
↓
FORGIVE EVERYTHING
↓
RELEASE EVERYTHING
↓
SELF-INQUIRY
"WHO AM I?"
↓
AWARENESS
↓
SELF REALIZATION

D. PROCESS LOOP PROGRESSION

TRIGGER → RELEASE → INQUIRE → AWARENESS → SELF

TRIGGER → INQUIRE → AWARENESS → SELF

TRIGGER → AWARENESS → SELF

TRIGGER → SELF

SELF

YOU ARE THAT!

THE SELF REALIZATION WORKBOOK

*A 16-Week Journey Into Inner Freedom, Love,
and the True Self*

PART I — FOUNDATIONS

1. The Nature of the Self
2. The Role of Love as the Base
3. How the Ego Obscures Reality
4. Overview of the Four Core Practices

PART II — 16-WEEK PROGRAM

Month 1: Love & Forgiveness (Weeks 1–4)

- Week 1: Opening the Heart
- Week 2: Forgiving the Past
- Week 3: Forgiving Yourself
- Week 4: Compassion in Action

Month 2: The Release Technique (Weeks 5–8)

- Week 5: Letting Go of Emotional Charge
- Week 6: Letting Go of Mental Positions
- Week 7: Letting Go of Control
- Week 8: Surrender to What Is

Month 3: Self-Inquiry (Weeks 9–12)

- Week 9: "Who Am I?"
- Week 10: The Witness
- Week 11: Seeing Through the Ego
- Week 12: Abiding as Awareness

Month 4: The Direct Path (Weeks 13–16)

- Week 13: Dissolving the Seeker

- Week 14: Resting as Emptiness
- Week 15: Direct Recognition of the Self
- Week 16: Integration & Natural Living

PART III — APPENDICES

- Worksheet Templates
- Dyad Guide
- Trigger-to-Release Map
- Daily/Weekly Checklists
- Additional Diagrams
- Glossary of Practice Terms

PART I

FOUNDATIONS

1. The Nature of the Self

You are not the body, mind, emotions, memories, or personality. You are the **awareness** in which all these appear.

Realization is not something to gain.
It is the recognition of what is already here.

2. The Base of Love

Before deep inquiry, the heart must be open.
Love dissolves fear, softens identity, and prevents ego backlash.

Love is the accelerator and stabilizer of awakening.

3. The Ego's Role

The ego is:

- A bundle of thoughts
- A habit of identification
- A defensive pattern
- A fear-based contraction

It is not real — but it *appears* real until seen through.

4. The Four Core Practices

1. Forgiveness

Dissolves resentment, guilt, and emotional density.

2. Release Technique

Let go of feelings, reactions, and attachments.

3. Self-Inquiry ("Who am I?")

Reveals the false self and the true Self.

4. Dyad Inquiry

A partner-based method for deep breakthroughs.

PART II

THE 16-WEEK PROGRAM

WEEKS 1–2 — OPENING THE HEART (Inner Cultivation)

Primary Goal

To gently open emotional awareness, soften self-judgment, and establish loving attention toward self and others.

Daily Core Practices

1. **Loving-Kindness Meditation — 10 minutes**

   ○ Begin with yourself → loved one → neutral person → all beings.

   ○ Simple phrases:

      ■ *May I be safe.*

      ■ *May I be peaceful.*

      ■ *May I live with ease.*

2. **Heart Coherence Meditation — 5 minutes**
   Three Steps:

   ○ Focus attention on the heart area

   ○ Breathe slowly: 5 seconds in / 5 seconds out

   ○ Recall a memory connected with one word:

■ *Care*

■ *Compassion*

■ *Gratitude*

■ *Appreciation*
Allow the feeling to be embodied, not forced.

3. **Heart Journaling — 5 minutes**
Choose one daily:

○ *What opened my heart today?*

○ *What closed it?*

○ *What did I feel but not express?*

4. **One Conscious Act of Kindness**

○ Small, intentional, and attuned.

○ Example: listening fully, helping quietly, offering warmth without expectation.

5. **Evening Gratitude Reflection — 3–5 minutes**

○ Write or name:

■ 3 gratitudes

■ 1 heart moment from the day

Weekly Reflection & Inner Inquiry (Once Per Week)

Worksheet Prompts

● What is love?

● What emotions resist love in me?

● Who is easiest for me to love? Why?

● Who is hardest for me to love? Why?

● Where do I withhold affection or compassion?

Heart Activation Exercise (2–3 times per week)

Write and complete:

"Today, I choose to love…"
Complete with **10 honest statements** (no perfection required).

WEEKS 3–4
COMPASSION IN ACTION (Embodied Love)

Primary Goal

To move love from inward cultivation into embodied service, relationship, and joyful engagement with others.

Daily Core Practices

1. **Heart Coherence Meditation — 8–10 minutes**

   ○ Alternate focus:

   ■ Day 1: Self-compassion

   ■ Day 2: Someone you love

   ■ Day 3: Someone neutral

   ■ Day 4: Someone difficult (gently)

   ■ Repeat cycle

2. **Loving-Kindness or Compassion Meditation — 5 minutes**

   ○ Emphasize:

> ■ *May you be free from suffering.*

> ■ *May you feel supported.*

> ■ *May your heart be at ease.*

3. **Relational Journaling — 5 minutes**

○ *Where did I practice compassion today?*

○ *Where did I avoid it?*

○ *What did I learn about myself in relationship?*

Service Practice (2–3 times per week minimum)

Choose **one form of service per week**:

● Physical help (errands, labor, caregiving)

● Emotional support (listening, checking in, comforting)

● Anonymous kindness

● Community or volunteer support

After Service — Journal:

"How did serving others open my heart today?"

Skill of the Week: Empathetic Joy (Mudita)

Practice **celebrating others without comparison or self-diminishment.**

Daily Mudita Practice

- Silently bless:

    - Someone's success

    - Someone else's happiness

- Say internally:

    - *May your joy continue to grow.*

Mudita Journal Prompt

- *When others succeed, what arises in me first? Joy, comparison, fear, contraction?*

- *What changes when I consciously choose joy for them?*

END OF PREPARATORY PHASE
(Final 2–3 Days)

Deep Reflection

- How has my relationship with love changed?

- Where am I softer?

- Where am I still guarded?

- What kind of love feels most natural for me now?

Embodiment Practice

- Choose one daily ritual you will **continue beyond the 4 weeks**:

  - ○ Heart coherence

  - ○ Loving-kindness

  - ○ Service

  - ○ Gratitude

MONTH 1 — FORGIVENESS

Purpose:
To dissolve resentment, guilt, blame, and emotional resistance

through systematic forgiveness, preparing the inner field for deeper release and Self-Inquiry.

WEEK 1 — RECOGNIZING GRIEVANCE

Theme: Bringing unconscious resentments into conscious awareness.

Daily Practices

- 10–20 minutes of written forgiveness inventory

- Silent reflection on emotional triggers

- Evening review of reactions

- Perform Forgiveness method as much as possible during weeks 1- 4

Exercise: Grievance Scan

Write freely:

- "What am I upset about?" Who is upset? Who is the I?

- "Who or what do I feel wronged by?" Who feels wronged? Who is the I?

- "Where do I feel blame toward myself?" Who feels blame? Who is the I?

Worksheet

- List the top 5 recurring grievances in your life.

- Note the emotional charge of each from 1–10.

Weekly Intention
"I am willing to see what I have been holding."

WEEK 2 — FORGIVING OTHERS

Theme: Releasing stored resentment toward people and situations.

Daily Forgiveness Script
Repeat slowly:
"I forgive you for what you did or failed to do.
I release you from my mind and
my heart. I choose to be free."

Practice

- Choose **one person per day** and forgive them deliberately.

- Forgive both **actual events and imagined offenses**.

- Perform Forgiveness method as much as
  possible during weeks 1 - 4

Worksheet

- List 5 people you feel unresolved with.

● For each, write:

  ○ What happened

  ○ What you felt

  ○ What you are now willing to release

Weekly Intention
"I no longer carry the past."

WEEK 3 — FORGIVING YOURSELF

Theme: Dissolving guilt, shame, and self-punishment.

Daily Practice

● 10–20 minutes of **self-forgiveness statements**

● Gentle reflection on past choices without judgment

● Perform Forgiveness method as much as possible during weeks 1 - 4

Exercise: Mirror Practice

Stand before a mirror. Look into your own eyes.
Say:

"I forgive you. I love you. You are enough."

Or

Look into your eyes and repeat:
"I forgive you for all perceived failures.
You did the best you could with the awareness you had."

This is often harder than forgiving others.

Reflection Questions

- What am I hardest on myself for?
- What wounds am I carrying?
- What quality in myself needs compassion?

Weekly Intention
"I release myself from self-condemnation."

WEEK 4 — FORGIVING LIFE & LETTING GO

Theme: Releasing anger toward life, fate, God, and circumstances.

Daily Practice

- Perform Forgiveness method as much as possible during weeks 1 - 4

- Forgiveness of:

  - Life

  - The body

  - Parents

○ Past conditions

○ Missed opportunities

Forgiveness Integration Statement
"I forgive life as it unfolded.
I let go of the past completely.
I choose peace over memory."

Journaling Prompt

● "What has life taken from me?"

● "What am I now willing to give back to life?"

Weekly Intention
"I am finished with the past."

BONUS — Forgiving the Past

Forgiveness Script

Repeat daily:

"I release the past.
I forgive everyone who has hurt me. I
forgive myself for all mistakes.
I am willing to be free."

Worksheet

● List 5 people you haven't forgiven.

- Write one sentence you wish they knew.

- Release each with "I let you go."

Remember always: it is the ego that needs to forgive. The Self is eternally whole and free—beyond judgment, beyond anger, beyond sorrow, untouched. You are THAT!

MONTH 2 — RELEASE TECHNIQUE

Purpose: remove emotional, mental, and energetic contractions.

WEEK 5 — RELEASE/LETTING GO

Release Technique

1. **Feel the emotion.**
2. **Ask:** "Can I let this go?"
3. **Ask:** "Would I let this go?"
4. **Ask:** "When can I let this go?
5. Bask in awareness

Worksheet

Describe a recent emotional event:

- What triggered it?

- What was felt?

- What softened after releasing?

WEEK 6 — RELEASING MENTAL POSITIONS

Exercise: Letting Go of Being Right

Notice when ego insists on correctness.

Ask:

- "Can I let go of being right?"
- "What am I defending?"
- "Who is the defender?"

WEEK 7 — LETTING GO OF CONTROL

Surrender Practice

Choose one area of life to stop controlling.
Examples:

- People
- Outcomes
- Timelines
- Perfectionism

Worksheet

1. What am I afraid will happen if I stop controlling?
2. Is that fear real?

WEEK 8 — SURRENDER TO WHAT IS

Main Teaching

Suffering = resistance to reality.

Exercise: Radical Acceptance

Whenever discomfort arises:

"Let this be here."

Reflection Questions

- Where did I resist this week?
- What happened when I surrendered?

MONTH 3 — SELF-INQUIRY

Purpose: dissolve the illusion of the separate self.

WEEK 9 — "WHO AM I?"

Self- Inquiry (Direct Path)

Return to these inquiries throughout the day:

- "Who am I?"

- "What is aware of this?"

- When a thought appears, ask:
  "To whom does this thought arise?"

Then rest as the silent presence that remains.

WEEK 9 — SELF-INQUIRY WORKSHEET

Use this worksheet to **point attention back to awareness**, not to analyze experiences.

1. Moments of Inquiry
Briefly note when inquiry was applied today:

- Situation:

- Inquiry used:

- Immediate shift (if any):

2. Recognition, Not Interpretation

- Was awareness noticed as separate from thought?

- Did any sense of "me" dissolve, even briefly?

3. The Sense of "I"

- After inquiry, what felt like "I"?

- Was it a thought, a feeling, a body-sense, or simple presence?

4. Resting as Awareness

- Did you rest as the silent knower after the question?

- For how long (brief / sustained)?

5. Subtle Seeing

Instead of "what did I see," reflect gently:

- What no longer felt solid?

- What felt unchanged and always present?

End-of-Week Contemplation

Sit quietly and ask once:
"Without referring to memory, role, or thought — what am I right now?"
Do not answer with words. Let attention fall back into awareness itself.

WEEK 10 — THE WITNESS

Theme: Disidentifying from experience by recognizing the one that is aware.

Core Practice: Awareness Notation (Witnessing)

In daily life, gently and silently note:

- "Thought"

- "Feeling"

- "Sensation"

- "Image"

After each notation, turn attention inward and ask:
"What is aware of this?"
Then rest as the awareness itself, without trying to answer.

WEEK 10 — SELF-INQUIRY WORKSHEET

Use this only to **support recognition, not analysis.**

1. Shifts in Identification

- Was there a moment today when experience was seen instead of owned?

- Did awareness feel separate from what was observed?

2. The Witnessing Position

- Did the sense of being a "doer" or "thinker" soften at any point?

- Was there a simple knowing without effort?

3. Stability of the Witness

- Was witnessing brief, intermittent, or steady?

- What seemed to pull attention back into identification?

4. Subtle Recognition

Instead of describing experiences, notice:

- What remained constant while thoughts and feelings changed?

- Did awareness itself ever change?

End-of-Week Contemplation

Sit quietly and observe whatever arises for a few minutes.
Then ask once:
"Am I what is observed, or what observes?"
Do not answer in words. Let the seeing happen through awareness.

WEEK 11 — SEEING THROUGH THE EGO

Theme: Exposing the assumed "me" through direct observation and inquiry.

Core Practice: Investigating the "Me"

When a reaction arises, pause and inquire:

- **"Whose reaction is this?"**

- **"Where is the one reacting?"**

● **"Can this 'me' actually be found?"**

Do not seek conceptual answers.
Let attention search directly for the one who seems to react.

WEEK 11 — SELF-INQUIRY WORKSHEET

Use this only to **support direct seeing**, not to reinforce identity.

1. Moments of Reaction
 Briefly note when a strong reaction appeared:

● Situation:

● Felt sense of the reaction (tightness, heat, movement, etc.):

2. Investigation

● Was a separate "me" located?

● Or only sensations, thoughts, and awareness? Does the awareness change?

3. Dissolution

● Did the reaction weaken, dissolve, or remain after inquiry?

● Was there a return to stillness or neutrality?

4. The Ego Assumption

Instead of listing "ego patterns," gently notice:

- What identity was implied in the reaction?

- Was that identity actually present upon inspection?

End-of-Week Contemplation

Sit quietly and ask:
"Without referring to any story, where is the 'I' right now?"
Rest as what cannot be found yet is undeniably present.

WEEK 12 — ABIDING AS AWARENESS

Theme: Shifting from moments of recognition into natural, effortless resting as Awareness.

Core Practice: Resting as the Background

Instead of directing attention to objects (thoughts, feelings, sensations), gently:

- Notice what is already aware

- Do not follow what appears

- Do not try to hold awareness

- Simply remain as the silent presence in which everything arises

There is **nothing to do** and **no state to achieve**.
Just **cease following experience** and remain as what is watching.

WEEK 12 — SELF-INQUIRY WORKSHEET

Use this only to **stabilize recognition**, not to evaluate progress.

1. Natural Abiding

- Were there moments when awareness rested without effort?

- Did being feel simpler, quieter, or more open?

2. Effort vs. Effortlessness

- Was there a sense of "doing awareness," or did awareness simply *be?*

- Did trying relax into just being?

3. The Background Sense

- Did awareness feel like a background that never moved?

- Did experiences come and go within that unmoving presence?

4. Return to Identification

- What most often pulled attention back into thought or role?

● Was that pull seen as an object in awareness?

End-of-Week Contemplation

Sit quietly and notice:
Thoughts may appear. Feelings may appear. Sensations may appear.
Yet something is effortlessly aware of all of this.

Ask once, without effort:
 "Is awareness doing anything to be aware?"

Then stop questioning and simply **remain as that**.

MONTH 4 — DIRECT PATH

Purpose: dissolve the seeker, rest in the Self, stabilize Self Realization.

WEEK 13 — DISSOLVING THE SEEKER

Main Teaching
The last illusion to fall is the one who seeks realization.

Inquiry Practice
Gently turn attention toward the sense of the one who is searching:

● "Who is seeking realization?"

● "Can the seeker be found in direct experience?"

● "Does the Self require effort to be itself?"

Do not look for answers in thought. Look for the *actual seeker*.

WEEK 14 — RESTING AS EMPTINESS

Meditation Practice
Rest in the natural gap between thoughts.
Notice the open space in which all experience appears.
Observe: no boundary, no center, no edge.

Contemplative Reflection
Describe **emptiness** as it is directly felt.
Describe **fullness** as it is directly felt.
Notice where they are not two.

WEEK 15 — DIRECT RECOGNITION OF THE SELF

Spontaneous Inquiry
Let attention relax back into what is already present:

- "What is here without effort?"

Reflection Questions

- What is always present?

- What never changes?

- What remains when everything is let go?

Rest as that.

WEEK 16 — INTEGRATION & NATURAL LIVING

Integration Practice
Without analysis, simply note:

- What has dissolved

- What has opened

- What remains true

Let realization express itself through ordinary life. Before enlightenment chop wood carry water, after enlightenment, chop wood carry water. The only difference is one is now identified as the awareness within and every experience becomes a meditation.

Closing Inquiry
"Who am I when I stop trying to be anything?"

Remain in silence.

EXTRA:

Dyad Guide

Two partners alternate:

One asks: **"Tell me who you are."**
The other answers with raw honesty for 5 minutes.

Switch.

Continue for 30–60 minutes.

SAMPLE DAILY PRACTICE CHECKLIST

✓ Forgiveness
✓ Release moments
✓ Self-Inquiry
✓ Meditation
✓ Service
✓ Gratitude

ABIDING AS WHAT YOU ARE

You have not arrived at the Self.

You have **stopped leaving It**.

From the very beginning, nothing was missing. Nothing needed to be added. What appeared as a journey was the gradual release of what never truly belonged to you—beliefs, identities, emotional conditioning, and the imagined seeker itself.

Through love, the heart softened.
Through forgiveness, the ego loosened its grip.
Through release, the emotional body emptied.
Through inquiry, the false self was seen through.
And now, what remains is not an attainment—
it is what has always been here.

Awareness does not come and go.
It is not improved through practice.
It is not damaged by thought.
It is not disturbed by emotion.

It simply **is**.

At this stage, there is nothing left to "work on."
Only one subtle habit may remain: the habit of turning awareness into an object, a state, or a personal achievement. Let even that dissolve.

There is no longer a practitioner.
There is only **natural presence knowing itself**.

LIVING AS THE SELF

Integration is not something you do—it is what happens when there is no separation between meditation and life.

You may still feel emotions. You
may still think thoughts.
You may still move through joy, grief, activity, and rest.

But they arise in a different context now.

They arise **in you**, not *as you*.

Life continues, but the center has fallen out of it.

There is functioning without friction.
Doing without a doer.
Witnessing without a witness.
Living without a separate "me" at the center of life.

This is not a special state.
This is **natural life without misidentification**.

THE END OF THE PATH IS THE END OF SEEKING

The spiritual path ends where it began:
In the simple, obvious fact of being aware.

No vision, no experience, no realization is greater than this:
You are that which is aware of all experience.

Nothing needs to be protected.
Nothing needs to be maintained.
Nothing needs to be defended.

If seeking arises again, let it be seen. If
doubt arises, let it be seen.
If the "I" returns, inquire gently.

But do not resume the posture of the seeker.

You are no longer moving *toward* truth.
You are resting *as* truth.

FINAL CONTEMPLATION

Sit quietly now.

Let the body breathe.
Let the mind be as it is.
Let the world appear.

And notice:

You are here.
You are aware.
Nothing else is required.

Ask once, softly, and then fall silent:

"What is it that is aware of this moment?"

Do not answer.

Remain.

FINAL WORDS

You did not become the Self through this program.
You simply stopped being convinced that you were not.

May this recognition deepen naturally.
May love remain your orientation.
May humility remain your doorway.
And may life unfold freely through what you are.

There is nowhere else to arrive.

You are Home.